BEST of the BEST
from
LOUISIANA

Selected Recipes from Louisiana's
FAVORITE COOKBOOKS

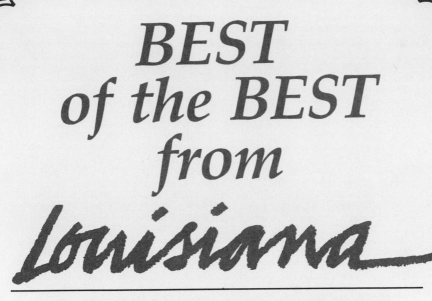

BEST
of the BEST
from
Louisiana

Selected Recipes from Louisiana's
FAVORITE COOKBOOKS

EDITED BY
Gwen McKee
AND
Barbara Moseley

Illustrated by Tupper Davidson

QUAIL RIDGE PRESS

CONTENTS

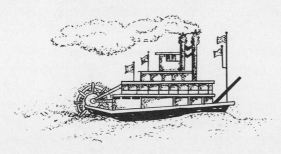

PREFACE

The preparing and consuming of food is, in most places, merely a *necessity* of life. In Louisiana, it is a *celebration* of life. Louisiana cooks seem to know that they're a part of a special tradition. This cookbook is an attempt to capture that remarkable heritage. *Best of the Best from Louisiana* is a collection of specially selected recipes from the leading cookbooks in the state. Readers and cooks everywhere are invited to have a "taste" of the unique flavor of Louisiana cooking.

The assembling of all these recipes was made possible by the remarkable cooperation of the individual authors and publishers plus the many charitable organizations that allowed their cookbooks to be included. We are indeed grateful to all these warm and wonderful Louisiana people. Their enthusiastic eagerness to participate in the development of this project has enabled us to gather together as nearly as is possible in one book, Louisiana's truly unique cuisine.

We have attempted to reproduce the recipes as they appear in their own books, changing only the typeset style for uniformity. There is a diversity among these books that made each one enjoyable to work with. Besides excellent recipes, many have beautiful Louisiana photographs, paintings, drawings, historical sketches, helpful kitchen hints, French and Cajun translations, and humorous stories and anecdotes. The books are enjoyable to read and look through as well as to cook from. A complete catalog of the contributing cookbooks begins on page 269.

We have included some definitions of words and terms which

may not have been known to all who read and use this book. Carol Mead worked very hard to research and compile the glossary, and we are grateful to her for her efforts. And thanks to Tupper Davidson, whose illustrations add such a delightful flavor to the book; and to Susan Hymel for writing the foreword and for allowing us to tap her wide knowledge of Louisiana cookbooks and cuisine; and to Bruce Morgan and the Louisiana Office of Tourism for their cooperation in providing open-door access to their wealth of pictures and information; and to Lois McKee, Janet Odom, Esther McLin, Tempe Crosby, Iris Bowman and Jean Harrison, who have helped us, hosted us, and encouraged us in so many ways through this monumental undertaking.

We invite you to partake of the celebration that is included in *Best of the Best from Louisiana.*

Gwen McKee and Barbara Moseley

FOREWORD

By Susan Hymel

"Sometimes cooks in other regions find that Louisiana's best seems to extend beyond reasonable limitations; the Creole repertoire is a formidable list, yet one that magnetizes those who like to cook." EVAN JONES—*American Food*

The Best of the Best from Louisiana is a whole magnetic field drawing from 50 tantalizing collections. Combining techniques with an abundance of resources, Lousiana boasts the only truly native American cuisine. To study the foods of any group of people is to taste their history. These cookbooks herald a love for food, folks, and fun!

Voilà! What a taste sensation we have here! *Louisiana's LEGACY* boasts a resourcefulness of her cooks from the *Cotton Country*, the *Plantation Country*, and the *Revel* of the northern part of the state.

Everyone in Louisiana seems to get into cooking. Almost anything *From a Louisiana Kitchen* would be a hit worldwide. The way *Louisiana Entertains* celebrates *Le Bon Temps* (the good times), *La Bonne Cuisine* (the good cooking), and *La Bonne Louisiane* (the good from Louisiana). The *Brennan's New Orleans Cookbook*, the *Buster Holmes Restaurant Cookbook*, *The Best of South Louisiana Cooking*, *The Asphodel Plantation Cookbook*, and *The Encyclopedia of Cajun and Creole Cuisine* leave no doubt as to why there are lines at the restaurants these books represent. They also demonstrate the house favorites, secrets, and tips. Two authors offer selections from various restaurants throughout the state, as well as share their own tested specials—Jude Theriot with *La Meilleure de la Louisiane* and *Paul Naquin's French Collections*.

Cookbooks have come from folks whose names we associate with Louisiana and her cooking. *Tony Chachere* gave us an all purpose seasoning and three *Cajun Country Cookbooks*. The *Justin Wilson Cook Book* has some serious offerings, though we laugh with its humorist/author. WWL radio made us drool in our homes and cars as Leon Soniat cooked over the airwaves and *La Bouche Creole* immortalizes those programs. *Frank Davis' Seafood Notebook* continued radio cooking and tips giving us a great reference book as well as an outstanding cookbook.

Louisiana is almost synonymous with water. Yet we seem to take the Mississippi River for granted—the river that both drains and irrigates so much of America. It's fitting that *River Road Recipes*, like its namesake, the "father of waters," is seen as the "mother of winners" in regards to what the Baton Rouge Junior League started over 25 years ago. Civic and church cookbooks have shared many a family secret and at the same time supported many a worthy cause. Success breeds company and lots of *Talk About Good, Cane River Cuisine, Recipes and Reminisenses of New Orleans, Pirate's Pantry*, and *Fellowship Church's Quickies for Singles*.

Even our natural resources have spawned namesake cookbooks—*Jambalaya* has elevated that grain to a celebrated staple while *Louisiana Crawfish* may make aquaculture history and *Turnip Greens in the Bathtub* could surprise a newcomer in our state.

Though so many recipes were perfected in black iron pots, Louisiana cooks have changed as ways of cooking have changed. Not to be outdone, they adopted the old favorites with *Southern Spice à la Microwave, Tout de Suite à la Microwave* and *Micro-wave Cajun Country Cookbook*.

Cookbooks are a *Louisiana Keepsake* and *'Tiger Bait'* to natives and visitors alike. Every time we share our *Foods à la Louisiane*, it calls for an *Encore* and shouts about *Louisiana's Largesse*. Cooks in Louisiana with various national heritages seem to always cook with *Chesta e Chida* ("a bit of this or a little of that") because we're *Cooking for Love and Life*.

Whether you're in *The Shadows-on-the-Teche*, or even in the "Big Apple," cooking and eating *Favorite New Orleans Recipes*, or enjoying *Opera on the Halfshell*, one thing is certain—you're involved in a celebration of tastes that are the *Best of the Best from Louisiana* and among the most enjoyed and talked about in the world. What a bounty! Let's eat! *SH*

Susan Hymel, educator, researcher, writer, caterer, cook, community activist, and TV personality, was listed in the Outstanding Young Women of America in 1980. A cookbook connoisseur, Susan buys, sells, reads, studies and uses them on her WBRZ-TV cooking show and in her cooking schools and seminars she hosts around the state and in her gourmet shop, Kitchen Works, in Baton Rouge.

CONTRIBUTING COOKBOOKS

*The Asphodel Plantation
  Cookbook*
*The Best of South Louisiana
  Cooking*
*Brennan's New Orleans
  Cookbook*
*The Buster Holmes Restaurant
  Cookbook*
Cane River Cuisine
Chesta e Chida
Cooking For Love and Life
The Cotton Country Collection
Encore
*The Encyclopedia of Cajun
  and Creole Cuisine*
Favorite New Orleans Recipes
Foods à la Louisiane
*The Frank Davis Seafood
  Notebook*
From A Louisiana Kitchen
Jambalaya
The Justin Wilson Cook Book
La Bonne Cuisine
La Bonne Louisiane
La Bouche Creole
La Meilleure de la Louisiane
Le Bon Temps
*The Louisiana Crawfish
  Cookbook*
Louisiana Entertains
Louisiana Keepsake
Louisiana Largesse
Louisiana LEGACY

*Louisiana's Original Creole
  Seafood Recipes*
Opera on the Half Shell
*Paul Naquin's French Collection
  I—Louisiana Seafood*
*Paul Naquin's French Collection
  II—Meats & Poultry*
*Paul Naquin's French Collection
  III—Louisiana Wild Game*
Pirate's Pantry
Plantation Country
Quickies For Singles
*Recipes and Reminiscenses
  of New Orleans I*
*Recipes and Reminiscenses
  of New Orleans II*
Revel
River Road Recipes I
River Road Recipes II
*The Shadows-on-the-Teche
  Cookbook*
Southern Spice à la Microwave
Talk About Good!
Talk About Good II
'Tiger Bait' Recipes
*Tony Chachere's Cajun Country
  Cookbook*
*Tony Chachere's Microwave
  Cajun Country Cookbook*
Tout de Suite à la Microwave I
Tout de Suite à la Microwave II
Turnip Greens in the Bathtub
*Voilà! Lafayette Centennial
  Cookbook 1884–1984*

Hors D'Oeuvres

A French Quarter courtyard. New Orleans.

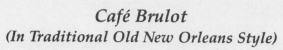

Café Brulot
(In Traditional Old New Orleans Style)

Long ago the Frenchman Talleyrand laid down the ground rules for coffee making when he insisted:—

Noir Commele Diable—Black as the Devil
Chaud Comme L'enger—Hot as Hades
Pur Comme un Ange—Pure as an Angel
Doux Comme L'amour—Sweet as Love

Peel of 1 orange, broken into 10 or 12 pieces
4 sticks of cinnamon, 4-inches long, broken into bits
10 cloves

3 demitasse coffee cups of Cognac
14 lumps of loaf sugar
10 demitasse cups hot strong black coffee

Place first 5 ingredients into the Café Brulot bowl. Fill 1 tablespoon with Cognac. Hold lighted match underneath spoon and ignite contents of bowl with burning Cognac. Ladle high for effect. Stir and ladle high. Pour in slowly from coffee pot the 10 demitasse cups of strong, hot, black coffee and ladle at once from bowl to the cups.

Opera on the Halfshell

 Café—French word for coffee. *Café au lait*—Coffee with milk.

Coffee Punch

Small jar instant coffee
4 cups sugar
4 cups boiling water

12 quarts milk
½ gallon chocolate ice cream
½ gallon vanilla ice cream

Mix coffee, sugar, and water. (This may be kept in refrigerator indefinitely.) Stir this mixture into milk and pour over ice cream when ready to serve. Serves 75.

Pirate's Pantry

Milk Punch I

1 quart vanilla ice cream or ice   ½ gallon milk
  milk   2 to 3 cups bourbon

In mixer, blend together softened ice cream and milk. Add bourbon and mix. Place mixture in freezer until ready to use. The mixture fits conveniently into two ½-gallon milk cartons. Take from freezer and place in refrigerator 3 or 4 hours before serving. Do not thaw completely—leave icy. Serve from silver pitcher. Makes approximately 1 gallon.

River Road Recipes II

Egg Nog

6 eggs, separated   ¼ teaspoon salt
¾ cup sugar, divided   1 (15-ounce) can evaporated milk
1 quart milk   Ground nutmeg (optional)

Beat egg whites with half of the sugar until stiff peaks form; set aside. Beat egg yolks with remaining sugar until thick and lemon-colored. Heat 1 quart milk on low heat until scalded. Remove from heat; add salt and evaporated milk. Let cool. Fold egg yolks into cooled mixture, then fold in beaten egg whites. Chill; sprinkle with nutmeg and serve. Serves 8.

Foods à la Louisiane

Bayless Special

3 parts gin   1 part fresh orange juice
1 part bourbon   1 part fresh lemon juice
½ part *Good* red grenadine

Shake over ice, strain and serve.

Be sure the grenadine is of a good variety. Add or subtract the grenadine to adjust the sweetness.

The Shadows-on-the-Teche Cookbook

Hurricane Punch
(from Pat O'Brien's)

2 ounces Jero's Red Passion Fruit
  Cocktail Mix
2 ounces fresh lemon juice

4 ounces good dark rum (Amber)
Crushed ice
Orange and cherry as decoration

Pour Jero's Mix, lemon juice and rum in a hurricane glass and fill the glass with crushed ice. Decorate with an orange and a cherry. Serves one.

La Meilleure de la Louisiane

Cherry-Orange Fizz

3 cups orange juice
½ cup red Maraschino cherry
  juice
1 tablespoon lemon juice
½ tablespoon lime juice

1 (12-ounce) bottle ginger ale
1 tray frozen orange juice cubes
Maraschino cherries and orange
  slices for garnish
Fresh mint

Mix first 4 ingredients in large pitcher. Chill. Add orange cubes and ginger ale before serving. Float cherries and orange slices. Add fresh mint to each glass as garnish. Serves 6.

Revel

Almond Punch

1 large can frozen orange juice
1 small can frozen lemon juice
1 large can pineapple juice
1 large can apricot nectar

½ cup sugar
½ to ¾ small bottle of almond
  extract

Dilute frozen juices according to directions. Mix all together and chill.

The Cotton Country Collection

Amaretto Freeze

½ gallon vanilla ice cream
⅔ cup Amaretto liqueur

½ cup Triple-Sec liqueur
½ cup Creme de Cacao

In food processor, using steel blade, put everything in the bowl and process until smooth. Chill.

Recipes and Reminiscences of New Orleans II

Mardi Gras Madness

1 ice ring
1 (40-ounce) bottle grape juice
1 (48-ounce) can unsweetened pineapple juice
1 (2-liter) bottle lemon-lime soft drink

1 fifth vodka or more, to taste
2 oranges or lemons
2 limes

Place ice ring in bottom of punch bowl. Add liquids in order given. Float slices of oranges and limes on top. Makes about 65 one-half cup servings. Makes 8–9 quarts.

Adds to the fun in true Carnival colors of purple, green, and gold!

Louisiana LEGACY

Crowd Pleasing Punch with "Punch"
(Punch garni pour contenter une foule)

Sugar substitute equal to 2 cups
sugar
2 unpeeled oranges, cut in half,
(cartwheels)*
2 cups boiling water
4 tea bags
½ teaspoon bitters

2 (⅘-quart) dry wine, chilled
4 cups fresh squeezed orange
juice, chilled
3 cups fresh squeezed lemon
juice, chilled
½ cup apricot flavored brandy
Ice

Sprinkle half of sugar substitute over orange halves in bowl (crush fruit slightly to extract some juice). Let stand 1 hour. Pour boiling water over tea bags. Steep 5 minutes. Remove tea bags. Add bitters and cool. Add remaining sugar substitute and chill. To serve in punch bowl, combine sweetened orange half cartwheels, tea mixture, wine, orange juice, lemon juice, brandy, and ice. Stir to blend.

Total: 32 (4-ounce) servings. Per serving: 50 calories
Exchanges per serving = 1¼ fruits
12½ grams carbohydrates

*To make cartwheels, slice orange in half, lengthwise. Place cut side down. Cut into thin slices.

Non-Alcoholic Variation:
Omit wine and brandy. Substitute 2 (28-ounce) bottles sugar free lemon/lime flavored soda and 2 cups cranberry juice cocktail. Stir to blend.

Total: 40 (4-ounce) servings. Per serving: 12 calories
Exchanges per serving = ¼ fruit
2½ carbohydrates

Cooking for Love and Life

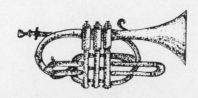

Frozen Punch

2 (3-ounce) packages lime jello or
    your choice of flavor
2 (46-ounce) cans pineapple juice
2 (8-ounce) bottles real lemon
    juice
5 cups sugar

16 cups water
Add these just prior to serving:
2 (32-ounce) bottles ginger ale
1 (2-ounce) bottle almond
    flavoring

Mix jello, pineapple juice, lemon juice, sugar and water until thoroughly dissolved. Put in two (5-quart) ice cream buckets and freeze. Remove from freezer 4 hours before serving. Add ginger ale and almond flavoring. It will be slushy. Serves 40. This is a favorite West Feliciana Punch served at many receptions. The flavor of jello can be coordinated with color scheme of your party.

Variation: Also called "Baptist Punch." Use half of each ingredient and add three small 7-Ups along with the ginger ale and almond extract when serving. This serves 20.

Plantation Country

Tex-Mex Dip

3 avocados
2 tablespoons lemon juice
Salt and pepper to taste
1 cup sour cream
½ cup mayonnaise
1 (1¼-ounce) package taco
    seasoning mix
2 (10½-ounce) cans
    jalapeno-flavored bean dip

1 bunch grean onions, chopped
2 tomatoes, chopped
1 (3½-ounce) can pitted ripe
    olives, drained and coarsely
    chopped
1 cup shredded Cheddar cheese
1½ cups shredded Monterey Jack
    cheese

Peel, pit, and mash avocados in medium size bowl. Add lemon juice and seasonings to taste. Combine sour cream, mayonnaise, and taco seasoning mix in separate bowl. To assemble: spread bean dip on a large shallow serving plate; top with seasoned avocado mixture; layer with sour cream-taco mixture. Sprinkle with chopped green onions, tomatoes, and olives. Cover with shredded Cheddar and Monterey Jack cheese. Serve chilled, with round tortilla chips.

From A Louisiana Kitchen

Ara's Shrimp Dip

2 (4½-ounce) cans small shrimp
2 (8-ounces) cream cheese
½ can of shrimp juice
Juice of 2 lemons

1 tablespoon grated onion
1 teaspoon pressed garlic
1 (6½-ounce) can crabmeat
Tabasco to taste

Drain shrimp and reserve the juice. Cream the cheese and combine with the shrimp juice. Add lemon juice, onion, crabmeat, and half of the shrimp. Add the last of the shrimp and fold in carefully. This is best served from a chafing dish with Ritz crackers but it is also good as a cold dip. It will keep for a week or two in the refrigerator and may also be frozen.

The Cotton Country Collection

Guacomole-Shrimp

½ pound cooked, deveined
   shrimp
2 medium, ripe avocadoes,
   peeled and sliced
2 canned chili peppers
1 small onion, thin sliced

1 clove garlic, minced
1 medium tomato, peeled and
   chopped
2 tablespoons lemon juice
1 teaspoon salt
1 tablespoon cooking oil

Combine all ingredients, except shrimp, blending until smooth. Chop shrimp coarsely, add to ingredients, keeping a few for garnish. Makes about 2 cups.

Louisiana's Original Creole Seafood Recipes

Hot Crawfish Dip

1 pound ground crawfish tails	1 teaspoon sugar
1 stick butter	3 tablespoons Sauterne wine
1 onion, chopped	1 (8-ounce) package cream cheese
3 stalks celery, chopped	¼ cup mayonnaise
1 bell pepper, chopped	1 teaspoon dry mustard
1 clove garlic, minced	Salt and pepper to taste

Sauté onions, celery, and bell pepper in butter. Add crawfish and cream cheese; cover and simmer until cream cheese is melted. Add mayonnaise, mustard, sugar, and wine. Simmer, add salt and pepper to taste.

Optional: You may add onion tops, parsley, and crawfish fat.

Paw sez: "Crawfish are like women . . . they're all good . . . but some are better than others."

The Louisiana Crawfish Cookbook

Crawfish Dip

½ cup butter	1 (10¾-ounce) can cream of
½ cup flour	mushroom soup
1 green pepper, chopped	2 pounds crawfish tails
1 bunch green onions, chopped	Salt and pepper to taste
3 large stalks celery, chopped	Cayenne to taste
1 onion, chopped	

In large skillet, melt butter, add flour, and mix well. Sauté all vegetables until tender, stirring constantly to prevent sticking. Add cream of mushroom soup, and mix well. Gently stir in crawfish tails. Cook until mixture is thoroughly heated. Season to taste. Serve warm, with chips or crackers.

From A Lousiana Kitchen

Hot Oyster Dip

½ stick butter
1 small onion, finely chopped
2 bunches shallots, chopped
½ bell pepper, finely chopped
1 (4-inch) piece of celery, finely chopped
3 dozen oysters

2 cans cream of mushroom soup
Salt, red and black pepper to taste
3 cloves of garlic, minced
3 pimentos, finely chopped
2 dozen tiny pastry shells

Simmer onions, shallots, bell pepper and celery in melted butter until soft. Cut oysters with scissors into small pieces. Heat in separate saucepan with oyster juice until they begin to curl. Drain oysters and reserve juice. Add oysters to onion mixture. Add mushroom soup, red and black pepper to taste, salt and garlic. Bring to a boil, stirring constantly. Remove from heat when boiling and add pimento. If mixture is too thick, thin with oyster juice. Serve from chafing dish in tiny pastry shells. Serves about 24.

Cane River Cuisine

Shallots—Mild onion-like herbs which are formed in small clusters rather than in large bulbs. Sometimes called scallions or green onions.

Mock Oyster Dip

1 package frozen chopped broccoli
1 large onion, minced
8 tablespoons butter or margarine

1 (6-ounce) roll of garlic cheese
1 can mushroom stems and pieces
Dash of hot sauce
1 can cream of mushroom soup

Cook broccoli in water (over done). Sauté onion in butter; add cream of mushroom soup, mushrooms and juice. Break up garlic cheese and add to mixture. Add hot sauce and broccoli. Mix well. Keep warm in chafing dish; eat with dipper potato chips. Can also be used in patty shells or over noodles as a casserole.

Recipes and Reminiscences of New Orleans I

Fried Monterrey Jack
(with Mexican Sauce)

SAUCE:

2 tablespoons peanut oil
⅓ cup scallions, sliced
1 clove garlic, crushed
1 (15-ounce) can tomato sauce

2 tablespoons green chilies, diced
2 teaspoons chili powder
½ teaspoon oregano leaves
¼ teaspoon ground cumin

1. MAKE SAUCE: In medium saucepan, over medium heat, heat 2 tablespoons peanut oil. 2. Sauté scallions and garlic until tender. 3. Stir in tomato sauce, green chilies, chili powder, oregano and cumin. 4. Cover and simmer 20 minutes, stirring occasionally. 5. Makes about 2 cups.

CHEESE:

Peanut Oil
2 (8-ounce) packages Monterrey
  Jack cheese, cut in half
  crosswise and cut into ½-inch
  thick slices

All-purpose flour
1 egg, beaten
46 corn crackers, finely rolled
  (about 1 cup crumbs)

6. FRY CHEESE: In a large skillet or electric skillet, heat a 1-inch depth of peanut oil to 375 degrees 7. Lightly coat cheese with flour. 8. Dip in egg, then coat completely with corn cracker crumbs. 9. Fry cheese, a few pieces at a time, 30 to 60 seconds, or until crust is golden and centers are melted. 10. Remove with slotted spoon; drain on paper towels. 11. Serve immediately with sauce. Makes about 16 pieces.

Louisiana Largesse

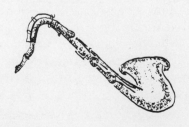

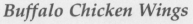

Buffalo Chicken Wings

24 wings (about 4 pounds)
4 cups peanut, vegetable or corn oil
4 tablespoons butter
2 to 5 tablespoons (1 [2½-ounce] bottle) Louisiana Red Hot Sauce

1 tablespoon white vinegar
Blue cheese dressing (recipe below)
Celery sticks
Salt, if desired
Freshly ground pepper

1. Cut off and discard the small tip of each wing. Cut the main wing bone and second wing bone at the joint. Sprinkle the wings with salt and pepper to taste. 2. Heat the oil in a deep-fat fryer or large casserole. 3. When it is quite hot, add half of the wings and cook about 10 minutes, stirring occasionally. When the chicken wings are golden brown and crisp, remove them and drain well. 4. Add the remaining wings and cook about 10 minutes, or until golden brown and crisp. Drain well. 5. Melt the butter in a saucepan and add 2 to 5 tablespoons (to taste) of the hot sauce. Add the vinegar. 6. Put the chicken wings on warm serving platter and pour the butter mixture over them. 7. Serve with blue cheese dressing and celery sticks, or bottled taco sauce. 8. Makes 4 to 6 servings.

BLUE CHEESE DRESSING:

1 cup mayonnaise
2 tablespoons onion, finely chopped
1 teaspoon garlic, finely minced
¼ cup parsley, finely chopped
½ cup dairy sour cream

1 tablespoon lemon juice
1 tablespoon white vinegar
¼ cup blue cheese, crumbled
Salt to taste, if desired
Freshly ground pepper to taste
Cayenne pepper to taste

1. Combine mayonnaise, onion, garlic, parsley, sour cream, lemon juice, vinegar, blue cheese, salt, pepper and cayenne in a mixing bowl. 2. Chill for an hour or longer. 3. Yields about 2½ cups dressing. 4. Serve with *Buffalo Chicken Wings.*

Editor's Note: This recipe is not native to Louisiana. The original was sent to us from Buffalo, New York, but when we find something good, we'll take it!

Louisiana Largesse

Celestial Chicken Wings

1 cup soy sauce
1 cup pineapple juice
1 clove garlic, pressed
2 tablespoons minced onion
1 teaspoon ground ginger
¼ cup brown sugar

1 (7-ounce) can beer
¼ cup butter or oil
2 packages drumettes (chicken
   wings, the part that looks like
   little drumsticks)

Combine first 8 ingredients and stir until dissolved. Pour over chicken and marinate overnight or at least 8 hours. Be sure sauce covers all pieces. Drain and save marinade. In a large skillet, heat a small amount of oil and brown chicken on all sides over medium heat. When brown, add ½ cup marinade; cover; reduce heat and simmer 15–20 minutes. Stir and add more marinade if necessary. This may be cooked a day ahead and then reheated in oven before serving. Add marinade to moisten before heating. Serve hot in a chafing dish. Serves 8–10.

Revel

Cold Pepper Steak

1 (4-pound) eye of round or flank
   steak

Garlic powder to taste
1 (1.87-ounce) bottle peppercorns

MARINADE:
½ cup soy sauce
1 (12-ounce) bottle cooking sherry

¼ cup Worcestershire sauce
¼ cup corn oil

Generously cover the meat with garlic powder. With a small paring knife, pierce the entire surface of the meat and stuff each hole with a peppercorn. Prepare the marinade. Place the meat in a deep dish and pour the marinade over it. Refrigerate the meat in the marinade for 24 hours, turning periodically. Remove the meat from the refrigerator and allow it to come to room temperature. Place the meat and the marinade in a roasting pan. Bake the meat at 500 degrees F., uncovered, for 30 minutes. *Reduce oven temperature* to 350 degrees F. and continue cooking, basting occasionally, for 1½ hours. Remove the meat from the oven, allow it to cool to room temperature, and refrigerate it. Serve the meat thinly sliced.

La Bonne Cuisine

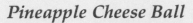

Pineapple Cheese Ball

2 (8-ounce) packages cream
   cheese, softened
1 (8½-ounce) can crushed
   pineapple, drained
2 cups chopped pecans

¼ cup [finely chopped green
   pepper
2 tablespoons finely chopped
   onion
1 tablespoon seasoned salt

In medium bowl beat cream cheese with fork until smooth. Gradually stir in crushed pineapple, 1 cup nuts, green pepper, onion and seasoned salt. Shape in 2 balls; roll in other cup of pecans. Wrap in foil. Refrigerate until well chilled (overnight). Serve with crackers. Serves 16.

Revel

Olive and Cheese Ball

1 (8-ounce) package cream
   cheese, softened
1 (8-ounce) package blue cheese,
   crumbled
¼ cup soft butter or margarine

1 (4½-ounce) can chopped ripe
   olives
1 tablespoon chopped chives
½ cup chopped pecans or
   walnuts

Blend cheeses and butter. Add olives and chives. Chill slightly for easier shaping. Form into ball and roll in chopped nuts, or press them on ball. Serve with assorted crackers. Makes 3 cups. Serves 18 to 20.

Cane River Cuisine

Mushroom Pâté

½ pound fresh mushrooms,
   chopped
2 tablespoons butter

1 (8-ounce) bar cream cheese
¾ teaspoon garlic salt

Sauté mushrooms in butter until tender and liquid has evaporated. Process all ingredients until smooth. Refrigerate, covered, for 3 hours before serving. Serve with Melba or toast points. Yield: 1½ cups.

The Shadows-on-the-Teche Cookbook

Pickled Mushrooms
(Champignons au vinaigre)

4 cups onions
1 cup water
1 cup vinegar
½ teaspoon leaf marjoram
¼ teaspoon whole cloves
½ teaspoon celery seed

½ teaspoon mustard seed
1 tablespoon salt
Few drops hot sauce
8 cups fresh mushrooms
¼ cup olive oil

Cut onions in 2-inch slices, and quarter. Cook in water, vinegar, and spices for 5 minutes. Add mushrooms and cook 5 minutes longer. Remove mushrooms and add olive oil to remaining liquid and onions. Bring to a boil and pour over mushrooms. Let stand for 3 hours or longer, and serve as hors d'oeuvre or a salad.

Total: 12 servings. Per serving: 70 calories
Exchanges per serving = 1 vegetable, 1 fat
5 grams carbohydrates, 2 grams protein, 5 grams fat
Cooking for Love and Life

Marinated Mushrooms

½ pound fresh or canned
  mushrooms
6 tablespoons olive oil
3 tablespoons wine vinegar
1 teaspoon dried tarragon
Dash celery salt

1 teaspoon grated onion
½ teaspoon salt
⅛ teaspoon freshly ground black
  pepper
1 clove garlic, crushed

Wash fresh mushrooms or drain canned mushrooms. Combine remaining ingredients. Pour over mushrooms. Stir to coat mushrooms with marinade. Cover, chill 6 to 8 hours, stirring gently several times. The mushrooms will darken. Serve on food picks.
Recipes and Reminiscences of New Orleans I

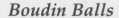

Boudin Balls

1 pound cooked boudin*	Seasoned bread crumbs
1 or 2 eggs, beaten slightly	Cooking oil

Remove the boudin from the casing. Form dressing into balls about the size of walnuts. Dip balls in beaten egg and then into seasoned bread crumbs. Deep-fry balls in cooking oil at about 325 degrees until lightly browned. Drain on paper towels. Serve hot with toothpicks. Yield: 20–25 servings.

This is a simple and excellent party appetizer or hors d'oeuvre and is excellent to serve to boudin lovers who might be reticent about eating boudin at social gatherings in the usual messy fashion.

*See *Boudin* recipe in meat section.

The Shadows-on-the-Teche Cookbook

Shrimp Puffs

1 pound boiled shrimp, peeled and finely chopped	1 cup flour
1 small onion, finely chopped	2 teaspoons baking powder
1 clove garlic, finely chopped	1 teaspoon salt
Black pepper	Dash of red pepper
	Milk

Mix together all ingredients except milk. Add milk a little at a time until mixture forms a stiff dough. Drop into hot grease about 3 inches deep, a teaspoon at a time. Fry fast until golden brown. Drain on paper towels. Yields 40–50.

Recipes and Reminiscences of New Orleans II

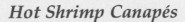

Hot Shrimp Canapés

1 cup chopped cooked shrimp
1 cup grated sharp Cheddar
  cheese
2 large kosher dill pickles, grated
½ cup mayonnaise
½ teaspoon Tabasco

½ teaspoon onion juice
½ teaspoon coarse black pepper
¼ teaspoon salt
1 clove garlic, pressed
50 (1½-inch) rounds of bread,
  toasted on one side

Combine first 9 ingredients and spread on toasted side of rounds. Bake 10 minutes at 350 degrees. Freezes well. Yield: 50.

Louisiana Entertains

Shrimp and Mushrooms
(Microwave)

Cooking Time: 9 minutes
Utensils: 2-quart glass dish
Serving: 6-8

¼ cup margarine
3 cloves garlic, minced
1 tablespoon parsley, chopped
¼ cup Vermouth or white wine

3 tablespoons lemon juice
1 teaspoon salt
½ teaspoon ground pepper
2 cups whole fresh mushrooms

1. Melt margarine in a 2-quart dish on HIGH (100%) 1 MINUTE. Stir in garlic, parsley, wine, lemon juice, salt and pepper. Add mushrooms and mix well. Microwave on HIGH (100%) 3 MINUTES.

1 pound medium large shrimp,
  peeled

2. Add shrimp. Cover. Microwave on HIGH (100%) 5 MINUTES until all shrimp are pink. Stir shrimp after half the cooking time. Let stand in sauce. When ready to serve, use a slotted spoon to remove shrimp and mushrooms to a serving dish. Sauce may be used as a dip for the shrimp and mushrooms. Serve with wooden picks.

Tout de Suite à la Microwave II

Marinated Crawfish Tails

2 pounds cooked and peeled
  crawfish tails
1 onion, chopped
1 cup vegetable oil
3 tablespoons white vinegar
2 tablespoons chopped sweet
  pickle

1 teaspoon dry mustard
1 teaspoon salt
¼ teaspoon pepper
2 teaspoons minced parsley
2 teaspoons minced chives
2 tablespoons drained capers

Layer crawfish and onions. Heat next 6 ingredients to boiling. Stir in remaining ingredients and pour over crawfish mixture. Cover and refrigerate at least 24 hours. Drain and serve with toothpicks.

Louisiana Entertains

Crabmeat Mornay

1 stick butter
1 small bunch green onions,
  chopped
½ cup finely chopped parsley
2 tablespoons flour
1 pint breakfast cream

½ pound grated Swiss cheese
1 tablespoon sherry wine
Red pepper to taste
Salt to taste
1 pound white crab meat

Melt butter in heavy pot and sauté onions and parsley. Blend in flour, cream, and cheese, until cheese is melted. Add other ingredients and gently fold in crab meat. This may be served in a chafing dish with Melba toast or in patty shells.

River Road Recipes I

 Mornay—A traditional French sauce made with white sauce and one or more kinds of melted cheese.

Artichoke-Oysters Bienvenue

¼ cup butter
1 bunch green onions, chopped
1 tablespoon lemon juice
2 tablespoons flour
2 dozen oysters
3 cups oyster liquid or oyster
   liquid and milk to make 3 cups

2 (7¾-ounce) cans artichoke
   bottoms, one can drained and
   sliced, the other drained only
Salt and pepper
Parmesan cheese

Sauté onions in butter until transparent. Add lemon juice and stir in flour. Add oysters and liquid, artichoke slices, salt and pepper to taste. Simmer for 10 minutes; sauce will thicken. Spoon mixture into whole artichoke bottoms, sprinkle with Parmesan cheese and run under the broiler for 2 to 3 minutes. Top with heavy serving of Bearnaise sauce. (If made the day before, bake in oven for 20 minutes at 300 degrees F. at serving time, or reheat in microwave for five minutes). Then top with sauce.

BEARNAISE SAUCE:
4 egg yolks
Juice of one lemon
2 cups melted butter

Salt and pepper
¼ cup chopped parsley
1 tablespoon tarragon vinegar

To make sauce, put egg yolks and lemon juice in top of double boiler and cook over low heat, never allowing water in bottom to boil. Slowly add melted butter, stirring constantly with a wooden spoon or wire whisk. Add salt, pepper, parsley and vinegar. Makes 2 cups. Serves 8.

This elegant hors d'oeuvre is nice if bottoms are placed in individual ramekins.

Louisiana LEGACY

 Bearnaise—A hollandaise sauce flavored with wine, shallots and herbs.

Red Fish Hors D'Oeuvre

1 (5 to 6-pound) red fish
Cheesecloth
1 quart mayonnaise (reserve
  enough for icing)
1 bottle horseradish
1 clove garlic, pressed
½ medium onion, grated
1 teaspoon dry mustard
1 large carrot, chopped fine or
  grated

1 large dill pickle, chopped
1 bottle capers, drained
Worcestershire sauce
Tabasco
Red pepper
Salt and black pepper
Juice of ½ lemon

Have the head removed from the fish. Place fish on the cheese cloth, tying at each end. Have the cloth long enough to extend out of the very large pot you will need to poach the fish. This is for easy removal. Poach the fish in well seasoned water, preferably seasoned with crab boil, salt, lemon, black and red pepper. When fish is done, remove, cool and flake. Mix the fish meat with the above listed ingredients, reserving enough mayonnaise to ice the fish after shaping. Check seasonings according to taste. The fish may be put in fish mold(s) or one large fish may be shaped on platter. Ice with mayonnaise and decorate with lemon slices for fins; a stuffed olive for the eye. Serve with crackers.

If red fish is unavailable, red snapper may be substituted. You may want to boil the fish head in seasoned water to make fish bouillon which may be frozen and used later.

Turnip Greens in the Bathtub

Salads

Parlange Plantation. New Roads.

Seafood Salad

2 pounds cooked seafood
  (shrimp, crawfish, crabmeat,
  tuna, or a combination)
½ cup French dressing
1½ tablespoons finely grated
  onion
½ cup finely grated green pepper
½ cup finely grated celery
1 teaspoon salt
½ teaspoon pepper
1 teaspoon Tabasco
1 teaspoon Worcestershire sauce
1 cup mayonnaise
2 hard-boiled eggs, chopped

In a large bowl, combine seafood with all ingredients except mayonnaise and eggs. Mix well and refrigerate 30 minutes. Fold in mayonnaise and eggs. Best made ahead. Serves 6 to 8.

Jambalaya

Wild Rice and Shrimp Salad with Curry Dressing

¾ pound fresh mushrooms,
  washed and sliced
4 tablespoons olive oil
1 pound raw shrimp, peeled
1 cup unseasoned wild rice,
  cooked and cooled
5 hard cooked eggs, diced
Salt and pepper to taste
8 green onions with tops, finely
  chopped
1 clove pressed garlic
4 tablespoons lemon juice
1 cup sour cream
1 cup mayonnaise
⅛ teaspoon oregano
1½ teaspoon thyme
1 to 2 teaspoons curry powder, to
  taste

Sauté mushrooms in olive oil until just soft. Add raw shrimp, and sauté for several minutes, until shrimp are just cooked. Remove from heat. Place cooled rice in a large bowl, and add mushrooms, oil, and shrimp mixture. Add diced hard cooked eggs, and mix gently. Season with salt and pepper.

Mix together remaining ingredients. Pour a spoonful of this dressing into the rice-shrimp mixture, blend gently, and chill. Chill remaining dressing. Serve on a bed of crisp lettuce with the dressing in a separate bowl to pass. Serves 8 to 10.

Le Bon Temps

Shrimp Salad
(Stretched)

SALAD:

1 pound well-seasoned boiled
  shrimp, peeled
3 small red potatoes, peeled,
  boiled in shrimp water

2 hard boiled eggs, peeled and
  chopped
2 tablespoons onion, chopped
¼ cup celery, chopped

Save the shrimp water to boil the potatoes in. If using crab boil bag to season shrimp, remove before boiling potatoes. Cube the potatoes. Mix all ingredients and add the following dressing:

DRESSING:

¼ cup (heaping) mayonnaise
3 teaspoons Durkee's dressing
  (more according to taste)
½ teaspoon salt

¼ teaspoon black pepper
Sprinkling of red pepper
Sprinkling dill weed

Combine ingredients. Mix dressing. Check seasonings for taste. Add to shrimp mixture. Chill. When ready serve on crisp lettuce leaf.

Turnip Greens in the Bathtub

Hot Shrimp-Avocado Salad

1 tablespoon butter
1½ teaspoons curry powder
1¼ teaspoons salt
1 medium tomato, chopped
1 medium onion, chopped

1½ pounds fresh shrimp, cleaned
  and well-drained
2 tablespoons lemon juice
1 cup dairy sour cream
3 or 4 avocados, peeled

Melt butter and stir in curry powder and salt. Add tomato, onion and shrimp, and sauté until shrimp are done and seasoning is soft. Add lemon juice. If mixture is a bit watery, drain some of the liquid at this point. Stir in sour cream and heat thoroughly. Serve hot as follows:

For a salad meal, halve avocados and scoop in shrimp mixture. For a salad accompaniment, spoon onto lettuce and surround with slices of avocado. Serves 6–8.

Looking for something different and mouth-watering? This is it!

Louisiana LEGACY

Wild Duck Salad

6 wild teal ducks
Water to cover
4 stalks of celery
2 large onions, quartered
2 tablespoons of salt
1 teaspoon pepper
2 bay leaves

2 sprigs of parsley
½ cup chopped green onions
¾ cup chopped celery
½ cup finely chopped chutney
Mayonnaise to desired
   consistency
Tabasco pepper sauce to taste

Place ducks in large pot and boil with first 7 ingredients. Simmer for 1 hour or until tender. Skin, debone and chop meat. Refrigerate. When cold, mix with green onions, celery, mayonnaise, Tabasco pepper sauce and chutney. May be served as a salad or with crackers as an hors d'oeuvre. Yield: 4 servings.

The Shadows-on-the-Teche Cookbook

Chicken Mousse

2 (2½-pound) chickens
1 teaspoon salt
1 rib celery, quartered
¼ teaspoon pepper
1 onion, quartered
1 bay leaf
1 carrot, sliced
2 envelopes unflavored gelatin

1 (8-ounce) package cream cheese
1 (10½-ounce) can cream of
   chicken soup
1 cup mayonnaise
2 cups chopped celery
2 tablespoons lemon juice
4 tablespoons chopped olives

In a large pot cover the chicken with cold water and add the next 6 ingredients. Bring the water to a rolling boil, reduce the heat, and simmer for 1½ hours, or until the chicken is tender. Reserve 1 cup of strained broth. When the chicken is cool, skin, bone, and cut it in small pieces. In a large bowl soften the gelatin in the chicken broth. In a saucepan blend the cream cheese with the chicken soup over low heat and add it to the gelatin mixture. To this mixture add the chicken and the remaining ingredients and mix well. Pour the mixture into a 9 × 13-inch pan. Refrigerate the mousse at least 24 hours. Cut the mousse into squares and serve it on lettuce leaves. The mousse may be topped with homemade mayonnaise. Serves 12–16.

La Bonne Cuisine

Hearts of Palm

1 (16-ounce) can Hearts of Palm
Romaine lettuce

Chill can of Hearts of Palm. Serve Hearts of Palm over Romaine with dressing below spooned over it. Serves 4.

DRESSING:

½ cup celery, chopped
6 ripe olives, chopped
¼ teaspoon capers
1 cup olive oil

¼ cup bell pepper, chopped
½ dill pickle, minced
¼ cup onion, chopped
2 cloves garlic, pressed

Mix all ingredients, except oil. Add oil and mix well. Let set in refrigerator for at least one day before using. Just before using, mix well and spoon over Hearts of Palm. It is best to let the dressing set out of refrigerator briefly before spooning over Hearts of Palm. Makes about 1 pint.

Paul Naquin's French Collection I—Louisiana Seafood

Layered Salad

1 small head lettuce, bite-size
  pieces
1 (10-ounce) package frozen peas,
  not cooked, rinsed in cold
  water
4 ribs celery, chopped
1 (8-ounce) can water chestnuts,
  sliced

1 cup mayonnaise
1 (8-ounce) carton sour cream
2 tablespoons sugar
1 cup Romano cheese, grated
Bacon bits
2 hard-boiled eggs, sliced

Layer lettuce in bottom of large bowl; layer peas, celery and water chestnuts. Combine mayonnaise and sour cream, mixing well. Spread on top of ingredients to edge of bowl, sealing completely. Do not stir. Sprinkle sugar and cheese on top. Cover. Chill 8 hours or overnight. Garnish with bacon bits and hard-boiled eggs. At serving time, toss lightly to coat with mayonnaise.

Easily made, can be made ahead and keeps well.

Encore

Cauliflower Salad

1 head lettuce, shredded
1 head cauliflower, thinly sliced
2 (10-ounce) packages frozen
    small green peas, thawed

1 pint mayonnaise
2 (1.3 ounce) packages dry Italian
    dressing mix
Parmesan cheese

In a salad bowl layer the lettuce, cauliflower, and peas. Cover the vegetables completely with the mayonnaise and sprinkle the top with the dry dressing mix and cheese. Cover the salad and refrigerate it overnight. Serves 8–10.

La Bonne Cuisine

Maw Maw Bennett's Potato Salad

8 red potatoes
6 eggs
3 large dill pickles
¼ cup salad oil

3 tablespoons mustard
½ cup mayonnaise
Salt and pepper to taste

Peel and cut potatoes in fourths and boil with eggs. Drain and peel eggs. Cut potatoes in small cubes and chop egg whites up small while hot. Chop dill pickles. Mash egg yolks, oil, mustard, mayonnaise and stir until smooth. Pour over egg-potato mixture, add salt and pepper and mix gently. Add more mayonnaise if too dry. Serves 8–10.

Plantation Country

Bean Salad

1 can cut green beans
1 can cut yellow wax beans
1 can red kidney beans
¼ cup chopped green pepper
1 medium onion, sliced thin

½ cup cider vinegar
⅔ cup cooking oil
½ cup sugar
1 teaspoon salt
1 teaspoon pepper

Drain beans, rinse well and drain again. Add green pepper and sliced onion to beans. Mix other ingredients and add to bean mixture. Mix well and marinate overnight in refrigerator. Serves 6.

Recipes and Reminiscences of New Orleans I

Red Apple Salad

6 apples
1 cup sugar
½ cup water

1 package cinnamon candy (Red Hots)
Red food coloring

STUFFING:
1 small package cream cheese
¼–½ cup fine chopped pecans
¼–½ cup fine chopped raisins

Few drops lemon juice
Milk

Peel and core apples. In saucepan boil sugar, water and candy until all candy melts. Add red food coloring and 2–3 apples at a time at slow boil until tender. Set aside in large pyrex dish to cool. Pour extra syrup over all to glaze. Mix stuffing ingredients with small amount of milk to desired consistency. Stuff each apple and refrigerate. Serve on lettuce. Serves 6.

Talk About Good II

Cranberry Salad

1–2 oranges
2½ cups fresh cranberries
1 (6-ounce) box orange flavored gelatin
3 cups boiling water
2 tablespoons lemon juice

1 cup sugar
Pinch salt
1½ cups finely chopped celery
1 cup crushed pineapple, drained
½ cup chopped pecans

Peel orange; put peelings and cranberries through a food grinder, or use a food processor to chop finely. Dissolve gelatin in boiling water. Add lemon juice, sugar and salt. Stir until sugar is dissolved. Add cranberry mixture, celery, pineapple and pecans. Mix well. Pour into large (10–12 cup) mold, or a large Pyrex casserole. Let set in refrigerator. Best if made at least 2 days ahead to enhance flavor. Serves 6–8.

Revel

Bing Cherry Salad

1 (17-ounce) can pitted dark
  sweet Bing cherries
1 (No. 2) can crushed pineapple
1 cup chopped pecans
1 envelope plain gelatin

1 can pineapple chunks
1 box black cherry flavored jello
1 (3-ounce) package Borden's
  cream cheese
1 cup Coca-Cola or port wine

Strain and drain fruit, heat liquid; pour over jello. Add softened gelatin. In individual molds, distribute pineapple pieces, pecans, cubed cream cheese and cherries. Add Coca-Cola to liquid while still fizzing, pour into molds. Use softened cream cheese with mayonnaise as a dressing or just plain mayonnaise.

Talk About Good!

Daiquiri Salad

1 (8-ounce) package Philadelphia
  cream cheese
1 small (3-ounce) box egg custard
  mix
1 can frozen Daiquiri mix or 1
  package of dry mix (mix
  according to instructions)

1 medium can crushed pineapple,
  drained
⅓ cup mayonnaise
1 + jigger of rum
1 envelope Dream Whip mixed
  according to directions
½ cup chopped nuts

Mix in mixer, blender or food processor omitting Dream Whip and nuts. Prepare whip. Fold into first mixture. Add nuts. Line 9 × 13-inch pan with wax paper. Freeze 3 hours. Serves 9.

Turnip Greens in the Bathtub

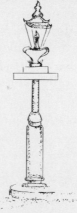

Delicious Tomato Aspic

3 (8-ounce) cans Campbell's
Home-Style tomato juice or 2
(12-ounce) cans
2 tablespoons gelatin dissolved
in ½ cup cold water
1 teaspoon salt
1 teaspoon sugar
½ teaspoon dried green parsley
½ teaspoon dried green onion
2 teaspoons Worcestershire
1 tablespoon onion juice or 1
teaspoon onion puree
(Progresso)
4 drops Tabasco
2 teaspoons lemon juice
1 tablespoon horseradish
½ cup finely chopped celery
½ cup sliced stuffed olives
1 avocado cut into chunks or 1
(14-ounce) can artichoke hearts,
drained
1 (4-ounce) can button
mushrooms (optional)
2 cups cooked shrimp (optional)

Heat tomato juice in a saucepan until it begins to boil. Add dissolved gelatin, salt, sugar, dried green onion and parsley. Allow mixture to cool and add Worcestershire, onion juice, Tabasco, lemon juice and horseradish. Adjust salt if needed. Add celery, avocado or artichokes and olives. If using artichoke hearts or mushrooms, marinate overnight in a good French dressing for a gourmet touch. This is optional. Serves 8. This is a highly seasoned salad and marvelous with any full bodied meat or seafood such as lamb, pork, ham or shrimp. You may use this as a main dish for a luncheon or for a cold supper by adding 2 cups of cooked shrimp.

Cane River Cuisine

Overnight Coleslaw

1 head cabbage, shredded
1 to 2 onions, thinly sliced
⅓ to ½ cup sugar
1 cup white vinegar
2 teaspoons dry mustard
2½ teaspoons salt
1 teaspoon celery seed
2 to 3 tablespoons salad onions
(optional)
1 cup salad oil

Layer cabbage and onions in a large container, sprinkling each layer with sugar. In a saucepan, bring next 5 ingredients to a boil. Remove from heat. Beat in oil. Heat again, but do not boil. Pour over cabbage mixture. Cover tightly and refrigerate at least 24 hours. Keeps well up to a week. Serve with a slotted spoon.

Louisiana Entertains

Wilted Spinach Salad
(Microwave)

Utensils: Large salad bowl
          Small casserole dish
          3-quart deep dish
Time: 16 minutes
Servings: 6

**1 (one-pound) package fresh
spinach**

1. Wash spinach. Drain and dry with paper towels. Set aside.

**6 slices bacon
½ cup green onions, chopped**

2. In small casserole, Micro bacon on HIGH 6 MINUTES, until crisp. Remove bacon and set aside. Add green onions. Micro on HIGH 2–3 MINUTES.

**1 (1-pound) package fresh
mushrooms, washed, drained,
and halved**

3. In 3-quart dish, put above bacon drippings and onions. Add mushrooms. Micro on HIGH 5 MINUTES, until partly sautéed.

4 tablespoons wine vinegar	**1½ teaspoons salt**
2 tablespoons lemon juice	**¼ teaspoon black pepper**
2 teaspoons sugar	**¼ teaspoon mustard**

4. Combine wine vinegar, lemon juice, sugar, salt, black pepper and mustard. Add crumbled bacon bits. Add this mixture to the above mushrooms in 3-quart dish. Micro on HIGH 3 MINUTES. Place spinach in large salad bowl. Pour hot mixture over spinach and mix until wilted. Serve hot.

Note: For variety you may add Parmesan cheese and 2 hard-cooked eggs, chopped.

Southern Spice à la Microwave

Sensation Salad Dressing

6 tablespoons (90 ml) Romano
   cheese, grated
2 tablespoons (30 ml) bleu
   cheese, grated
2 cloves garlic, pressed
Juice of one lemon, more if
   desired

⅓ cup (80 ml) olive oil
⅔ cup (160 ml) vegetable oil
¼ teaspoon (1.2 ml) black pepper
½ teaspoon (2.5 ml) salt

Grate cheeses and mix together. Set aside. Combine remaining ingredients. For each individual serving of tossed green salad sprinkle with 1 tablespoon (15 ml) of the mixed cheeses and 3 tablespoons (45 ml) dressing.

Hint: Freeze bleu cheese to grate.

'Tiger Bait' Recipes

Special Salad Dressing

(from La Provence)

1 ounce garlic
3 ounces prepared mustard
2 tablespoons oregano
½ cup lemon juice
3 ounces anchovies

4 eggs
½ cup wine vinegar
Salt and pepper
4 cups oil

Blend together garlic, anchovies, prepared mustard, eggs and oregano. Then add wine vinegar, lemon juice, and salt and pepper to taste. Slowly add oil and mix well. Serve over fresh lettuce, preferably two or three different kinds of lettuce tossed together.

Paul Naquin's French Collection II—Meats & Poultry

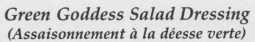

Green Goddess Salad Dressing
(Assaisonnement à la déesse verte)

1 clove crushed garlic
2 tablespoons chopped green
 onion
2 tablespoons lemon juice
3 tablespoons tarragon wine
 vinegar

½ cup low fat sour cream
1 cup low fat mayonnaise
½ cup chopped parsley
Salad and coarse black pepper to
 taste

Mix in the order given, and chill. Serve over your favorite vegetable salad.

Total: 18 (2-tablespoon) servings. Per serving: 45 calories
Exchanges per serving = 1 fat
5 grams fat

Cooking for Love and Life

Bread
and Breakfast

Oak Alley Plantation. Between St. James and Vacherie.

New Orleans Creamed Eggs

2 tablespoons butter
2 tablespoons flour
½ teaspoon salt
¼ teaspoon pepper
1 cup milk

1 teaspoon Cognac
4 slices hot toast
4 hard-cooked eggs, sliced
8 anchovy fillets

Melt butter in top of double boiler. Stir in flour, salt, and pepper until smooth. Let cook 1 or 2 minutes. Add milk gradually. Stir and cook until slightly thickened. Stir in Cognac. Arrange toast on serving plates and cover with sliced egg (1 egg per serving). Spoon hot sauce on top. Crisscross 2 anchovy fillets on each serving. Serves 4.

The Buster Holmes Restaurant Cookbook

Baked Spanish Eggs

4 tablespoons green pepper, chopped fine
4 tablespoons onion, chopped fine
4 tablespoons butter or margarine
8 to 10 eggs
¾ cups grated processed Cheddar cheese

½ cup day-old bread crumbs
1 cup beer
Paprika
Salt
Pepper
Tabasco sauce

Sauté onion and green pepper in butter until tender. Pour into shallow baking dish, season lightly with black pepper, salt and a dash of Tabasco sauce. Stir. Carefully break eggs into dish without breaking yolks. Mix bread crumbs with cheese and sprinkle over eggs. Spoon beer over eggs; sprinkle with paprika. Bake in moderate oven, 350 degrees, about 12 or 15 minutes, or until eggs are set as you like them. Serve with hearty vegetable and accompany with your favorite beer or ale. Delightful for brunch. Serves 6 or more.

Note: Fresh tomato or Ro-Tel tomatoes may be added to onions and peppers while simmering, if desired. If Ro-Tel tomatoes are used, leave out Tabasco sauce.

Talk About Good!

Eggs Bourguignonne

⅓ cup finely chopped onion
⅓ cup finely chopped shallots
2 tablespoons minced garlic
2 tablespoons butter
¼ cup flour
1 cup whole canned tomatoes

¼ cup liquid from snails
1 (4½-ounce) can snails
¼ cup diced, cooked carrots
Salt and pepper to taste
6 eggs

In a 9-inch skillet over medium heat, sauté onion, shallots and garlic in butter. Stir in flour and brown thoroughly over low heat. Blend in tomatoes and liquid from snails. Add snails, carrots, salt and pepper, cook slowly 10 to 15 minutes, stirring constantly. Yield 1½ cups.

Make three 2-egg omelets and fold ¼ cup sauce into each omelet. Roll omelet onto luncheon plate and spoon sauce beside it. Yields 3 servings.

Brennan's New Orleans Cookbook

Eggs Sardou

4 artichoke bottoms
1 tablespoon chopped green
  onion
2 tablespoons butter
2 tablespoons flour
1 cup Half-and-Half cream
1 (10-ounce) package frozen
  chopped spinach, cooked and
  drained

2 teaspoons lemon juice
3 tablespoons Parmesan cheese
Salt and pepper to taste
4 eggs, poached
¾ cup Hollandaise Sauce*
Paprika

In a small saucepan warm the artichoke bottoms in salted water and place them in a greased baking dish. In a separate saucepan sauté the green onion in the butter; blend in the flour, stirring constantly. Gradually pour in the cream and cook until thickened. Combine the spinach, lemon juice, cheese, salt, and pepper, add to the cream sauce, and mix well. Place ¼ of the spinach mixture on each artichoke bottom and keep them warm in the oven. Poach the eggs and place 1 egg on each filled artichoke bottom. Serve the eggs immediately topped with the Hollandaise Sauce and sprinkled with paprika. The Hollandaise Sauce may be kept warm by placing the blender jar in tepid water. Serves 2.

*See Lagniappe section.

La Bonne Cuisine

Garlic Cheese Grits

1 cup grits
4 cups water
1 teaspoon salt
1 roll garlic cheese

1 stick butter
2 eggs, well beaten
¼ cup milk
Salt and pepper to taste

Cook grits in water with salt added. After grits are cooked, add one roll garlic cheese (Kraft). Break in pieces and add 1 stick of butter, 2 eggs well beaten, salt and pepper to taste, milk. Put in a casserole (1½-quart) and bake 40 minutes to 1 hour at 300 to 350 degrees.

Variation: Separate eggs and folds in 2 stiffly beaten egg whites before putting in casserole to bake.

Talk About Good!

Jambalaya Grits

2 tablespoons bacon grease
2 tablespoons flour
½ cup chopped onion
1 green pepper, chopped
½ cup chopped celery

1 cup quick grits
3 fresh tomatoes, peeled and
    chopped (approximately 1 cup)
1 cup ground ham
Bacon, cooked and crumbled

In a heavy skillet, heat bacon grease and gradually add flour, stirring constantly, until roux becomes light brown. Add onion, green pepper and celery; cook 5 minutes. Cook grits according to package directions and add to roux. Add tomatoes and ham. Sprinkle with bacon and serve immediately. Serves 6.

Jambalaya

Mère's Couche Couche

1½ cups white corn meal
½ cup flour
2 teaspoons salt
1½ cups very hot water

2 eggs
2 teaspoons baking powder
2 tablespoons oil

Sift together corn meal, flour and salt. Add the hot water to make a light batter. Break 2 eggs into the mixture and beat well. Add the baking powder. Put the oil in a heavy iron skillet. When very hot, pour in the batter, lower the heat, and cover tightly. Cook 5 minutes (until crust is formed at the bottom of the pot). Stir occasionally until cooked, but not dry. Yield: 4–6 servings.

The Shadows-on-the-Teche Cookbook

Never Fail Biscuits

2 cups flour
4 teaspoons baking powder
½ teaspoon salt, scant
6 tablespoons oleo

2 tablespoons sesame seed
¼ teaspoon cream of tartar
Milk

Preheat oven to 450 degrees. Place large iron skillet in oven. In mixing bowl, mix dry ingredients. Cut in oleo with pastry cutter. Add milk to desired consistency. (I usually make mine very soft and use about 1 to 1⅓ cups milk and then I drop them.) Remove skillet from oven and place enough oleo to coat the bottom of the pan. Sprinkle 1 or 2 tablespoons sesame seeds on the bottom of the skillet. Drop biscuits and bake 12 to 15 minutes or until golden brown. Remove and invert. These are delicious. The hotter the skillet the browner and more crisp the bottoms of the biscuits will be.

Chesta e Chida

Louisiana Pecan Waffles

2 cups (500 ml.) sifted flour
4 teaspoons (20 ml.) baking
  powder
½ teaspoon (2.5 ml.) salt
1 tablespoon (15 ml.) sugar

1½ cups (375 ml.) milk
3 large eggs, separated
4 tablespoons (60 ml.) melted
  butter
1 cup (250 ml.) chopped pecans

Beat egg yolks into milk. Sift together flour, baking powder, sugar, and salt; add dry ingredients to milk and eggs, mixing thoroughly to remove lumps. Add melted butter and blend well again. Beat egg whites until stiff. Fold in pecans and add egg whites to batter. Heat waffle iron. Pour enough batter to bake proper-sized waffle. Bake until iron stops steaming and waffle is golden brown. Yield: 12 small or 6 large waffles.

Favorite New Orleans Recipes

Couche-couche—Also spelled "coush-coush" or "cush-cush." A crusty Creole bread dish made with corn meal. It is often served with milk and sugar or with cane syrup and crisp bacon.

King Cake

CAKE:

1 stick plus 1 tablespoon butter
⅔ cup 99% fat free skim
  evaporated milk
½ cup sugar
2 teaspoons salt
2 packages dry yeast

⅓ cup warm water
4 eggs
1 tablespoon grated lemon rind
2 tablespoons grated orange rind
6 cups flour

In a saucepan, melt 1 stick butter, milk, ⅓ cup sugar, and salt. Cool to lukewarm. In a large mixing bowl, combine 2 tablespoons sugar, yeast, and water. Let stand until foaming, about 5 to 10 minutes. Beat eggs into yeast; then milk mixture and rinds. Stir in flour, ½ cup at a time, reserving 1 cup to flour kneading surface. Knead dough until smooth, about 5 to 10 minutes. Place in large mixing bowl greased with 1 tablespoon butter; turning dough once to grease top, cover and let rise in a warm place until doubled, about 1½ to 2 hours.

FILLING:

½ cup dark brown sugar, packed
¾ cup granulated sugar

1 tablespoon cinnamon
1 stick butter, melted

For filling, mix sugars and cinnamon. Set aside.

TOPPING:

1 egg, beaten
1 cup sugar, colored (⅓ cup each
  of yellow, purple, and green)

2 (¾-inch) plastic babies or 2
  beans

For topping, tint sugar by mixing food coloring until desired color is reached. For purple, use equal amounts of blue and red. A food processor aids in mixing and keeps the sugar from being too moist!

When dough has doubled, punch down and divide in half. On a floured surface, roll half into a rectangle 30 × 15. Brush with half of melted butter and cut into 3 lengthwise strips. Sprinkle half of sugar mixture on strips, leaving a 1-inch lengthwise strip free for sealing. Fold each strip lengthwise toward the center, sealing the seam. You will now have three 30-inch strips with sugar mixture enclosed in each. Braid the 3 strips and make a circle by joining

CONTINUED

CONTINUED

ends. Repeat with other half of dough. Place each cake on a 10 × 15 baking sheet, cover with a damp cloth, and let rise until doubled, about 1 hour. Brush each with egg and sprinkle top with colored sugars, alternating colors. Preheat oven to 350. Bake 20 minutes. Remove from pan immediately so sugar will not harden; while still warm, place 1 plastic baby* in each from underneath. Makes two 9 × 12-inch cakes. Preparation time—5½ hours. Freezes well.

To freeze: Wrap cooled cake tightly in plastic. Before serving, remove plastic and thaw.

*In New Orleans, this cake is served during Carnival season from the Feast of Epiphany (January 6) until Mardi Gras (the day before Ash Wednesday). The person receiving the baby (or the bean) is considered lucky; by custom that person must also supply the next King Cake.

Jambalaya

Beignets
(French Market Doughnuts)

½ cup boiling water
2 tablespoons shortening
¼ cup sugar
½ teaspoon salt
½ cup evaporated milk

½ package dry yeast
¼ cup warm water
1 egg, beaten
3¾ cups sifted flour
Confectioners' sugar

In a large mixing bowl pour the boiling water over the shortening, sugar, and salt. Add the milk and let stand until warm. In a small bowl dissolve the yeast in the warm water and add to the milk mixture with the egg. Stir in 2 cups flour and beat. Add enough flour to make a soft dough. Place the dough in a greased bowl turning to grease the top. Cover with wax paper and a cloth and chill until ready to use. On a lightly floured surface roll the dough to ⅛-inch thickness. Do not let dough rise before frying. Cut into 2-inch squares and fry, a few at a time, in deep hot fat (360 degrees F.). Brown on 1 side, turn and brown on the other side. Drain on paper towels. Sprinkle with the confectioners' sugar and serve hot. Makes 30 doughnuts.

La Bonne Cuisine

Mock Beignets

2 cans refrigerated biscuits
(plain)

Hot grease
Sifted powdered sugar

Cut biscuits in half and roll flat with a rolling pin. Drop in hot grease, a few at a time. Turn once. Watch carefully as they brown quickly. Drain on absorbent paper. Sprinkle with powdered sugar. Yield: 40 doughnuts.

Recipes and Reminiscences of New Orleans I

Beignets—Small, square French pastries fried like doughnuts and covered with powdered sugar.

Stuffed Crawfish Beignets

⅓ cup butter
½ cup chopped celery
½ cup chopped onion
2 cloves garlic, minced
Salt and pepper to taste
1 pound crawfish tails
¼ cup shredded Cheddar cheese

¼ cup shredded Swiss cheese
1½ tablespoon chopped green
  onion
1½ tablespoons chopped parsley
Vegetable oil for frying
Dough (recipe follows)

Sauté onion and celery in butter until tender. Add garlic, seasoning and crawfish tails. Simmer for 8–10 minutes or until all liquid is absorbed. Set aside and let cool completely. Add cheese, green onions and parsley. Prepare dough.

BEIGNET DOUGH:
2 cups Biscuit mix
¾ cup water

Mix together with a fork. On a well-floured surface roll out dough. Cut with a 4-inch circle cutter. Place filling on half of dough. Fold circle in half; seal edges with fork dipped in flour. In deep pot, heat oil to 350 degrees. Fry the beignets until they are golden brown. Serve warm. Makes about 16 beignets. May be frozen before being fried. Thaw for 10 minutes and fry as usual.

   To make this dish quick, try using a can of refrigerated biscuits. Use same filling and frying method.

The Louisiana Crawfish Cookbook

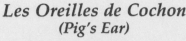

Les Oreilles de Cochon
(Pig's Ear)

Don't let the name "pig's ear" disturb you. This really is a delicious pastry. This is a combination of recipes that I tried to work out as I had only had the pastry once in Lafayette, Louisiana, and couldn't find anyone except Eleonora Carter (a wonderful pastry cook) who was willing to try them. We were working on a committee (food, naturally) for the Campus Club at LSU for a morning coffee featuring Louisiana foods. I will give my recipe and the variation of Eleanora's. Mine looks more like a pig's ear and Eleanora's more like eating.

2 cups flour	**½ block butter (¼ cup)**
½ teaspoon baking powder	**2 eggs, beaten**
½ teaspoon salt	**1 teaspoon white vinegar**

Mix ingredients as for pastry. Divide into 26 to 30 small pieces about 1½ to 2 inches. Roll each very thin. Fry in hot oil, bending one end with tongs or fork to resemble pig's ear. Drain on paper towels. In meantime, have syrup hot on stove. (Cane is recommended in Louisiana but having some honest-to-goodness Vermont maple syrup bought on a trip there, we find this is very good.) Drizzle over hot pastry. (Important that both pastry and syrup are hot.) I drizzle syrup lightly as I prefer it not too sweet. Powdered sugar may be substituted for the syrup. The difference being those made with powdered sugar should be served warm and immediately. The ones with syrup can be frozen. However, the flavor is best restored by heating before serving. The cooked pastry can be frozen, thawed, reheated and sprinkled with powdered sugar before serving.

Eleanora's method:
When we compared, we found our recipes the same, but Eleanora's finished product was different. She rolled the dough thin and cut in triangles. She made a slit at the large end and pulled the point through, then fried in hot oil. She used cane syrup, cooking it to the soft ball stage, then drizzled over the hot triangles and sprinkled with chopped pecans.

Turnip Greens in the Bathtub

Lost Bread
(Microwave)

Pain Perdu in French literally means "lost bread" which refers to the fact that stale bread might be lost if not made into this delightful breakfast toast, also called French Toast. Bread is dipped into a seasoned egg mixture, then cooked until brown on each side and sprinkled with confectioners sugar before serving.

Cooking Time: 6 minutes
Utensil: Browning skillet
Servings: 3–4

3 large eggs	**½ teaspoon cinnamon**
¾ cup sugar	**10–12 slices white bread, stale**
1 cup evaporated milk	**(French bread is preferred)**
1 tablespoon vanilla	

1. In a 10-inch glass pie plate, whisk eggs. Beat in sugar and add milk, vanilla and cinnamon. Dip bread slices in mixture until soaked.

3 tablespoons butter, melted

2. Preheat browning skillet on HIGH 4 MINUTES. Pour 1 tablespoon of butter in skillet, quickly put in 4 slices of soaked bread. Turn immediately to brown both sides. Cover with wax paper and microwave on HIGH 1 MINUTE. Turn slices over, cook on HIGH 1 MINUTE. Repeat process for next 4 slices. Serve plain or with powdered sugar or syrup.

Micro Memo: Pain Perdu can be made ahead and wrapped individually in plastic wrap. Heat in wrap on HIGH 1 MINUTE per slice.

Tout de Suite à la Microwave I

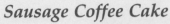

Sausage Coffee Cake

1 pound bulk sausage
½ cup chopped onions
¼ cup grated Parmesan cheese
½ cup grated Swiss cheese
1 egg, beaten
¼ teaspoon Tabasco
1½ teaspoons salt

2 tablespoons chopped parsley
2 cups Bisquick
¾ cup milk
¼ cup mayonnaise
1 egg yolk
1 tablespoon water

Brown sausage and onions; drain. Add next 6 ingredients. Make batter of Bisquick, milk and mayonnaise. Spread half of batter in 9 × 9 × 2-inch greased pan. Pour in sausage mixture, then spread remaining batter on top. Mix egg yolk and water and brush top. Bake at 400 degrees for 25 to 30 minutes or until cake leaves edges of pan. Cool 5 minutes before cutting into 3-inch squares. This recipe doubles easily in a 9 × 13-inch pan. Freezes well.

Louisiana Entertains

Swedish Puff Coffee Cake

PART I:
1 cup flour
1 stick margarine or butter
1 tablespoon water

Combine flour and margarine and add water, blending as for a pie crust. Place in a round tin (cake pan serves well), or divide in half and spread on baking sheet in 2 long (3 × 12-inch) strips, 3 inches apart.

PART II:
1 cup water
1 stick margarine or butter
1 cup flour

3 eggs
1 teaspoon almond flavoring
Cardamom

Bring water and margarine to a boil, remove from heat. Add flour, beating vigorously with a wooden spoon. Add eggs, 1 at a time, beating after each. Add flavoring. Spread this over first mixture and sprinkle with cardamom. Bake at 400 degrees F. for 45 minutes.

PART III:
Confectioners sugar
Almonds, toasted

While coffee cake is still warm, coat lightly with confectioners sugar and sprinkle with toasted almonds. Serve at once. Serves 8.
   Makes a very showy dessert.

Pirate's Pantry

Pumpkin Bread
(Microwave)

Cooking Time: 7 minutes per loaf
Utensil: 2-cup glass measuring cup
Servings: 5 loaves

3 cups sugar	1 teaspoon nutmeg
1 cup vegetable oil	1 teaspoon allspice
4 eggs, beaten	1 teaspoon cinnamon
⅔ cup water	1 teaspoon vanilla
3½ cups all-purpose flour	1 (16-ounce) can pumpkin, solid
1½ teaspoons salt	pack
2 teaspoons baking soda	1 cup pecans, chopped

1. Combine sugar and oil in a large mixing bowl. Stir in eggs and mix well. Add water and flour, slowly. Add salt, baking soda, nutmeg, allspice, cinnamon, vanilla, pumpkin and pecans. Mix until blended. Line bottom of a 2-cup Pyrex measuring cup with a circle of wax paper (cut 5 or 6 circles for additional loaves). Pour 1⅓ cups batter in a 2-cup measure. Cover with vented plastic wrap. Microwave on MEDIUM (50%) 7 MINUTES, rotating cup ½ turn after 3 minutes.

2. Bread is done when no unbaked batter appears on sides of cup and center springs back when touched lightly. Cool uncovered 5 minutes. Remove from cup. Microwave 4 or 5 more loaves with remaining batter, using same measurements and timing. Serve warm. To reheat, place slices on plate. Cover loosely with plastic wrap. Microwave on HIGH (100%) 30 SECONDS. Loaves freeze well.

Tout de Suite à la Microwave II

Banana Nut Bread
(Microwave)

Cooking Time: 12 minutes
Utensils: Glass loaf pan
Yield: 1 loaf bread

1 stick butter or margarine	2 eggs, slightly beaten
1 cup sugar	1 teaspoon lemon juice
2 large ripe bananas, well mashed	½ cup chopped nuts
1 tablespoon baking soda	2 cups flour
2 tablespoons boiling water	¼ cup chopped nuts

1. In mixing bowl, cream together sugar and butter until light and fluffy. Add bananas. Place soda in hot water.

2. Add dissolved soda, eggs, lemon juice, ½ cup chopped nuts, and flour. Stir just enough to combine ingredients.

3. Line bottom of glass loaf pan with wax paper. Spread batter into glass loaf pan and sprinkle with ¼ cup chopped nuts.

4. Shield ends of glass loaf pan with 2-inch wide strips of foil, covering 1 inch of batter and molding around the ends of the glass loaf pan. Place loaf pan on inverted saucer in microwave oven.

5. Microwave on 50% POWER FOR 10 to 11 MINUTES or until set. Remove foil from ends of loaf pan.

6. Microwave on HIGH FOR 2 to 3 MINUTES or until toothpick inserted near center comes out clean. Let stand 5 to 10 minutes before removing from loaf pan.

Tony Chachere's Microwave Cajun Country Cookbook

Strawberry Bread

3 cups all-purpose flour
2 cups sugar
1 teaspoon ground cinnamon
1 teaspoon salt
1 teaspoon soda

4 eggs
1¼ cups Wesson oil
1 cup chopped pecans
2 (10-ounce) packages frozen
    strawberries, thawed

Preheat oven to 350 degrees. In large mixing bowl, sift together flour, sugar, cinnamon, salt, and baking soda. Set aside. In small bowl, beat eggs and Wesson oil. Add pecans and strawberries. Add strawberry mixture to dry ingredients. Grease and flour two 9×5×3-inch loafpans; pour mixture in loafpans and bake at 350 degrees for 1 hour. (Bake 45 to 50 minutes for smaller pans.) Yield: 2 large loaves or 4 small loaves.

Foods à la Louisiane

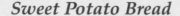

Sweet Potato Bread

½ cup butter
½ cup granulated sugar
¾ cup brown sugar
2 eggs, beaten
1 cup flour

1 teaspoon baking powder
1 teaspoon cinnamon
1 teaspoon nutmeg
⅛ teaspoon salt
3 cups grated raw sweet potatoes

Cream butter and sugars in large mixing bowl. Blend in eggs. Add flour, baking powder, cinnamon, nutmeg and salt. Fold in grated sweet potatoes. Pour into a well-greased 8-inch black iron skillet. Bake in preheated 350-degree oven 1 hour or until tester comes out clean. Yield: 6–8 servings.

Voilà! Lafayette Centennial Cookbook 1884–1984

Sweet Rice Cakes
(Belles Calas Tout Chauds, old recipe)

½ cup rice
½ cake dissolved yeast
½ cup sugar
½ teaspoon nutmeg

3 cups boiling water
3 eggs, well beaten
1 heaping tablespoon flour
Powdered sugar

Cook a half cup of rice in the boiling water until mushy. When cold, mash well and mix in a half-cake of dissolved yeast. Set to rise overnight.

The next morning, add the eggs, continue beating, and add the sugar and spoonful of flour. Beat into a thick batter. Let it rise for 15 minutes, then add ½ teaspoon nutmeg. From a large spoon, drop the batter a spoonful at a time into hot lard (400 degrees F.) and fry. When brown, take out, drain, and wrap in cloth to keep hot.

Sprinkle with powdered sugar and serve with *café au lait* for breakfast.

The old cala women used to take them piping hot, wrapped in a clean towel, in a basket through the streets, crying, *"Belles calas, tout chauds!"*

Louisiana Keepsake

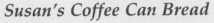

Susan's Coffee Can Bread

4 cups flour, unsifted
1 package dry yeast
½ cup water
½ cup milk
1 stick oleo

¼ cup sugar
1 teaspoon salt
2 eggs, beaten
Shortening

Mix 2 cups flour with yeast. Combine water, milk, oleo, sugar and salt; heat till oleo melts; cool 5 minutes. Add to flour and yeast mixture; add eggs and remaining flour. Dough will be stiff. Knead on floured board till smooth and elastic. Grease 2 (1-pound) coffee cans; divide dough in ½; place in cans. Cover with plastic tops. Let rise to ½ inch from top of can. Remove lid. Bake 350 degrees 35–40 minutes. Brush tops of bread with shortening. Remove from cans. Serve hot or cold. Easily made!

Encore

Challa
(Egg Twist Bread)

3 ounces yeast
2½ cups warm water
1 cup oil
1 teaspoon salt

5 eggs
1 cup sugar
5 pounds plain flour

Dissolve yeast in lukewarm water. Add sugar, salt and oil. Mix well. Add flour and knead until smooth and satiny. Place in large bowl. Grease top of dough lightly. Cover with waxed paper and let rise in warm place until triple in size.

Break off baseball-sized pieces, 3 at a time. Roll each into a banana-shaped piece and plait the 3 together. Place in greased pan and allow to rise for one hour more until doubled in size.

Beat 1 egg and brush tops of loaves. Sprinkle with poppy seeds (optional). Bake in 350-degree oven until brown. Makes 8 to 9 loaves.

The Best of South Louisiana Cooking

Rural Homestead Cornbread

1½ cups cornmeal	½ teaspoon salt
½ cup flour	3–5 tablespoons fat*
2 teaspoons baking powder	Approximately 1 cup plus 2
1 teaspoon sugar	tablespoons milk**

Sift all the dry ingredients together. Add enough milk to make the mixture soupy. Too little milk makes the bread dry. Melt fat in a 9-inch skillet. Pour half into the cornbread. Pour mixture into the hot skillet. Bake 450 degrees for about 25 minutes. Serves 8.

*It takes a little more if you want to bake it in cornstick pans.
**Stoneground meal takes more milk than commercial meal.

Origin of "Homestead Cornbread":

Each spring, St. Francisville presents for the public a Pilgrimage, recreating the period when John James Audubon lived here and did at least 80 of his famous bird and wildlife folios.

One year it was decided that "crafts" of that era would be of great interest, and Dot Wilson, Chairman that year, invited me to serve on her committee. She asked if our family's wood-burning stove might be used in the craft display. I later suggested that it may be more authentic if we actually cooked on the stove.

Although the first cornbread was only for display, the demand to buy and taste was so great that at present we literally bake hundreds of cornbread sticks during the Pilgrimage.

Plantation Country

Corn Bread

1 cup yellow corn meal	1 teaspoon sugar
1 cup flour	1 slightly beaten egg
4 teaspoons baking powder	1 cup milk
¾ teaspoon salt	2 tablespoons melted shortening

Melt shortening in heavy skillet. Sift dry ingredients into bowl. Add the egg and milk and mix well. Pour into the same skillet and stir again to mix the shortening in with the batter. Bake at 425 degrees for 25 minutes.

Talk About Good!

Tony's Ole-Fashioned Creole Corn Bread

2 cups yellow cornmeal	1 cup cream style corn
1 cup all-purpose flour	1½ teaspoons salt (to taste)
1 cup sour cream	½ cup bacon fat
3 tablespoons baking powder	Milk
2 eggs	

Mix all ingredients together until well blended. Add enough milk to make the mixture pour easily. Place in greased muffin tins or baking pan. Place in preheated 400-degree oven until golden brown, about 20 to 30 minutes. Serve with butter and pure cane syrup (made in open kettle). Now you can sop your way to the Promised Land!

Tony Chachere's Cajun Country Cookbook

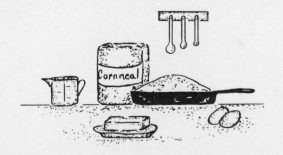

Gougère

2 cups milk	6 ounces plus 8 tablespoons
½ cup margarine, cut up	Gruyère or Swiss cheese
2 teaspoons salt	2 cups flour (sift before
Sprinkling of black pepper	measuring)
8 eggs	

Scald milk, cool and strain. Add margarine, salt, and black pepper. Bring mixture to rolling boil. Add all at once 2 cups sifted flour. Cook paste over low heat, beating briskly with wooden spoon until mixture forms ball and leaves sides of pan clean. Remove from heat. Beat in eggs, one at a time. When paste is shiny and smooth, mix in 6 ounces of Gruyère or Swiss cheese cut in fine cubes. Have ready two buttered cookie sheets. Use soup spoon to drop blobs, forming a circle on each sheet (about 12 blobs per sheet). With teaspoon put small blob on top. Brush with milk and sprinkle each circle with 4 tablespoons of finely diced cheese. Bake in preheated 375-degree oven for 45 minutes or until well puffed and brown.

This bread can be served as an hors d'oeuvre. Since this recipe makes 2 rings, I often make 1 ring, then make individual blobs to freeze (raw). However, the cooking time is different. I quick freeze on a cookie sheet and package in plastic bags. When ready to serve, remove from the freezer and place on buttered cookie sheet. Bake in preheated 425 degree oven for 10 minutes; reduce heat to 375 degrees and bake 15 or 20 minutes longer. Watch carefully as any recipe with cheese can burn. This baking time also applies to the frozen ring. As an hors d'oeuvre you may want to fill with a favorite ham or chicken mixture.

Turnip Greens in the Bathtub

Gougère—A pastry mixed with cheese which originated in Burgundy, France.

Jalapeño Hushpuppies
"The World's Best"

2 cups cornmeal
1 cup flour
2 eggs, beaten
3 teaspoons baking powder
1½ teaspoons salt
1 small can cream style corn

3 jalapeño peppers, chopped
¼ bell pepper, chopped
1 small onion, minced
Buttermilk
Pinch of soda

Mix all ingredients. Use enough buttermilk to make this the consistency of cornbread batter. Test batter by scooping up a portion on a spoon and with your thumb push portion into medium hot grease. *The object of this recipe is to have light, fluffy hushpuppies.* If heavy and do not rise enough, use more baking powder. If hushpuppies are greasy and break apart, add more flour. If you want more tang, add some jalapeno pepper juice.

The Cotton Country Collection

Hush Puppies for Seafood

1 cup flour
2 cups corn meal
2 tablespoons baking powder
1 egg
1 tablespoon sugar

1 teaspoon salt
1 tablespoon onions, finely
   chopped
Milk

Mix all ingredients with enough milk to make a thick dough. Wet fingers and roll into balls and fry in deep fat. Remove when brown.

Louisiana's Original Creole Seafood Recipes

Hush puppies—Fried cornmeal fritters. They usually accompany seafood.

Speidini

1 long loaf French bread
1 pound Mozzarella cheese,
  grated

½ pound bacon, fried and
  crumbled
1 stick butter, melted

Slice bread on diagonal into about 20 slices. Do not slice through the bottom crust. Place on long sheet of heavy foil and stuff the cheese and bacon into the slices. Pour the melted butter slowly over the bread. Wrap the foil to enclose the loaf and bake at 350 degrees about 25 minutes. Serves 8–10. Delicious with soup and a green salad.

Plantation Country

Herb Stix

4 slices bread
¼ cup butter, creamed
⅛ teaspoon thyme

⅛ teaspoon paprika
⅛ teaspoon salt
Dash cayenne pepper

Toast bread lightly on both sides. Mix creamed butter thoroughly with remaining ingredients. Spread on both sides of toast. Cut each slice into 5 strips. Bake on baking sheet at 250 degrees F. for about 20 minutes, or until crunchy. May be frozen, or kept in airtight container for several weeks. Makes 20 stix.

Good with soups, salads, or as cocktail food.

Pirate's Pantry

Cheese Soufflé Sandwiches

1 pound butter
4 (5-ounce) jars Kraft Old English
  cheese
1 teaspoon Tabasco
1 teaspoon onion powder
1½ teaspoons Lea and Perrins
  sauce

1 teaspoon Beau Monde
  seasoning
1½ teaspoons dill weed
2½ loaves thin sliced bread

Soften butter and cheese. Beat with a mixer until fluffy, then add rest of ingredients. Remove crusts from bread. Spread 3 slices with mixture and stack; spread sides and cut into 4 or 6 pieces. Spread cut sides and continue with remaining bread. Place on wax paper and freeze. Then place in plastic bags to store. When ready to use, place on cookie sheet and bake at 325 degrees until done. If thawed, bake for 10 to 15 minutes or until edges are brown: Yields 80 pieces.

The Cotton Country Collection

Mushroom Sandwiches

1 pound fresh mushrooms, sliced
3 tablespoons butter
1 tablespoon minced fresh
  parsley
3 tablespoons minced green
  onions

¼ teaspoon Worcestershire sauce
⅛ teaspoon Tabasco
1 teaspoon garlic salt
½ cup homemade mayonnaise
1 loaf very thin bread

Sauté mushrooms, parsley, and green onions in butter until most of the liquid has evaporated (about 5 minutes). Add Worcestershire, Tabasco, and garlic salt. Cool. Put mixture in food processor with the mayonnaise, and chop with the steel blade. Do not pureé.

Remove crusts from the bread, spread with the mixture, and cut into finger sandwiches. These will keep in the refrigerator for several hours if tightly sealed. Makes about 40 finger-size sandwiches.

Le Bon Temps

Sandwich Surprise

2 cups crumbled, crisp bacon
1 cup finely chopped or shaved
  pecans

¼ cup finely chopped or shaved
  bell pepper
Mayonnaise

Mix first 3 ingredients together. Add enough mayonnaise to bind
the mixture and to make it spreadable on bread. Terrific! Propor-
tions can vary according to individual taste. Yield: 10–12 sandwiches.

Talk About Good II

Po-Boys

1 large loaf New Orleans French
  bread (approximately 36 inches
  or about 1 meter)
36 large oysters

Cooking oil
Corn meal
Salt and pepper
Sliced lettuce and tomatoes

At least ½ hour before using, drain oysters. Flour with corn meal,
salt, and pepper. In large kettle, pour 3 inches (7.5 cm.) oil. Heat
to 390 degrees F (198 degrees C). Gently lower oysters and deep
fry until golden. Drain on absorbent paper and keep warm. Slice
bread lengthwise. Arrange lettuce and tomatoes on bottom slice.
Add oysters and cover with top slice. Slice loaf into 6 equal parts.
Serve with mayonnaise or tomato ketchup.

Note: If Shrimp Po-Boy is served, use:

36 fresh, peeled, deveined,
  medium shrimp

1 egg beaten with salt and pepper
  and 1 tablespoon (15 ml.) water

Dip shrimp in egg mixture. Dredge in bread crumbs. Deep fry in
same manner as oysters. Assemble Po-Boy as above. Leftover
cold roast beef can be used in same manner. Serves 6.

Favorite New Orleans Recipes

Opelousas Oyster Loaf
(Microwave)

Cooking Time: 3 minutes
                8 minutes to preheat skillet
Utensils: Microwave browning skillet
Yield: 4 to 6 servings

1 loaf French bread, unsliced	1 egg
1 dozen select oysters, large	½ cup cream
1 cup seasoned bread crumbs,	2 tablespoons cooking oil
can use crumbs from inside of	Dill pickles
loaf of French bread	Lemon
½ teaspoon salt	Catsup
¼ teaspoon pepper	Butter

1. Slice off top of the French bread and reserve. Scoop out insides and toast the bread under the broiler. Butter inside generously and wrap in terry cloth towel to keep warm.

2. Dry oysters on paper towel. In small bowl, combine salt, pepper, and egg. Beat well. Add cream and mix well. Place oysters in egg mixture.

3. Place bread crumbs in plastic bag, add oysters, and shake to coat each piece.

4. Preheat microwave browning skillet on HIGH FOR 8 MINUTES. Pour cooking oil into preheated skillet. Place oysters in oil.

5. Microwave on HIGH 1 MINUTE. Turn over.

6. Microwave on HIGH FOR 1 to 1½ MINUTES or until browned. Drain on paper towel. Fill in hollow of French bread with fried oysters. Garnish with sliced dill pickles, lemon wedges, and dabs of catsup. Replace top, wrap in terry towel, and place in microwave.

7. Microwave on 70% POWER FOR 45 to 60 SECONDS or until warm. Serve at once.

Tony Chachere's Microwave Cajun Country Cookbook

Soups
and Gumbos

Evangeline. St. Martin's Courtyard. St. Martinville.

Cream of Broccoli Soup
(Potage de broccoli à la crème)

1 quart chicken stock*
1 cup dry white wine
4 cups fresh broccoli
1 tablespoon lemon juice
½ teaspoon salt

½ teaspoon red pepper
1 tablespoon Worcestershire
  sauce
1 cup evaporated whole milk
8 teaspoons low fat oleo

Combine all ingredients, except oleo and milk, in saucepan. Bring to boil, then lower heat and simmer for about 1 hour, until broccoli spears fall apart. Allow to cool and purée in blender. When ready to serve, add oleo and milk. Heat just to boiling or until oleo is melted. Serve with thin slices of toasted French bread.

Total: 8 servings. Per serving: 130 calories
Exchanges per serving = 2 vegetables, 1 fat
10 grams carbohydrates, 4 grams protein, 5 grams fat, 5 grams alcohol

Cooking for Love and Life

*Use recipe from *Cooking for Love and Life*.

Cold Cucumber Soup

1 pint good chicken stock
  (preferably homemade, the
  kind that jells)
2 large cucumbers, peeled,
  seeded, cut in chunks
1 piece of onion, size of a golf
  ball, cut in chunks
¼ teaspoon tarragon

Freshly ground pepper
Salt
1 small (8-ounce) carton sour
  cream
Chives, chopped or parsley,
  chopped
Paprika

Place first 6 ingredients in blender; blend well. Leave in blender. Chill. Just before serving, blend again; add sour cream; blend. Serve in chilled cups garnished with chopped parsley, chives or paprika.

At the point where mixture has been blended and before the sour cream has been added, freeze for later use. Make use of a bountiful cucumber crop!

Encore

Cauliflower Soup
(Microwave)

Cooking Time: 21 minutes
Utensils: Paper plate
         3-quart casserole
Servings: Makes 8 cups

**1 medium head cauliflower (1½–2
  pounds)**

1. Rinse, then place whole cauliflower on a small paper plate. Cover cauliflower and plate with plastic wrap. Microwave on HIGH (100%) 4 MINUTES. Turn cauliflower package over and continue to cook on HIGH (100%) 4 MINUTES. Keep covered while preparing the next step.

1 cup onion, chopped
½ cup celery, chopped
3½ cups chicken stock or 2
  (13¾-ounce) cans chicken broth
½ cup water

1 teaspoon salt
1 teaspoon celery salt
¼ teaspoon white pepper
1 teaspoon Worcestershire sauce

2. Wilt onion and celery in a 3-quart casserole covered with plastic wrap on HIGH (100%) 3 MINUTES. Add chicken stock, water, salt, celery salt, white pepper and Worcestershire sauce. Cut cauliflower in flowerets and add to liquid. Cover and microwave on HIGH (100%) 8 MINUTES. Pour a small amount of hot mixture into blender and purée until all is blended. Return soup to the 3-quart casserole.

**1½ cups light cream or
  evaporated milk**

3. Stir in light cream and microwave on HIGH (100%) 2 MINUTES or until hot.

Tout de Suite à la Microwave II

Red Bean Soup

2 cups dried red kidney beans
¼ cup butter
1 medium onion, finely chopped
3 cloves garlic, finely chopped
2 ribs celery, finely chopped
1 tablespoon Worcestershire
 sauce
1 bay leaf
1 teaspoon dried thyme leaves
½ pound ham, finely ground
Salt and pepper to taste
½ cup claret wine
2 hard-boiled eggs, finely
 chopped
1 lemon, thinly sliced

Soak the beans overnight in 1 quart of water. In a heavy Dutch oven melt the butter over medium heat. Add the onion, garlic, and celery and sauté until brown. Add 2 quarts of water, beans, Worcestershire sauce, bay leaf, and thyme. Simmer for 2 hours, or until the water has reduced to 1 quart. Strain the mixture and reserve the liquid. Force the beans through a sieve. Return the beans and liquid to the pot. Add the ham, salt, and pepper and simmer for 5 to 10 minutes. Pour the soup into a heated tureen. Stir in the wine and garnish with the chopped egg and lemon slices. Serves 6–8.

La Bonne Cuisine

Curried Lima Bean Soup

1 (10-ounce) package frozen lima
 beans
2 tablespoons butter or margarine
⅓ cup sliced green onions
1 teaspoon curry powder
½ teaspoon salt
⅛ teaspoon pepper
½ teaspoon tarragon
4 sprigs parsley
1½ cups chicken broth
½ cup cream

In a saucepan combine beans, butter, onions and curry powder with the amount of water directed on package and cook until soft. Purée in blender with salt, pepper, tarragon and parsley. Return to saucepan, add chicken broth and cream, and heat gently. Serve hot or cold. Louisianians often serve appetizer soups in a *demitasse* before coming to the table. Yield: 28 ounces.

Louisiana Entertains

Corn And Crabmeat Soup
(Acadian)

1 pound lump crabmeat	1 cup fresh yellow corn
¼ cup butter	¼ cup all-purpose flour
2 cups chicken stock	2 cups half-and-half cream
Salt and pepper	Garlic powder

Canned or frozen corn may be used. Cut fresh corn from cob and save scrapings and milk. Set aside. Melt butter in saucepan. Add flour and blend well. Add chicken stock, stirring constantly. Cook until thick and smooth. Stir-in cream, crabmeat, corn and seasonings. Cook over low fire until corn is tender.

The Best of South Louisiana Cooking

Clam Chowder

4 medium potatoes, pared and sliced	3 cups milk
¼ pound bacon or 3 tablespoons bacon drippings	1 cup bottled clam juice or substitute additional cup of milk
1 cup chopped onion	3 (6-ounce) cans minced clams, undrained
1 cup chopped celery	
5 tablespoons margarine or butter	½ teaspoon thyme
5 tablespoons flour	Salt and pepper to taste

Using a 3-quart pot, cover potatoes with salted water, boil until done, 10–15 minutes, and drain. While potatoes cook, fry bacon in large pot until crisp. Set bacon aside on toweling to drain and retain drippings to wilt, do not brown, onions and celery over medium heat. When onions and celery are soft, add butter, mix in flour, add milk and clam juice and stir constantly until thickened. Add boiled potatoes, clams, thyme, salt and pepper. Heat thoroughly. *Do not boil.* Serve hot and garnish with bacon bits. Serves 4–6.

Talk About Good II

Turtle Soup

1 gallon hot water
5 pounds turtle meat cut into
   cubes 1-inch thick
1½ cups flour
1½ cups oil
5 chopped onions
1 block butter
1 small jar sweet pickles
1 small jar sour pickles
3 chopped bell peppers

1 small jar of Heintz chow chow
1 pack chopped green onions
1 package chopped celery
4 garlic pods (not chopped)
3 lemons (chop peeling fine) use
   juice to taste
4 bay leaves
Lea & Perrins sauce
Salt & pepper to taste

Using flour and oil, make roux and brown well. Add turtle meat and cook well so that water evaporates. Add onions and let fry with meat. Add water gradually. Add block of butter. Next, add celery, green onions, bell peppers, garlic, bay leaves, lemon peel chopped fine, pickles, chow chow, and salt and pepper to taste. If soup is too dark, add a few tablespoons of tomato paste. Just before serving, add a few tablespoons of Lea & Perrins sauce.

The Encyclopedia of Cajun and Creole Cuisine

Catfish Courtbouillon (Coo-Bee-Yon)

1 large (3 to 6 pound) catfish
8 medium onions, chopped
4 cups green onions, chopped
1 cup celery, chopped
½ cup chopped bell pepper
1 clove garlic, chopped fine
½ cup parsley, finely chopped
   (using dried parsley, use ¼
   cup)

1 cup flour
½ cup olive oil
Salt and pepper (black and
   cayenne pepper)
2 cups water

Heat cooking oil. Add flour and brown. Add chopped seasoning. Simmer 1 hour. Cut up fish in large pieces. Season with salt and both peppers. Add to the above sauce. Add water. Cover and cook over low heat about 1 hour. Serve over rice. Serves 6 to 8.

The Justin Wilson Cook Book

Courtbouillon—A fish soup or stew cooked with vegetables and served over rice.

Oyster-Artichoke Soup

1 stick butter	1 teaspoon red pepper flakes
2 bunches green onions	1 teaspoon anise seed
2 garlic cloves	1 teaspoon salt
3 (8 to 10 count) cans artichoke hearts	1 tablespoon Worcestershire sauce
3 tablespoons flour	1 quart oysters
4 cans chicken stock	

In a 4-quart heavy pot, melt butter and sauté chopped green onions and garlic until soft. Wash and drain artichokes; cut each into 4 pieces and add to onions. Sprinkle with flour and stir to coat well. *Do not brown.* Add chicken stock, red pepper, anise seed, salt, and Worcestershire. Simmer for about 15 minutes. While mixture cooks, drain oysters, reserve the liquor, and check oysters for shells. To chop oysters put in blender and without removing hand from switch, turn motor on and off twice. Add oysters and oyster liquor to pot; simmer for about 10 minutes. *Do not boil.* This soup improves with age. Make it at least 8 hours before serving. Refrigerate; reheat to serve. Keeps well for 2 to 3 days. This is excellent served in mugs for an appetizer. Serves 8 for first course. Fantastic!

The Cotton Country Collection

Artichoke Soup

3 (14-ounce) cans artichoke hearts, drained	1 pint whipping cream
3 (10¾-ounce) cans cream of mushroom soup	2 cups chicken broth
	½ cup dry white wine
	6 drops hot pepper sauce

Place about ⅓ of the artichokes in the bottom of a blender or food processor. In a large bowl, combine the soup, whipping cream, broth, white wine, and hot pepper sauce. Add part of this liquid mixture to the artichokes and blend until puréed. Repeat with remaining artichokes and liquid until all has been puréed. Pour puréed soup into a large saucepan and heat over a low heat. Serve hot. Yield: 6 to 8 servings.

Note: People will think you spent hours in the kitchen preparing this soup.

From A Louisiana Kitchen

Green Onion and Potato Soup

2 bunches green onions, chopped
4 medium-sized potatoes, peeled
  and diced
3 tablespoons butter or margarine
3 tablespoons flour

2 quarts water
Cream (1 tablespoon per each
  plate)
Salt and pepper to taste

Sauté the green onions in the butter for 5 minutes. Add the flour and stir, mixing well. Slowly pour in the water; bring the mixture to a boil. Add the potatoes, salt, and pepper. Cook until the potatoes are tender (about 20 to 25 minutes).

When ready to serve, put about 1 tablespoon of cream in the bottom of each plate and pour the soup over it. Serves 6 to 8.

La Bouche Creole

Susie's Onion Soup

4 or 5 large onions
3 tablespoons butter
¼ teaspoon peppercorn, crushed
  (if available)
1 tablespoon flour
3 cans condensed beef broth
2 cans water

6 to 8 slices French bread toasted
  (top each slice with a pat of
  butter)
1 cup grated Swiss cheese or ½
  cup grated Swiss and ½ cup
  grated Mozzarella

1. Chop onions. Heat butter in heavy saucepan. Add onions and peppercorns. Cook stirring frequently until onions are light brown.

2. Sprinkle onions with flour. Cook 1 minute, stirring constantly. Add beef broth and water. Bring to a boil. Then simmer for 30–40 minutes. Correct seasoning.

3. While soup is simmering, toast bread and grate the cheese.

4. Turn soup into oven-proof soup tureen. Place toast on top and sprinkle with cheese. Place broiler at 400 degrees until cheese turns golden.

Plantation Country

Roux

LSU's yearbook is named *The Gumbo* for the state's most famous soup. Gumbo is more than a soup. It is a meal made of bits of either seafood, game or fowl and creole seasonings cooked together and served over rice. There are as many ways to make gumbo in Louisiana as there are cooks, but basically gumbo is of two types, depending upon whether it is thickened with okra or filé powder. Okra, an African vegetable, came to Louisiana with the Negro slaves. The Choctaw Indians, natives of the swamp land, ground sassafras leaves to make the filé powder. The settlers concocted the soups thickened with both ingredients. Perhaps you will want to try both, but first, you make a roux. Not only gumbos but many other creole dishes begin with a roux. A recipe follows.

3 tablespoons (45 ml) bacon drippings or shortening
3 tablespoons (45 ml) flour

Heavy black iron pot or heavy skillet

Melt fat in heavy skillet and stir in flour. Continue to stir over low heat until flour is dark brown. (The slow dry heat fragments the starch molecules in the flour and develops a nutlike flavor that gives body to soups and stews. It also reduces thickening power of the flour.) A roux is used as a base for most creole dishes. The quantity of fat and oil may vary from recipe to recipe, but the method of cooking remains the same.

'Tiger Bait' Recipes

Buster's Famous Creole Gumbo

1 stick margarine
1 cup chopped onions
½ cup chopped green peppers
3 cloves garlic, minced
3 quarts water
2 green onions, chopped
1 tablespoon Worcestershire
2 tablespoons Louisiana hot
  sauce

4 cleaned crabs, quartered
2 pounds peeled shrimp
2 dozen oysters
1 pound smoked bite-size
  sausage
½ cup chopped chicken gizzards
Filé

In a large pot sauté vegetables in margarine. Add all ingredients except seafood. Make roux and add to desired thickness. Cook 1 hour. Add seafood. Cook 30 minutes. Serve over rice with a dash of filé.

The Buster Holmes Restaurant Cookbook

Creole Crab Gumbo

1 pound cooked crab meat
1 pound okra, cut up
½ cup sliced onion
4 tablespoons butter
4 tablespoons flour
5 cups canned tomatoes

1 cup diced green pepper
2 garlic cloves, crushed
1 teaspoon ground nutmeg
2 teaspoons salt
Freshly ground black pepper

Sauté onion in butter 10 minutes. Stir in flour and brown. Add crab meat and other ingredients plus 2 cups water. Bring to a boil, reduce heat, cover, simmer for 1 hour. Serves 6.

Louisiana's Original Creole Seafood Recipes

Z'herbes Gumbo

1 pound pickled pork
1 cabbage
2 large bunches fresh spinach
1 bunch turnip tops
1 bunch mustard greens
1 heaping tablespoon vegetable
  shortening

2 tablespoons flour
2 large onions, chopped
4 cloves garlic, chopped
2 tablespoons vinegar
1 pod hot red pepper, chopped
Salt and pepper to taste

Cover salt meat with water to boil until tender (salt meat and pickled pork are the same). At the same time, break up the cabbage, stem spinach, turnip tops and mustard greens and put them in the pot with enough water to cover. When the greens are cooked to tenderness, place in a colander and drain. After well drained, chop very fine. Place a deep iron pot on the fire. When it is hot, add the vegetable shortening and stir in the flour slowly to make a dark roux. Add chopped onions and garlic and brown. Put in the chopped salt meat and add the greens. Allow to cook 5 minutes, stirring all the time. Add 1½ quarts of water and let cook slowly until it becomes a thick purée. Put in vinegar, a pod of red pepper broken up and salt to taste. Serve with grits. Yield: 6 servings.

The Shadows-on-the-Teche Cookbook

Seafood Gumbo

Cooking Time: Roux—12 minutes
     Gumbo—45 minutes
Utensils: 4-cup glass measuring cup
   5-quart dish
Servings: 10–12

ROUX:
⅔ cup flour
⅔ cup oil

1. Mix flour and oil together in a 4-cup measure. Microwave on HIGH 6½ TO 7 MINUTES. Stir. Roux will be dark caramel.

2 cups onion, chopped   **½ cup green bell pepper,**
1 cup celery, chopped   **chopped**

2. Add onion, celery and pepper. Sauté on HIGH 3 MINUTES. Stir.

½ cup green onion tops, chopped
¼ cup parsley, chopped
4 cloves garlic, minced

3. Add onion, parsley and garlic. Sauté on HIGH 2 MINUTES. Add hot water to bring mixture to 4-cup mark. Pour into a 5-quart dish.

1½ quarts hot water
1 tablespoon salt
1 teaspoon cayenne pepper

4. Add hot water, salt and pepper. Cover and cook on HIGH 15 MINUTES.

2 pounds shrimp, raw and peeled **1 pint oysters with liquid**
1 pound crabmeat or 8 small
 boiled and cleaned crabs

5. Add shrimp and crab. Cover and cook on MEDIUM 20 MINUTES. Add oysters and liquid—cook on MEDIUM 10 MINUTES. Serve with rice and filé.

Put away the heavy black iron pot.

Tout de Suite à la Microwave I

Seafood Gumbo II

½ cup salad oil
½ cup flour
1 large onion, chopped
2 to 3 garlic cloves, minced
1 (1-pound) can tomatoes, undrained
1½ pounds frozen okra or equivalent fresh
Oil for frying okra
2 quarts hot water
3½ tablespoons salt

¾ teaspoon red pepper
1 large bay leaf
¼ teaspoon thyme
8 to 10 allspice berries
Few grains chili pepper
2 pounds headless raw shrimp, peeled
1 pound claw crab meat, picked
1 pint oysters
½ cup chopped green onions
½ cup chopped parsley

Make a very dark roux in a large heavy pot. Add onions and garlic. Cook slowly until onions are transparent. Add tomatoes and cook on low heat until oil rises to the top (about 30 minutes) stirring frequently. In separate skillet, fry okra in oil on moderately high heat, stirring constantly until okra is no longer stringy. Add the okra to the other mixture, stir and simmer about 10 minutes. Add water, salt and pepper. Simmer partially covered for 45 minutes. Add other seasonings and simmer an additional 20 minutes, then add shrimp—simmer 15 minutes; then add crab meat, simmering 15 minutes more. Add the oysters the last 5 minutes of cooking. Taste carefully for seasoning, adding more if necessary. Remove from fire and stir in green onions and parsley. Serve over rice. Variations may be made by adding different seafoods, sausages or poultry. Serves 8 to 10.

River Road Recipes II

Chicken-Andouille Gumbo A La Rosina

1 large stewing chicken
*1 pound andouille, sliced in
  ¼-inch slices (gumbo sausage)
6 large white or yellow onions,
  chopped
1 small bunch green onions, cut
  fine
1 small bell pepper, chopped
1 tablespoon chopped celery

1 tablespoon finely chopped
  parsley
1 clove garlic, chopped
Salt, black pepper and red
  cayenne pepper
¾ cup all-purpose flour (for roux)
1 cup cooking oil
6 cups hot water

Cut up chicken, wash and season with salt and pepper. Heat 1 cup oil in heavy skillet and fry chicken until brown. Remove chicken and put aside. Pour remaining oil into large heavy pot for making roux.

After roux is made, lower heat and add all chopped ingredients, except green onions, garlic, and parsley. Cover and simmer until onions are clear, stirring occasionally.

Add sliced andouille and chicken to roux mixture, cover and let simmer about ½ hour. Stir often during this process. Keep heat low through this point.

Add water, garlic, parsley and green onions. You may increase heat until mixture begins to boil. Now lower heat to simmer, cover and cook 1½ to 2 hours or until chicken is tender.

This has a lot of liquid and is served on rice, over which ¼ teaspoon filé has been sprinkled. It's even better next day.

Variations: This same recipe may be used for duck, rabbit, squirrel. In making seafood gumbo, such as shrimp, crab or oysters, the only exception, of course, is that there will be no frying of the particular seafood being used.

*You are probably wondering what andouille is. Well, I'm gonna tell you. It is a special sausage we French people make, of chopped pork and seasoned especially for use in gumbo. It is pronounced "ohn-dewey." Ask your butcher to get you some. You'll love it. If for some reason, your butcher was not educate in south Louisiana, an' he don' know somethin' about andouille, forgot about it—an' him. You gonna have damn good gumbo anyhow.

The Justin Wilson Cook Book

Lenten Shrimp & Egg Gumbo

¾ cup vegetable oil
¾ cup all-purpose flour
2 medium onions, finely chopped
1½ bell peppers, finely chopped
3 large cloves garlic, minced
1 pound raw shrimp with shells
1 bay leaf and onion peelings
Cheesecloth

3½ quarts water
1½ tablespoons salt
1½ teaspoons cayenne pepper
½ teaspoon black pepper
10 hard cooked, peeled eggs
¼ cup chopped green onion
¼ cup chopped parsley

Heat oil in Dutch oven and add flour. Stir to make a dark brown roux. Add onion, bell pepper and garlic. Cook until vegetables are soft. Peel shrimp. Wrap shells in cheesecloth square with onion peelings and bay leaf. Tie securely. Place shells along with 3½ quarts water in large pot. Bring to boil and boil 20 minutes. Discard bag of shells and add shrimp stock slowly to roux. Add salt and pepper. Simmer 40 minutes. Add shrimp and simmer 10 minutes. Add peeled whole eggs. Simmer 5 minutes. Check seasoning and add green onion and parsley. Yield: 10 servings.

Voilà! Lafayette Centennial Cookbook 1884–1984

Ray Hay's Gumbo for a Crowd

ROUX:
12 cups flour
5 cups Wesson Oil

Heat oil first, then add flour as needed. Stir constantly until dark brown, being careful not to burn.

6 pounds onions	16 bay leaves
3 stalks of celery	1⁶⁄₁₀ can crushed whole tomatoes
2 pounds bell pepper	8 pounds okra
4 bunches of green onions	5 gallons water
4 ounces granulated garlic	10 pounds shrimp
12 ounces salt	6 pounds dark crab meat
¼ ounce ground red pepper	¼ cup Kitchen Bouquet
8 tablespoons gumbo file'	

Chop all vegetables. Put green onion in ½ cup of oil, let cook for 2 minutes. Then put all vegetables except okra into large pot. Add pepper, salt and garlic, then roux, and turn butter on high. Let this cook for 15 to 20 minutes, stirring constantly. Add 1 gallon of water at a time until 5 gallons have been added, stirring constantly. Let boil, then add okra, shrimp, crab meat, bay leaves, and Kitchen Bouquet. Let cook slowly for 3–4 hours. Makes 12 gallons.

The Encyclopedia of Cajun and Creole Cuisine

 Filé—A kind of powder made from sassafras leaves, it is added to gumbo just before serving to thicken the liquid.

Jambalayas,
Dressings,
Pasta, Quiches

Indian Creek Resevoir. Woodworth, south of Alexandria.

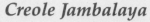

Creole Jambalaya

1½ pounds raw, peeled and deveined shrimp
2 tablespoons margarine or butter
¾ cup onion, chopped
½ cup celery, chopped
¼ cup green pepper, chopped
1 tablespoon parsley, chopped
1 clove garlic, minced
2 cups fully cooked ham, cubed
1 (28-ounce) can tomatoes, undrained, cut up

1 (10½-ounce) beef broth plus 1 can water
1 cup uncooked long grain rice
1 teaspoon sugar
½ teaspoon dried thyme leaves, crushed
½ teaspoon chili powder
¼ teaspoon pepper

1. Melt margarine in Dutch oven. Add onion, celery, green pepper, parsley and garlic. 2. Cover and cook until tender. 3. Add remaining ingredients, except shrimp. 4. Cover and simmer 25 minutes or until rice is tender. 5. Add shrimp and simmer uncovered to desired consistency and until shrimp are cooked, about 5 or 10 minutes. 6. Makes 6 to 8 servings.

Editor's Note: Jambalaya, a traditional "Louisiana dish" grew out of early French and Spanish Louisiana. (Jambalaya comes from jamba which means ham [but not necessarily] and Spanish paella.) Jambalaya is cooked in big black iron pots—originally for boiling syrup from sugar cane. Jambalaya is always cooked over an open wood fire outdoors, and boat oars are used for stirring. Don't let that deter you, jambalaya can be cooked at home on the range. It's a lot easier.

Louisiana Largesse

Jambalaya—A Creole dish of seasoned rice mixed with meat or seafood in which rice is the main ingredient.

Duck and Sausage Jambalaya

¼ cup cooking oil
3 large or 4 small ducks
2 pounds pork sausage links
3 large onions (cut into large pieces)
½ cup chopped celery
1 stick butter
½ cup chopped bell pepper
½ cup green onion tops
2 tablespoons chopped fresh parsley
½ teaspoon salt
½ teaspoon pepper
4 cups cooked rice

Cut ducks into serving pieces and cut sausage into ½-inch lengths. In a Dutch oven or large cooker, cook sausage until brown on both sides. Remove sausage. Salt and pepper duck pieces. Brown duck pieces on all sides. Add onions, celery and sausage to cooker. Cover and cook on low fire for 30 minutes, stirring occasionally. Add bell pepper, green onion tops and butter. Stir well and cook covered 15 minutes longer on low fire. Add rice, parsley, salt and pepper. Mix well. Cover and cook very low for 30 minutes. Serves 8.

Paul Naquin's French Collection III—Louisiana Wild Game

Turkey Jambalaya

2 tablespoons salad oil
1 cup green pepper, chopped
1 cup onion, chopped
1 clove garlic, minced
2 teaspoons salt
Pepper to taste
2 teaspoons (or more) Worcestershire
¼ teaspoon thyme or marjoram, or both
3 cups water
1½ cups uncooked rice
1 to 2 cups cubed cooked turkey or chicken
1 to 2 cups cubed cooked ham
1 small can mushrooms

Heat oil and cook green pepper, onion, and garlic until tender. Stir in seasonings and water and simmer for 10 minutes. Mix in rice, turkey, and ham. Cook covered over low heat for 25 minutes or until rice is done. Add mushrooms with a little of their liquid. Cook about 5 minutes longer. Serves 6.

River Road Recipes I

Shrimp and Eggplant Jambalaya
(Microwave)

Cooking Time: 35 minutes
Utensils: Clay simmer pot (3-quart)
Yield: 6 to 8 Servings

2 tablespoons oil
1 medium eggplant, peeled and diced
½ cup chopped onions
½ chopped celery
½ cup chopped bell pepper
1 clove garlic, chopped

2 cups water (warm)
1 (16-ounce) can whole tomatoes
2 teaspoons salt
½ teaspoon pepper
1 cup raw rice
1 pound peeled shrimp

1. Soak the clay simmer pot in cold tap water for 10 minutes.

2. In bottom of the clay simmer pot, combine oil, eggplant, onions, celery, bell pepper, and garlic. Mix well.

3. Microwave on HIGH FOR 5 to 6 MINUTES or until soft but not brown. Add warm water, tomatoes, salt, and pepper. Cover with water-soaked lid of clay simmer pot.

4. Microwave on HIGH FOR 10 MINUTES or until water boils. Add rice and shrimp. Stir well and cover with lid of clay simmer pot.

5. Microwave on 50% POWER FOR 20 to 25 MINUTES or until rice and shrimp are done. Let stand, covered, 5 minutes before serving.

Tony Chachere's Microwave Cajun Country Cookbook

Chicken and Sausage Jambalaya

1 small fryer
1 rib celery with leaves
1 onion, halved
1 clove garlic
2 cups converted long grain rice
1 pound smoked sausage, sliced
   into ½-inch pieces
1 pound ham, cubed
½ stick butter
1 cup chopped yellow onion

¾ cup chopped green pepper
¼ cup chopped fresh parsley
2 cloves garlic, minced
1 (6-ounce) can tomato paste
1 large bay leaf
¼ teaspoon thyme
2 teaspoons salt
½ teaspoon pepper
¼ teaspoon Tabasco

In a large pot, cover chicken with water; add celery, onion, garlic; boil until tender, about 1 hour. Reserve stock. Remove meat from bones. In 5 cups stock, cook rice until all liquid is absorbed, about 25 minutes.

In a Dutch oven, fry sausage and ham until lightly browned, about 3 to 5 minutes. Remove meat. Add butter to pan and sauté onion, pepper, and parsley until tender, about 3 minutes. Add chicken, sausage, and ham; stir in garlic, tomato paste, bay leaf, thyme, salt, pepper, and Tabasco. Add rice and mix thoroughly. Cook over low heat 15 minutes, stirring frequently. Remove bay leaf and serve. Serves 8 to 10.

Jambalaya

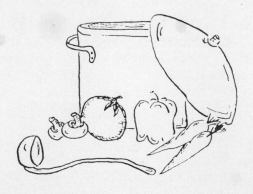

Rice Dressing with Oysters

2 tablespoons shortening
Giblets from fowl, chopped
1 package frozen chicken livers, chopped
2 large onions, chopped
3 large ribs celery, chopped
1 small bell pepper, chopped
½ cup chopped green onions
¼ cup chopped parsley

Salt, red pepper, black pepper, sage to taste
Thyme, bay leaf and basil, optional
25 to 100 oysters, as desired
1½ cups raw rice
1 egg, beaten
Corn meal for frying oysters

Fry chopped livers and giblets until brown. Fry onions, celery, bell peppers and fry with giblets until light brown. Add a cup of liquid (use oyster liquid as part) and cook covered on a low fire until tender. Roll oysters in corn meal and fry. Drain. Add oysters, parsley and onion tops to first ingredients. Season somewhat highly to take care of rice to be added. Cook rice. Add cooked rice and beaten egg; mix into dressing. Serve hot.

Louisiana's Original Creole Seafood Recipes

Eggplant Rice Dressing

2 medium eggplants (2 pounds), peeled and diced
1 large onion, chopped
1 cup chopped celery
2 medium bell peppers, chopped
8 cloves garlic, minced
1 teaspoon salt

1 cup water
3 cups cooked rice
1½ pounds ground pork
2 teaspoons salt
1 teaspoon black pepper
½ teaspoon red pepper
Bread crumbs for sprinkling

Boil eggplant, onion, celery, bell pepper, garlic, salt and water in Dutch oven until vegetables are tender. Cook rice in separate pot. Place meat in small skillet, brown in its own fat. Drain and add to cooked vegetables. Cook meat and vegetables to a thick consistency. Add rice, salt, black and red pepper. Place in buttered 2-quart round glass casserole dish. Sprinkle top with bread crumbs. Bake in preheated 350-degree oven 15 minutes. Yield: 12 servings. Microwave shortcut: After mixture has been placed in 2-quart glass dish, microwave on HIGH (100%) 4 MINUTES.

Voilà! Lafayette Centennial Cookbook 1884–1984

Dressing in a Skillet

¼ cup crumbled cornbread
¼ cup cooked rice
1 hardcooked egg, chopped
¼ cup chicken broth
Salt and pepper to taste

2 tablespoons chopped celery
1 tablespoon chopped onion
2 tablespoons butter
½ teaspoon chopped parsley

Crumble cornbread in a medium-size bowl and combine with rice, egg and chicken broth. In a small skillet, sauté onion and celery in butter until onion is transparent. Add and mix all ingredients together. Brown slightly, stirring as it cooks—about 20 minutes in 350-degree oven or over medium heat on top of stove. If dressing becomes too dry, add a small amount of chicken broth or water. Serve with baked or boiled chicken pieces, cranberry sauce and vegetable of choice. Try this with 2 slices of stale bread or ½ cup croutons in place of cornbread. Serves 1–2.

Quickie Tip: Instant bouillon can be bought granulated as well as in cubes for making just the right amount of broth. One teaspoon instant bouillon granules or 1 bouillon cube added to 1 cup of boiling water equals 1 cup bouillon broth.

Quickies for Singles

Corn Bread Dressing

1 pound chicken gizzards
1 pound lean ground meat (½ pork and ½ beef)
2 sticks margarine
4 chopped onions
4 sticks chopped celery
2 cloves minced garlic
1 tablespoon Worcestershire sauce

2 (10-ounce) cans chicken bouillon
4 cups corn bread
½ cup chopped green onion tops
Tony's Creole Seasoning or salt and pepper

In a Dutch oven, fry meat in margarine until brown. Add onions, celery and garlic. Sauté five minutes; add bouillon soup, Worcestershire; season to taste. Bring to boil and simmer for 2 hours. Mix in 4 cups corn bread and ½ cup onion tops. Bring seasoning up to taste. Makes 10 servings. Tony's Special!

Tony Chachere's Cajun Country Cookbook

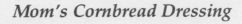

Mom's Cornbread Dressing

CORNBREAD:

1 cup (250 ml) yellow cornmeal
1 cup (250 ml) sifted all-purpose
 flour
4 teaspoons (20 ml) baking
 powder

½ teaspoon (2.5 ml) salt
1 egg
1 cup (250 ml) milk
¼ cup (60 ml) shortening

Preheat oven to 425 degrees F (220 degrees C). Sift dry ingredients together into a mixing bowl. Add egg, milk and shortening. Beat one minute at low speed of electric mixer or 300 vigorous strokes by hand. Bake in a greased 8-inch (20-cm) square baking pan for approximately 20 to 25 minutes. Let cornbread cool. The cornbread can be made a day in advance.

DRESSING:

1 cup (250 ml) chicken livers
½ cup (125 ml) chopped onion
½ cup (125 ml) chopped parsley
½ cup (125 ml) chopped green
 pepper
3 tablespoons (45 ml) margarine
 or butter
Crumbled cornbread from
 ingredients above

2 cups (500 ml) cooked rice
3 eggs, boiled and chopped
12 ounces (340 grams) oysters
1 cup (250 ml) chicken broth,
 more if needed
Salt and pepper to taste
Dash Tabasco, if desired
⅛ teaspoon (0.6 ml) monosodium
 glutamate, if desired

Boil chicken livers in enough water to cover for 10 minutes. Cool livers, then chop fine. Sauté onions, parsley and green peppers in margarine. Crumble cornbread fine and mix with cooked rice, chopped boiled eggs, sautéed vegetables, chopped livers and oysters. Add enough broth to form a very moist dressing. Season to taste. Bake at 325 degrees F (165 degrees C) in a shallow casserole for approximately 30 to 45 minutes.

Editors' Note: For a richer dressing, two raw eggs may be mixed into ingredients before baking.

'Tiger Bait' Recipes

Sausage Bread Dressing

Giblets from 18–22 pound turkey, cleaned
1 onion, peeled
2 ribs celery
2 pounds lean bulk sausage
½ cup butter or margarine
5 medium onions, finely chopped
1 large bell pepper, finely chopped
4 ribs celery, finely chopped
4 medium pods garlic, minced
1 bunch green onions, finely chopped (about ⅔ cup)
3 cups water
4 chicken bouillon cubes, dissolved in
3 cups boiling water
2 (8-ounce) bags bread stuffing mix
3 bay leaves, crushed
1 bunch parsley, chopped (about ¾ cup)
1 teaspoon pepper
2 teaspoons salt
¼ teaspoon thyme
2 eggs, beaten

Boil giblets with the peeled onion and celery in just enough water to cover. Cook for 1 hour, adding the liver during the last 15 minutes. Meanwhile, cook sausage in a large pot until just brown. Remove sausage with a slotted spoon, and drain off grease. Put in butter, along with the chopped onions, green pepper, celery, garlic, and green onions. Sauté until vegetables are limp.

Finely chop cooked giblets and return cup of them to the water in which they were boiled. (Reserve this for the gravy.) Add remaining giblets to sautéed seasonings, along with drained sausage, bouillon, stuffing mix, parsley, crushed bay leaves, pepper, salt, and thyme. Stir to blend well. Add beaten eggs and more broth (if the dressing seems too dry). The dressing may then be stuffed into an 18- to 22-pound turkey, or baked for 45 minutes at 350 degrees F. in a large casserole. Yields 24 servings.

Louisiana LEGACY

Fettucini Bun-Nutza

1 (16-ounce) package fettucini
  noodles
2 sticks butter
1 cup whipping cream
½ cup grated Parmesan cheese
½ cup Romano cheese

1 pint fresh mushrooms—caps
  only
¼ cup fresh parsley
Crushed garlic to taste
Salt and fresh black pepper to
  taste

Cook the noodles and set aside with 1 stick of butter. Whip the cream and add the Parmesan and Romano cheese. Sauté the mushroom caps with the other stick of butter. Mix the noodles, cream-cheese mixture and mushrooms and butter together; lightly mix. Add the parsley, garlic and salt and pepper to taste. Serve at once. Delicious. Serves 6.

La Meilleure de la Louisiane

Lenten Lasagna

2 tablespoons butter
2 tablespoons flour
2–3 green onions, chopped
2 cups milk or light cream
1 (16-ounce) carton cream style
  cottage cheese
1 egg

1 (12-ounce) package lasagne
  noodles, cooked, drained
1½ pounds white cheeses,
  assorted (Swiss, Mozzarella,
  Provolone, etc.)
1 cup mixed grated Parmesan and
  Romano cheeses

Preheat oven to 350 degrees F. In a saucepan, melt butter over low heat and stir in flour. Do not brown. Add onions and cook lightly. Cool slightly, then add milk, increase heat to medium, and cook, stirring, until thickened. Mix egg with cottage cheese in the carton. Pour a little sauce on the bottom of a 1–2-quart loaf pan. Layer half the noodles, white cheeses (in any order), cottage cheese, and Parmesan cheese, then repeat. Bake about 1 hour, covered, then remove cover and bake until brown on top. Serve hot. Serves 6–8.

No meat, but plenty of nutrition, flavor and heartiness! This will become a tradition at your house.

Louisiana LEGACY

Macaroni and Cheese
(Microwave)

Cooking time: 11 minutes
Utensil: 2-quart glass casserole
Servings: 4

1½ cups uncooked macaroni, #24
  large elbow
1 tablespoon dehydrated chopped
  onion
1½ tablespoon all-purpose flour
1 tablespoon pimiento, chopped

1 teaspoon salt
2 cups water
⅓ cup instant dry milk powder
2 tablespoons margarine
1 teaspoon paprika

1. In a 2-quart casserole combine dry macaroni, onion, flour, pimiento, salt, water, dry milk, margarine and paprika. Cover with a tight-fitting lid or plastic wrap. Microwave on HIGH (100%) 5–6 MINUTES until mixture boils. Stir and let stand covered 5 minutes.

1¼ cups processed Old English
  Cheddar cheese, shredded

2. Stir in cheese, cover and microwave on MEDIUM-HIGH (70%) 5 MINUTES. Stir then let stand covered 5 minutes before serving.

A speedy stir-together dish.

Tout de Suite à la Microwave II

Pasta Con Loga Laglie
(Pasta with Oil and Garlic)

Cook one package of pasta according to directions. Drain. Add 3 or 4 pods of garlic that have been mashed and 2 tablespoons oil. Stir in salt and lots of pepper. Toss. Serve immediately, topped with grated Italian cheese.

Chesta e Chida

Quiche Lorraine

½ pound bacon
1 large onion, chopped
3 eggs
1 (13-ounce) can evaporated milk
½ teaspoon salt
½ teaspoon dry mustard

Black pepper and cayenne pepper
  to taste
1 (10-inch) unbaked pie shell
½ pound Swiss cheese, grated
2 tablespoons butter

In skillet, brown bacon. Remove and crumble. In bacon grease, sauté onion until clear. Remove with slotted spoon. With fork, beat together eggs, milk and seasonings. Put bacon in bottom of pie shell. Put onions on top and then put a layer of Swiss cheese. Pour milk mixture over all and dot with butter. Bake at 375 degrees for 35 minutes or until brown and bubbly and crust is golden brown. Let stand 15 to 20 minutes before cutting. Good served either hot or cold. It is a perfect luncheon dish. Also good served in small wedges as an appetizer or baked in an oblong pan and cut into small squares as an hors d'oeuvre. Serves 6 as a main dish or 10 as an appetizer.

River Road Recipes II

Chicken Asparagus Quiche

2 unbaked (9-inch) pie shells
1½ pounds fresh asparagus or 2
  packages (10-ounce) frozen
  asparagus
2 green onions and tops, chopped
½ pound Swiss cheese, grated

2 cups cooked chicken, cut fine
1 (2-ounce) jar sliced pimientos
4 eggs, beaten
1½ cups light cream or
  homogenized milk
Salt and freshly ground pepper

Snap off and discard woody portion of fresh asparagus; cook in boiling salted water till tender crisp. If using frozen asparagus, cook according to directions; cook till tender crisp. Divide onions, Swiss cheese and chicken evenly between the 2 pie shells; cut asparagus spears so that each spear fits from the edge of the pie shell to the center. Arrange spears evenly in spoke fashion on top of quiche ingredients, tips to edge, ends to center. Sprinkle sliced pimiento among asparagus spears. Salt and pepper to taste. Combine eggs and milk, beating well. Pour over ingredients. Bake 375 degrees 40 minutes or till knife inserted comes out clean. Let stand 5 minutes before serving. Serves 8–10.

This is as pretty as it is good.

Encore

Seafood

The Toledo Bend Resevoir. Western Louisiana border.

Crawfish Étouffée

Along about June, M'sieu "Le Mud Bug" was just about ready to bid us goodbye for the season, fold his claws, and silently swim away. But before he left, we would gracefully move into summer with the euphoric feeling of having polished off a bowl or two of wonderful Creole *Crawfish Étouffée*. First, we had to get our "crawfish picking" hands on about 10 pounds of live crawfish.

Mamete, my mother, used to say that June crawfish were the hardest to peel and the most delicious to eat. It seemed that about this time of year, the shells got much thicker, making them more difficult to crack, but the crawfish were more mature and more full flavored. The more formidable the obstacle, the greater the reward.

To make this delicious étouffée, first you need 10 pounds of crawfish to boil. (If you don't want to start from scratch, you can begin with 1 pound of crawfish tails.) Wash the live crawfish well a couple of times, then leave them for about 15 minutes in salted water to "purge." Even before you start this, though, have the courtbouillon in which the crawfish will boil cooking on the stove. Put about 3 gallons of water in a pot and add to this 1 chopped onion, a few ribs of celery, 4 bay leaves, 1 chopped lemon, 1 teaspoon black pepper, ½ teaspoon cayenne or Tabasco, and ½ cup salt. Let this boil while you clean the crawfish.

When the crawfish are ready, dump them into the pot. Bring to a boil again, and cook for no longer than 10 minutes before you remove the crawfish. Cool the crawfish and peel. Set aside 1 cup of the courtbouillon for later. (If you decided to buy the crawfish tails from your friendly seafood dealer, ask him for about 1 pint of the water in which he made his crawfish "boils.")

To assemble the étouffée, first you need the crawfish, and also:

¼ pound butter	¼ teaspoon ground cloves
2 onions, chopped	¼ teaspoon chili powder
2 ribs celery, chopped	1 tablespoon lemon juice
3 toes garlic, minced	½ cup crawfish water
1 bell pepper, chopped	½ cup water
2 tablespoons flour	½ cup chopped green onions
1 tablespoon tomato paste	2 tablespoons minced parsley
¼ teaspoon thyme	Salt and pepper to taste
½ teaspoon basil	

CONTINUED

CONTINUED

First, melt the butter in a large, heavy skillet. Add the onions, celery, garlic, and bell pepper and sauté over low heat for about 20 minutes, or until the vegetables are very soft. Add the crawfish tails, tomato paste, thyme, basil, cloves, chili powder, lemon juice, crawfish water, and water. Mix well and cook for about 15 minutes. Add salt and pepper to taste. Cover and let simmer for another 10 minutes. Add the green onions and parsley.

Remove from the heat and let stand for about 10 minutes, covered, to allow the seasonings to blend. All you need now is some rice to serve it over and a hunk of crisp French bread.

La Bouche Creole

Crawfish Étouffée II

2 tablespoons butter
2 medium onions, chopped fine
2 bell peppers, chopped fine
4 ribs celery, chopped fine
1 clove garlic, minced
1 can tomato sauce
1 package dry spaghetti mix
   (McCormick)

1 teaspoon chili powder
1 tablespoon Worchestershire
1 tablespoon Louisiana Hot Sauce
Salt and pepper to taste
1 pound crawfish tails

Heat butter in large skillet. Add onions, bell pepper, celery, and garlic. Sauté the ingredients. Add tomato sauce, spaghetti mix, chili powder, Worcestershire, hot sauce, salt and pepper to taste. Let simmer for 30 minutes. Add crawfish; cover tightly and cook on low heat about 1 hour. Serve over rice. Serves 4.

The Louisiana Crawfish Cookbook

 Étouffée—Stewed or braised. Usually crawfish or shrimp cooked slowly with vegetables.

Crawfish Étouffée à la Arceneaux
(Microwave)

Cooking Time: 17 minutes
Utensil: 3-quart glass dish
Servings: 4

½ cup margarine
1½ cups onion, finely chopped
¾ cup green bell pepper, finely chopped

1 clove garlic, minced or ¼ teaspoon garlic powder

1. Micromelt margarine in a 3-quart dish on HIGH (100%) 1 MINUTE. Add onion, bell pepper and garlic. Sauté on HIGH (100%) 6 MINUTES or until tender.

2 tablespoons flour
2 heaping tablespoons undiluted cream of celery soup
1 (10-ounce) can Ro-tel tomatoes and green chilies, puréed with liquid

1 cup beer
2 teaspoons salt
1 teaspoon cayenne pepper

2. Add flour and celery soup. Stir in puréed Ro-tel, beer, salt, and pepper. Microwave on HIGH (100%) 6 MINUTES.

1 pound peeled crawfish

3. Add crawfish. Cover. Microwave on HIGH (100%) 4 MIN-UTES. Serve étouffée over rice.

Tout de Suite à la Microwave II

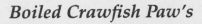

Boiled Crawfish Paw's

35 to 40 pounds crawfish
  (or 4 dozen crabs)
3 gallons water
3 garlic, whole, broken into
  cloves
1 bunch fresh parsley, chopped
1 bunch green onions, chopped
1 dozen lemons, quartered

3 yellow onions, chopped
1 box crushed red pepper
1 box ground red pepper
1 small box black pepper
1 small jar of mustard
1 bottle of Louisiana Hot Sauce
1½ boxes salt

Put water in huge pot and add all seasonings. Stir well, put crawfish in and stir again. Light fire. When water comes to rolling boil, time five minutes. Let soak five minutes. Crawfish with small claws (early) feeds 5–7 people. Crawfish with large claws (late–after June 15) feeds 3–4 people.

The Louisiana Crawfish Cookbook

Spicy Fried Crawfish Tails

6 tablespoons flour
2 teaspoons salt
1 teaspoon black pepper
2 tablespoons liquid crab boil
2 eggs, beaten

2 tablespoons milk
2 pounds crawfish tails
½ teaspoon salt
¼ teaspoon Cayenne pepper
1 quart oil

Preheat oven to 250 degrees. In bowl, mix flour, salt, pepper, crab boil, and eggs. Add milk, a teaspoon at a time, until batter is thick. Season crawfish with salt and Cayenne. Add to batter and let stand at least an hour.

In Dutch oven, heat oil until a wooden kitchen match floating on top ignites. Drop crawfish into hot oil, a handful at a time, making sure to separate them as they cook. Fry until golden brown, about 1 minute. Drain on a platter lined with paper towels, and keep warm in oven. When all crawfish have been fried, serve immediately. Serves 6.

Jambalaya

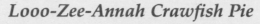

Looo-Zee-Annah Crawfish Pie

There are probably more recipes floating around for crawfish pie than there are politicians campaigning in Baton Rouge! And I don't think I've ever eaten any I didn't like! But this one—I do have to admit that I may be prejudiced—seems to be head and shoulders ahead of all the others. I mean, this one has *body*. This one has *intensity*. This one is *gooood*.

1 frozen, unbaked double pie shell	**3 tablespoons shredded carrots**
2 pounds crawfish tails with fat	**¼ cup parsley**
1 stick butter	**2 tablespoons paprika**
2 medium white onions, finely chopped	**½ teaspoon cayenne pepper**
¼ cup finely chopped shallots	**½ teaspoon white pepper**
½ cup finely chopped celery	**1 teaspoon salt**
½ cup finely chopped bell pepper	**2 hard-boiled eggs, chopped**
3 cloves garlic, finely chopped	**2 tablespoons heavy cream**
	1 egg yolk, beaten

Start by thawing the pie crust until it becomes pliable and easy to work with. Then place it in your refrigerator until you have your filling prepared. Here's how that's done:

For the best possible texture in this dish, you should separate the crawfish tails into two portions, leave one portion whole, and run the other portion through the grinder or food processor until the tail meat is finely chopped. Only by preparing the tails this way will you get uniform crawfish flavor throughout the pie. (Oh—grind the fat into the tails, too.)

Then get out a large skillet—the 12-inch size works best—and melt the butter over medium heat. At this point sauté the onions, shallots, celery, bell pepper, garlic, and carrots, and continue to cook them until they turn *just tender. Do not overcook* the ingredients or they will lose texture in the pie. Just 4 minutes should do nicely.

When the vegetables are wilted, remove the skillet from the fire and begin adding the remaining ingredients as follows, stirring all the while: Put in the parsley, then the paprika, then the two kinds of pepper, then the salt, then the chopped eggs, and then the heavy cream. Between each addition, be sure you thoroughly mix the ingredients together for uniformity. And now the coup de

CONTINUED

CONTINUED

grace: *You pour this mix into the bowl containing the whole and ground-up crawfish tails.* With a fork you begin working the seasonings evenly into the crawfish. When it's mixed just right, you're ready for your pie crust. Oh—better preheat your oven to 375 degrees, too.

Take the crust (you should have a bottom and a top) and begin spooning the filling into it. As you add the mix, take the spoon and pack the filling tightly across the bottom of the pie. Note: You want the filling to be rounded at the top, rather than level with the edge of the crust. When the pie is filled, place the top crust over the filling, crimp the edges with a fork, and make a 1-inch slit in each quarter of the top crust (4 slits in all).

Finally, reduce the oven temperature to 350 degrees, liberally brush the top crust with the egg yolk, and bake in the oven for about 40 minutes (or until the crust is golden brown and flakes easily). With a crisp tossed salad and a cold beer, this is one *Looo-zee-annah* dish you just won't be able to beat. Incidentally, crawfish pie should be served piping hot.

The Frank Davis Seafood Notebook

Gouda Crawfish

2 tablespoons butter
1 pound crawfish tails
½ cup chopped green onions
½ cup chopped fresh parsley
2 cloves garlic, crushed
⅓ cup heavy cream
3 tablespoons Parmesan cheese

½ cup dry Vermouth
1 tablespoon seafood seasoning
½ package frozen puff pastry
1 pound round Gouda cheese, cut
    into large slices
Melted butter

Simmer butter, crawfish, onions, parsley, and garlic until crawfish are tender. Add cream, Parmesan cheese, Vermouth, and seasoning. Simmer until liquid is consumed. Set aside to cool.

Defrost ½ package of puff pastry to room temperature. Place one pastry on baking sheet. Add Gouda cheese in center. Add crawfish mixture on top of cheese. Fold pastry over cheese and crawfish. Seal edges. Brush with melted butter. Bake at 350 degrees for 30 minutes. Serves 10.

The Louisiana Crawfish Cookbook

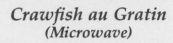

Crawfish au Gratin
(Microwave)

Cooking Time: 11 minutes
Utensil: 2-quart casserole
Servings: 6

2 tablespoons butter
1 bunch green onion tops,
   chopped

1. Sauté onions and butter in a 2-quart casserole on HIGH 3 MINUTES.

2 tablespoons flour   **1 teaspoon cayenne pepper**
½ cup whipping cream   **¼ teaspoon Tabasco**
¼ cup white wine   **¼ teaspoon garlic powder**
1 teaspoon salt

2. Add flour, cream and wine, salt, pepper, Tabasco and garlic. Cook on HIGH 1½–2 MINUTES.

6 ounces American cheese, grated
3 ounces Swiss cheese, grated
1 pound peeled crawfish tails

3. Stir cheese into hot mixture until it is melted. Add crawfish. Cover with wax paper and cook on HIGH 6 MINUTES. Stir halfway through cooking time.

Serve as a dip with Melba rounds or as an entrée in pastry shells.

Tout de Suite à la Microwave I

Spanish Rice-a-Roni Crawfish

2 tablespoon butter   **4 cloves garlic**
1 pound crawfish tails   **½ teaspoon salt**
½ cup onion, chopped   **1 package Spanish Rice-A-Roni**
¼ cup bell pepper, chopped

Sauté crawfish, butter, onion, bell pepper, garlic, red pepper and salt until crawfish are done. Use package directions for preparing Rice-A-Roni. Fold in crawfish mixture. Serve hot.

The Louisiana Crawfish Cookbook

Crawfish Tortellini Loupé

1 (7-ounce) box tortellini with
  Parmesan cheese
1 stick butter
1 medium onion, finely chopped
2 pods garlic, minced

¼ to ½ cup Parmesan cheese
Whipping cream (enough to
  create a heavy cream sauce)
1 pound crawfish tails
⅛ cup parsley, chopped

Sauté onions and garlic in butter. Add crawfish. Continue to cook for approximately 5 minutes. Add Parmesan cheese, parsley and whipping cream.

Prepare tortellini as directed and fold into crawfish mixture. Season with plain salt and red pepper. (Spinach tortellini may be used.) Delicious!!

We've found that Parmesan cheese and crawfish complement one another very well.

The Louisiana Crawfish Cookbook

Crawfish Stew

3 tablespoons fat or shortening
2 small onions, chopped
½ green pepper, chopped
2 stalks celery, chopped
½ clove garlic, minced
2 tablespoons all-purpose flour
½ cup tomato sauce
¼ teaspoon hot pepper sauce

1 tablespoon Worcestershire
  sauce
Salt and pepper to taste
Cayenne pepper to taste
1½ cups water
2 pounds peeled crawfish tails
Hot cooked rice

In an iron pot, heat fat until melted. Add onion, green pepper, celery, garlic; sauté until clear. Add flour, stirring well to blend. Gradually add tomato sauce, seasonings, water, and crawfish tails. Simmer on low heat for 30 minutes. Serve over hot rice. Serves 8.

Foods à la Louisiane

Boiled Crabs in a Chest

Tony's Creole Seasoning or 1 box
  salt mixed with
1 (4-ounce) bottle red pepper

4 dozen live crabs
1 ice chest big enough to hold 4
  dozen crabs

Plunge crabs in boiling water, boil for 11 minutes. Remove and immediately place (while hot) 1 layer crabs in bottom of ice chest. Sprinkle generously with seasoning, then place another layer of crabs. Season and repeat process until all crabs are placed and covered with seasoning. Cover with newspaper and close top securely. Heat will steam crabs and melt seasoning for flavor. After 1 hour, take out and eat. Crabs will keep hot for 5 or 6 hours. Serves 8.

Note: You can do this with crawfish or shrimp the same way. Use a styrofoam chest—it will not warp.

Tony Chachere's Cajun Country Cookbook

Opelousas Barbecued Crabs

1 dozen fresh cleaned crabs
1 cup chili powder
1 cup black pepper
⅓ cup salt
1 stick margarine

1 (14-ounce) bottle catsup
Juice of one lemon
1 teaspoon Tabasco
A few drops of liquid smoke

Roll cleaned crabs in mixture of equal parts, by weight, salt, black pepper and fresh chili powder. Fry in deep fat, 375-degrees, until they float, about 7 minutes.

Make a sauce with melted margarine or butter, catsup, lemon juice, Tabasco and a few drops of liquid smoke. Pour this sauce over the crabs and serve hot. Serves 2.

Louisiana's Original Creole Seafood Recipes

Crabmeat Caroline

2 tablespoons butter
2 tablespoons flour
¼ cup minced green onions
¼ cup minced green pepper
1 clove garlic, minced
⅛ teaspoon rosemary
1 tomato, peeled and chopped
¼ cup dry white wine
1 cup heavy cream

1 teaspoon salt
¼ teaspoon Tabasco
⅓ cup grated Gruyère cheese
⅛ teaspoon dry mustard
1 pound lump crabmeat
3 tablespoons grated Mozzarella cheese
3 tablespoons grated Parmesan cheese

Preheat oven to 350 degrees. In a large skillet melt butter and gradually blend in flour. Cook 2 minutes, stirring constantly. Add onions, green pepper, garlic, rosemary, and tomato; sauté 2 to 3 minutes. Add wine and continue cooking until vegetables are tender. Lower heat, and gradually add cream, salt, and Tabasco. Blend well. Remove from heat and stir in Gruyère cheese and mustard. Gently fold crabmeat into sauce and spoon into individual buttered ramekins. Combine cheeses and sprinkle on top. Bake 10 to 15 minutes, until browned and bubbly. Serves 4.

Jambalaya

Crabmeat Mousse

2 tablespoons gelatin
8 ounces cream cheese
1 cup mayonnaise
2 tablespoons lime juice
2 tablespoons lemon juice
1 tablespoon each chopped parsley and green onions

½ teaspoon garlic salt
Salt to taste
¼ teaspoon red pepper
¼ teaspoon Tabasco
1 pound crabmeat
¾ cup heavy cream, whipped

Soften gelatin in 3 tablespoons cold water. Heat to dissolve. Add cream cheese until melted. Cool to room temperature. Then add remaining ingredients. Pour into lightly greased mold and chill overnight. Soak mold in warm water for about 10 seconds to loosen the mold.

La Bonne Louisiane

Crabmeat in the Garden

6 green onions, chopped,
  including tops
2 fresh, slightly green tomatoes
2 medium green peppers,
  coarsely diced
6 or 8 large fresh mushrooms,
  sliced

¾ stick butter
¼ cup salad oil
3 cups cooked rice
¼ cup toasted slivered almonds
¼ cup minced parsley
1 pound back fin lump crabmeat
Salt and pepper

Line up all ingredients. Seasonings chopped, sliced, or whatever. Crabmeat picked over for bits of shell. The whole process takes all of five minutes, so if you have to pause to prepare anything the rest will overcook.

Heat oil in a large, heavy (preferably black iron) skillet. The pan should be very, very hot and beginning with oil will keep the butter from burning too quickly. When oil is smoking hot, add butter and melt. When butter is hot add in the following order all prepared ingredients. Each should be just about heated before the next one goes in. You are in a race against overcooking.

1. Green onions; stir around. 2. Tomatoes; give these a few seconds longer. 3. Green peppers; continue stirring. 4. Mushrooms. Stir and cook about a minute or two.

Add rice, crabmeat, almonds and parsley. Mix well but gently, so as not to break crabmeat. Taste for salt and pepper. Serve the minute everything is thoroughly hot.

The Asphodel Plantation Cookbook

Crabmeat Au Gratin

½ cup celery, chopped fine
1 cup onion, chopped
¼ teaspoon red pepper
½ cup flour
2 egg yolks

1 teaspoon salt
1 pound lump crabmeat
1 stick butter
1 (14-ounce) can evaporated milk
8 ounces grated Cheddar cheese

Sauté onions and celery in butter until soft. Add flour to this mixture. Add milk gradually, stirring constantly. Add egg yolks, salt, red and black pepper. Cook for 10 minutes. Put crabmeat in a bowl and pour sauce over the crabmeat. Blend well and place in a lightly greased casserole and sprinkle with grated cheese. Bake at 375 degrees. until browned, approximately 15 minutes. Serves 4 to 6.

Paul Naquin's French Collection I—Louisiana Seafood

Crabmeat Soufflé

1 onion, chopped
½ cup chopped green pepper
4 green onions, chopped
½ pound fresh mushrooms, sliced
¼ cup butter
14 slices white bread, crusts removed
½ pound Monterey Jack cheese, shredded

½ pound Cheddar cheese, shredded
1 pound white crabmeat
12 eggs
3¼ cups milk
⅛ cup white wine
Salt and pepper to taste
Several dashes of hot pepper sauce
1 teaspoon Worcestershire sauce

In medium skillet, sauté onion, green pepper, green onions, and mushrooms in ¼ cup butter until tender. Set side. Line bottom of a 3-quart casserole with bread. Put the onion mixture on top of the bread. Then sprinkle with the Monterey Jack cheese and the Cheddar cheese. Spread the crabmeat evenly over the cheese. Beat the eggs, milk, white wine, and seasonings together. Pour over the crabmeat. Cover with plastic wrap and refrigerate over-night. Bake at 325 degrees for 1 hour. Yields 8 to 10 servings.

From A Louisiana Kitchen

Soufflé—A light, puffed dish made with eggs, which may contain cheese, fruit, fish, minced meat or vegetables.

Blend of the Bayou Seafood Casserole

1 (8-ounce) package cream cheese
1 stick margarine or butter
1 pound shrimp, peeled
1 large onion, chopped
1 bell pepper, chopped
2 ribs celery, chopped
2 tablespoons butter
1 can mushroom soup
1 can mushrooms, drained
1 tablespoon garlic salt
1 teaspoon Tabasco
½ teaspoon red pepper
1 pint crab meat
¾ cup cooked rice
Sharp cheese, grated
Cracker crumbs

Melt cream cheese and butter using double boiler. Sauté shrimp, onion, pepper, and celery in 2 tablespoons butter. Add to the first mixture. Add soup, mushrooms, seasonings, crab meat, and rice. Mix well, place in 2-quart casserole, and top with cheese and cracker crumbs. Bake at 350 degrees F. about 20–30 minutes until bubbly. Freezes. Serves 8.

Pirate's Pantry

Black Pepper Shrimp

2 pounds headless fresh shrimp
  unpeeled
2 sticks margarine
1 (2-ounce) can ground black
pepper

Place shrimp in a baking pan and completely cover with the black pepper, then with sliced margarine. Cover and bake in 400-degree oven until shrimp turn red. Turn over once and cook the other side. When done, mix in juices and serve hot.

When peeled, they get the flavor of black pepper but not the hot taste.

Try this on your friends, you won't be disappointed. Serves 4.

Tony Chachere's Cajun Country Cookbook

Boiled Shrimp

5 pounds (2.3 kg) unpeeled raw
shrimp
1 large onion, peeled and
quartered
3 cloves garlic
½ cup (125 ml) vegetable oil
½ cup (125 ml) catsup, optional

½ teaspoon (2.5 ml) Tabasco
½ teaspoon (2.5 ml) black pepper
1 lemon, sliced
¼ cup (60 ml) vinegar
1 tablespoon (15 ml) liquid crab
boil
¾ cup (185 ml) salt

Wash shrimp. Half fill a 6-quart (6-liter) pot with water; bring to a boil. Add all ingredients except shrimp, crab boil and salt; return to a boil; add shrimp and crab boil. Boil 5 minutes; remove from heat. Add salt; stir to dissolve. Let set covered for 30 minutes for shrimp to absorb flavor. Remove shrimp. May be served immediately or chilled. The water may be used for boiling potatoes. Technique based on some research done at LSU. Excellent!

'Tiger Bait' Recipes

French Fried Shrimp

4 eggs
Milk
1 cup Parmesan cheese
2 large onions
1 clove garlic
1 cup Sauterne wine
1 bell pepper

1 tablespoon Lea & Perrins
　Worcestershire
1 teaspoon hot sauce (Louisiana)
Pancake flour
3 pounds shrimp (deveined)
Salt

Slice onions, garlic, bell (sweet) pepper and blend in blender. Place in large bowl over shrimp. Beat 4 eggs, adding Sauterne wine slowly while beating. Pour this over shrimp, adding Lea & Perrins and hot sauce. Stir this mixture well. Add milk to cover shrimp. Stir until milk mixes well. Salt to taste. Marinate overnight.

　　Place pancake flour (as much as needed) in brown paper sack, adding a little salt. Drain shrimp a few at a time and shake in pancake flour. Fry in deep fat. Serves 4 to 6.

The Justin Wilson Cook Book

Barbecued Shrimp

200 raw unpeeled shrimp,
　medium-sized (about 4
　pounds)
1½ cups salad oil
¼ cup Worcestershire
½ cup dry red wine
¾ cup soy sauce

¼ cup vinegar
⅓ cup lemon juice
1 teaspoon salt
1 teaspoon pepper
4 cloves garlic, pressed
2 tablespoons dry mustard
¼ cup parsley flakes

Peel and devein shrimp, and place in a large bowl. Mix all remaining ingredients in blender, and immediately pour over the shrimp. Marinate 2 hours.

　　Fashion a foil tray with sides. Drain marinade from shrimp, and place shrimp in foil tray on top of hot coals in barbecue grill. Cook 3 minutes per side, and serve hot. Serves 35 as a cocktail pick-up or 4 to 6 as a main course.

Le Bon Temps

Shrimp and Rice Rockefeller

1 cup chopped onions
2 tablespoons butter
12 ounces raw shrimp, peeled
and cut in half
1 (10¾-ounce) can mushroom
soup, undiluted
1 cup grated Swiss cheese
¼ cup sherry wine
3 cups cooked rice
1 (8-ounce) can water chestnuts,
drained and chopped

2 (10-ounce) packages frozen
chopped spinach, cooked
1 tablespoon lemon juice
¼ cup grated Parmesan cheese,
divided
1 teaspoon salt
1 teaspoon red pepper
½ teaspoon black pepper

In a 3-quart sauce pan sauté onions in butter. Add shrimp, cook until pink. Stir in mushroom soup, cheese and sherry. Heat thoroughly until mixture is warm. Add cooked rice, water chestnuts, drained spinach, lemon juice and 2 tablespoons Parmesan cheese. Add salt, red and black pepper. Pour into a greased shallow 2-quart dish. Sprinkle remaining Parmesan cheese over top. Bake in preheated 350-degree oven 30 minutes. Yield: 6-8 servings.

Voilà! Lafayette Centennial Cookbook 1884–1984

Shrimp and Artichokes

1 (No. 2) can artichoke hearts,
drained
¾ pound cooked shrimp
1 small can mushrooms or ¼
pound fresh mushrooms, sliced
2 tablespoons butter

1 tablespoon Lea & Perrins
¼ cup dry sherry
1½ cups cream sauce
Salt, pepper and paprika
¼ cup grated Parmesan cheese

Arrange artichoke hearts in a buttered baking dish. Spread the shrimp over the artichokes. Slice mushrooms and sauté in butter for 6 minutes and add to baking dish. Mix Lea & Perrins with sherry and cream sauce. Pour into baking dish. Sprinkle top with Parmesan cheese and paprika. Bake at 375 degrees for 30 to 40 minutes. Serve hot and garnish with parsley.

Cane River Cuisine

Shrimp Creole

3 pound peeled, deveined
   medium shrimp
4 tablespoons butter
1 tablespoon oil
6 tablespoons flour
1 (16-ounce) can tomato sauce
1 cup chopped onions
1 cup chopped celery

1 cup chopped bell pepper
6 cloves chopped garlic
½ cup hot water
Juice of 1 lemon
4 bay leaves
½ teaspoon sugar
Salt and cayenne pepper to taste
½ cup chopped green onions

In a heavy pot, melt butter. Add oil. Sauté all seasonings until done (approximately 5 minutes). Add flour and blend well. Add tomato sauce, hot water, and sugar. Cook over medium heat approximately 30 minutes. Season to taste. Add shrimp, cook 30 minutes longer.

The Encyclopedia of Cajun and Creole Cuisine

Creole—A type of French, Spanish, Indian and African cuisine which originated in the Gulf States, especially Louisiana. The word also refers to a red sauce which is often used in Creole cookery. The sauce is made of tomatoes, peppers and other spices, and it is usually served over rice.

Shrimp Rémoulade Sauce

10 ounces olive oil
5 ounces vinegar
7½ ounces Dijon mustard or
   Creole mustard
5 ounces tomato catsup

5 tablespoons fresh horseradish
   (from dairy case)
5 cloves garlic
1 teaspoon Tabasco sauce
Salt to taste

Blend ingredients as listed. Serve over boiled shrimp. Mix with shredded lettuce and finely sliced celery. Enough for 10 servings.

Tony Chachere's Cajun Country Cookbook

Rémoulade—A piquant cold sauce for cold poultry, meat or shellfish, made of mayonnaise with chopped pickles, capers, anchovies, and herbs.

Rockefeller Sauce

3 (10-ounce) bags fresh spinach
1 bunch green onions
Leaves from ½ bunch of celery
1 whole bulb garlic, peeled and
   separated
1 bunch fresh parsley
4 cups water
1 cup grated Parmesan cheese
1 cup bread crumbs
1 pound butter, melted
1 jigger Pernod (anise liqueur)

In a large pot, boil spinach, onions, celery leaves, garlic, and parsley in water 20 minutes. Drain and chop in a food processor. Return to pot and add cheese, bread crumbs, and melted butter. Mix. Add Pernod and stir. Serve over oysters. Freezes well. For 5 dozen oysters.

Jambalaya

Oysters Rockefeller—A dish of oysters on the half-shell with a purée of spinach, onions or shallots, and celery. According to one source, the dish is named Rockefeller because of its richness.

Oysters Aunt Nellie

2 tablespoons butter
2 tablespoons minced parsley
2 tablespoons minced celery tops
   and leaves
2 tablespoons minced green
   onion tops
½ cup catsup
2 (or more) dashes Tabasco
1 tablespoon Worcestershire
   sauce
Juice of ½ lemon
1 pint oysters, well-drained

Drain oysters well. Dry on paper towels. Sauté vegetables in butter about 5 minutes. Stir in remaining ingredients, except oysters and cook 2 or 3 more minutes. Add oysters and simmer just until edges curl. Serve in ramekins or shells with toast points or crackers to dip in sauce.

Doubles easily. (Sauce may be made the day before and refrigerated.)

This is a favorite dish in my family and almost always served as a first course on Thanksgiving and Christmas.

Plantation Country

Oysters Oregano

¼ cup butter
1 large onion, chopped
½ teaspoon thyme
¾ teaspoon oregano
3 cloves garlic, finely chopped
2 tablespoons chopped parsley

¼ teaspoon red pepper
Salt and pepper to taste
4 dozen oysters with liquor
1 cup Italian-style bread crumbs
½–¾ cup Parmesan cheese

In a skillet melt the butter. Add the onion and sauté until limp. Add all of the seasonings and mix well. Add the oysters and when the edges curl, add the oyster liquor. Fold in the bread crumbs. Transfer the mixture to a buttered casserole. Sprinkle the dish heavily with Parmesan cheese. Bake at 350 degrees F. for 15 to 20 minutes. Serves 4.

La Bonne Cuisine

Oysters Ellen

½ stick butter
1 green onion, chopped
2 tablespoons celery, chopped
2 tablespoons fresh parsley,
  chopped

½ pound fresh crabmeat
¼ pound boiled shrimp, chopped
1 large fresh lemon
Salt and pepper to taste
20 medium oysters

Place cleaned oyster shells on rock salt in baking plates. Lightly sauté green onion and celery. Add crabmeat, boiled shrimp, salt and pepper to taste. Cook slowly 5 minutes. Place raw oysters in shells and put equal amounts of crab and shrimp over oysters. Squeeze lemon juice over each oyster. Place in 350-degree oven for 15 minutes. Sprinkle parsley over each oyster and put back in oven for 5 minutes. Serves 4.

Paul Naquin's French Collection I—Louisiana Seafood

Bienville—Oysters baked with a roux-based sauce.

Oysters Bienville
(Microwave)

Cooking Time: 16 minutes
             2½ minutes per plate
Utensils: 2-quart batter bowl
           36 oyster shells
           6 microwave-safe serving plates
Yield: 6 servings

3 dozen oysters and juice
3 dozen oyster half-shells
6 serving plates half-filled with
**   rock salt**
½ cup butter or margarine
4 tablespoons flour
1 pint Half & Half cream
1 (4-ounce) can mushrooms
1 cup chopped shrimp

¼ cup chopped parsley
¼ cup chopped onions
¼ cup dry white wine
½ teaspoon thyme
¼ cup grated Parmesan cheese
1½ teaspoons Tony's Creole
**   Seasoning**
6 egg yolks

1. In 2-quart batter bowl, place butter.

2. Microwave on 70% POWER FOR 1 to 1½ MINUTES or until melted. Stir in flour. Add cream and stir well.

3. Microwave on HIGH FOR 2 MINUTES, stir.

4. Microwave on HIGH FOR 2 MINUTES, or until thickened. Add mushrooms, shrimp, parsley, onions, wine, thyme, Parmesan cheese, and Tony's Creole Seasoning. Mix well. Cover with plastic wrap.

5. Microwave on HIGH FOR 1 to 2 MINUTES or until warm and cheese has melted. Beat in egg yolks.

6. On microwave-safe serving platters, place rock salt and oyster shells, six shells per plate. Microwave one plate at a time.

7. Microwave on HIGH FOR 1½ to 2 MINUTES or until hot. Place 1 oyster on each shell, cover with sauce, and sprinkle with Parmesan or Cheddar cheese if desired. Cover with wax paper.

8. Microwave on HIGH FOR 1 to 1½ MINUTES or until hot and cheese has melted. Repeat steps 6, 7, and 8 for remaining oysters and plates. Serve hot.

Tips: If no rock salt is available, you can place oyster shells on folded terry cloth, place 1 oyster on each shell, cover with sauce, sprinkle with cheese, and cover with wax paper. Then microwave on HIGH FOR 1 to 1½ MINUTES or until hot.

Tony Chachere's Microwave Cajun Country Cookbook

Oyster Spaghetti

6 dozen oysters
1 clove garlic
1 bunch green onions
1 cup chopped parsley
¼ cup olive oil

1 cup sliced mushrooms, optional
½ teaspoon basil
1 pound spaghetti
½ cup Parmeasan cheese
Salt and pepper to taste

Drain oysters well. Reserve liquid. You may need it if spaghetti is too dry. Sauté garlic, onions, parsley in olive oil. Add mushrooms and oysters. Cook over low heat until oysters curl. Add basil. Toss oyster mixture with cooked spaghetti and Parmesan cheese. If spaghetti is too dry you may add olive oil or oyster liquid. If spaghetti has too much liquid you could add Italian bread crumbs and/or more Parmesan cheese. Serves 6 generously.

Talk About Good II

Louisiana Pasta

4 tablespoons butter
4 tablespoons green onion, chopped
4 teaspoons garlic, minced
1 pound shrimp

2 (10-ounce) containers oysters
Salt, red and black pepper, lemon pepper, garlic powder to taste
Cooked pasta to serve 4

1. Peel and devein shrimp. 2. Melt butter (or half butter and half olive oil). 3. Stir in onion, garlic and shrimp and cook until shrimp turns pink, stirring often. 4. Add drained oysters and continue cooking until edges of oysters curl. 5. Pour over hot pasta and serve immediately. 6. Makes 4 servings.

Louisiana Largesse

Oyster Stew

2 or 3 dozen small oysters with
   liquid
6 green onions (scallions),
   chopped fine
1 rib of celery, chopped fine
2 sprigs parsley, minced
1 quart milk

1 stick butter or margarine
2 tablespoons flour
Salt and pepper
Worcestershire sauce
Slices of toast bread cut into
   croutons

Sauté chopped vegetables in margarine and flour. Drain oysters and add liquid to vegetables. Add pre-heated milk, then oysters and simmer until oysters are plump and edges begin to turn. Add salt, pepper, Worcestershire sauce to taste. Serve with croutons. Sprinkle with parsley. Serves 4.

Louisiana's Original Creole Seafood Recipes

Paul Prudhomme's Blackened Redfish

The last recipe in this section (of my cookbook) is, in my opinion, the very best there is for fish. And it is the creation of my very good friend, Chef Paul Prudhomme. If there ever was a Cajun who could cook, m'frien', it's this man! I've had the opportunity over the past 20 years to talk with and cook with lots of culinary talent, but none I've met approach the creative genius of Chef Paul. So much of what I've learned to do in the kitchen is because of my relationship with Paul, and I truly consider him the unequalled master of food preparation.

Consequently, of all the dishes I prepare, this one, Paul's recipe for Blackened Redfish, is my absolute favorite. Thank you, m'frien', for a real masterpiece. Here's why I like it so much. . . .

6 (9-ounce) redfish fillets
12 bay leaves, finely crushed
2 teaspoons paprika
¼ teaspoon basil
¼ teaspoon oregano
¼ teaspoon thyme
½ teaspoon granulated onion

½ teaspoon granulated garlic
3 teaspoons salt
¼ teaspoon black pepper
½ teaspoon white pepper
½ teaspoon cayenne pepper
2 sticks butter, melted

Start off by drying the redfish fillets and chilling them in the refrigerator. Redfish is, by far, the best species to use for this recipe, but when I can't get redfish I use other heavy-bodied firm fish (drum, sheepshead, bass). The one important thing to remember is the *size* of the fillet. It cannot weigh less than 8 ounces or more than 12 ounces; otherwise it doesn't cook properly.

When you're ready to cook, place a black-iron Dutch oven on the burner and turn the heat up to high. *You must use an iron oven; no other metal can take the heat.* In fact you really should prepare this recipe outside because it makes lots of smoke. You want to get the pot almost *white hot*, hot enough to see a "flame circle" in the center. Remember, there is nothing in the pot—no oil, no shortening, no nothing. Just bare metal.

Lay the fillets on a sheet of waxed paper. Mix the bay leaves, paprika, basil, oregano, thyme, onion, garlic, salt, black pepper, white pepper, and cayenne in a small bowl. Sprinkle the mix over the fillets. *Do it lightly, but distribute the mixture evenly.* Then dip

CONTINUED

CONTINUED

the fillets in the melted butter so that they are completely coated. And *immediately* drop them into the hot Dutch oven. I suggest you do them one at a time.

I can tell you that the fish will sputter and jump and sizzle and smoke, but that's what it is supposed to do! And it's gonna do it quick, too. Because in just 30 to 40 *seconds*, the side down against the metal will be cooked and it will be time to flip the fillet over. The cooked side should be dark brown, almost charred. That's the way you want it. Cook the flip side another 30 to 40 seconds and remove the fillet from the black pot. Your *blackened redfish* is done!

The texture is unbelievable! Crispy brown on the outer crust, but light, tender, and ultramoist on the inside. It is one of the finest fish dishes you will ever eat. I recommend you serve it with cole slaw or potato salad, and some hush puppies, and a tall, frosted glass of the coldest beer you can get your hands on. If your mouth doesn't *run water* after your first bite, you've swallowed your taste buds!

The Frank Davis Seafood Notebook

Coach's Barbecued Redfish

6 redfish fillets (scales and skin left on)	Creole seasoning Lemon-pepper seasoning

1. First and most important is to fillet redfish and leave the scales and skin on. *Do not* remove the scales; leave them on. (They protect the fish and serve as an insulator and pan for the fish as it cooks). 2. Season fillets with Creole seasoning and lemon-pepper seasoning. (Season as you would sprinkle salt on meat.) 3. Be careful with the Creole seasoning—too much is not best—but you can be heavy on the lemon-pepper seasoning. 4. Let it sit for 1½ hours. 5. Light fire in your barbecue pit. Get fire ready as if you were fixing steaks the size of your fish fillets.

SMOKE GRUB BUB SAUCE:

2 sticks butter	1 tablespoon Creole seasoning
1 ounce white wine	¼ teaspoon garlic powder
1 ounce lemon juice	1 tablespoon Worcestershire
1 tablespoon lemon-pepper seasoning	sauce

1. Melt sauce mixture in a saucepan. (This can be done on the stove or in the microwave.) 2. By this time your fire should be ready. Take the redfish and place on grill fleshside down, scales up (put the top down on the pit if you have one). 3. Let cook for 4 minutes. 4. Turn fillets over, scale-side down, and baste with *Smoke Grub Bub Sauce.* 5. Continue basting 3 or 4 times while cooking. 6. When done, the fish will be tender and come away from the skin easily. Do not worry about the scales burning crisp. They will form a good protective coating for the fish. 7. When done, eat with a few drops of lemon juice.

Editor's Note: Barbecue sauce can be substituted for *Smoke Grub Bub Sauce.*

Louisiana Largesse

Pan Broiled Trout

6 whole cleaned trout	6 lemon slices
Lots and lots of butter	Milk
A little salad oil	Flour
Juice of 2 lemons	Salt and pepper

Wash and dry fish very well. Salt and pepper inside and out. Roll in flour to give a thin dusting, dip in milk, then again in flour. To keep butter from browning too fast start the heavy skillet which you are going to use by coating with 2 tablespoons of salad oil. When that has become very hot add at least one stick of butter.

Brown on both sides in hot butter. Turn gently; fish breaks easily when cooked. Set aside in a medium oven while you add 1 stick of butter and the lemon juice to the pan in which you have broiled the fish.

To serve, garnish each fish with a lemon slice and pour butter sauce over.

To make almondine, add slivered almonds to the second butter and brown slightly before adding lemon juice.

Dinner make-up: This can be a pretty fancy dinner. Try Brabant potatoes and oyster-stuffed artichokes if your kids aren't home.

The Asphodel Plantation Cookbook

Baked Crunchy Trout

2 pounds trout fillets
1 onion, chopped
1 (8-ounce) bottle Creamy
  Italian Dressing
2½ cups crushed potato chips

Lay trout fillets in the bottom of a buttered 3-quart baking dish. Sprinkle with chopped onion. Spread dressing over onion to cover fish. Put crushed potato chips on top to cover completely. Bake at 350 degrees for 35 minutes. Yield: 4 servings.

Note: Easy and very good.

From A Louisiana Kitchen

Stuffed Flounder

1 ounce olive oil
4 (1-pound) flounder
¾ stick butter
¼ cup chopped celery
¾ cup chopped onion
1 small clove garlic, minced

1 pound white crabmeat
3 teaspoons green onion tops
3 teaspoons chopped bell pepper
⅓ cup bread crumbs
1½ ounces white wine
¼ teaspoon each, salt and pepper

Use baking dish large enough to accommodate flounder when completely spread out. Head of flounder may be left on or removed. Split flounder from behind gills to tail and lift skin and meat one side at a time while running filet knife along backbone until total backbone is exposed. Backbone is then completely removed. Oil bottom of baking dish. Place flounder in dish dark side up. Open sides of flounder and apply lemon to all meat. Salt and pepper. Add stuffing to cavity and pull sides of flounder over stuffing. Place thin lemon slices over entire fish. Lightly salt and pepper. Cover with foil and bake in 350-degree oven for 20 minutes. Remove foil and bake for additional 10 minutes. Serves 4.

FLOUNDER STUFFING:

In melted butter, sauté onions, garlic, green onion tops and bell pepper. Add salt and pepper and wine. Simmer 5 minutes. Add crabmeat and bread crumbs. Mix well and place directly into flounder cavity.

Paul Naquin's French Collection I—Louisiana Seafood

Red Fish Fillets
(Microwave)

Cooking Time: 49 minutes
Utensils: 8-cup glass measuring cup
         4 or 5-quart casserole
Servings: 8

2 tablespoons olive oil	**½ cup celery, chopped**
2 cups onions, chopped	**¼ cup bell pepper, chopped**

1. Sauté onions, celery, bell pepper and oil in an 8-cup measure on HIGH 10 MINUTES.

½ cup green onions, chopped
2 cloves garlic, minced
½ cup parsley, chopped

2. Stir in green onions, garlic and parsley. Sauté on HIGH 4 MINUTES.

1 (6-ounce) can tomato paste	**½ teaspoon pepper**
½ lemon sliced thin	**½ teaspoon cayenne pepper**
2 cups water	**4 or 5 drops Tabasco sauce**
2 teaspoons salt	**5 pounds red fish fillets**

3. Stir in tomato paste. Cook on HIGH 10 MINUTES. Add lemon, water and seasonings. Cover with plastic wrap, cook on HIGH 10 MINUTES.
Place fillets, seasoned with cayenne pepper, in a 4 or 5-quart casserole dish. Pour hot sauce over fish. Cover with lid or plastic wrap. Cook on HIGH 15 MINUTES.

Tout de Suite à la Microwave I

Pompano en Papilloté

3 green onions and tops, chopped
3 ounces mushrooms, chopped
1 tablespoon butter
2 tablespoons flour
2 cups stock
Salt and pepper to taste
⅓ cup white wine

2 pounds pompano fillets
1 cup crabmeat
4 tablespoons butter
1 tablespoon white wine
½ teaspoon salt
1 egg yolk
1 lemon, sliced

Brown mushrooms and onions lightly in butter, mix in flour; add stock; season and boil 5 minutes. Add wine (¼ cup). Sauté fillets and crabmeat separately in butter for 5 minutes. Add wine, salt, and slightly beaten egg yolk to crabmeat and cook until thickened, stirring constantly. Place some of the crab meat mixture on half of each fillet; fold other half on top; cover with sauce; fold well in parchment cooking paper, or place in paper bag and bake at 425 degrees. for about 10 minutes. Arrange on platter garnished with lemon. Serves 6.

Louisiana's Original Creole Seafood Recipes

En papilloté—A dish that has been made using a thin parchment paper or foil made for baking.

Fish Casserole

Bass fillets, enough to cover
   bottom of flat 2-quart casserole
Milk, enough to cover fish
Flour
1 stick butter
1 bell pepper, diced
5 or 6 green onions, diced
2 cans shrimp soup

1 small can shrimp, deveined
1 can mushrooms, sliced; save
   juice
Juice of 1 lemon
⅓ cup sherry
Salt
Red pepper
Worcestershire

Soak fish (bass especially good) fillets in milk 2 to 3 hours. Dip in flour and brown in butter. Put into baking dish. Brown bell pepper and onion in butter until limp. Add shrimp soup, can of shrimp, mushrooms and ⅓ of mushroom juice, juice of lemon, sherry, salt, red pepper and Worcestershire to taste. Pour over fillets and bake 350 degrees for 30 to 40 minutes. Serves 6 generous portions.

The Cotton Country Collection

Caper Sauce Fish

3–4 pounds red snapper
1 onion
2 ribs celery

¼ teaspoon pepper
1 teaspoon salt

Poach fish with ingredients until done (about 15–20 minutes). Be sure to use head when poaching so that stock will gel. Remove fish from bones and place on platter in shape of fish; fill in with small pieces. Boil stock down to about 1 cup and pour over fish. Cover with plastic wrap and place in refrigerator until it congeals.

CAPER SAUCE:

1 dozen eggs, hard-boiled
4 cups mayonnaise
1 (2½-ounce) bottle small
  imported capers

1 tablespoon lemon juice
5 drops Tabasco

Mash egg yolks and add to mayonnaise with remaining ingredients. Cover fish with a portion of sauce, reserving some to pass when serving. Be sure to have plenty of sauce, even if you have to make more. Decorate fish with some of the grated egg whites. A stuffed olive may be used for the eye, strips of pimiento for the mouth and tail, and parsley to make gills. *Garnish the platter with lettuce and tomato or beets. Serves 6–8.*

Revel

Salmon Florentine

2 cups canned salmon, drained
(save liquid)
Milk
¼ cup butter, melted
¼ cup flour
½ teaspoon dry mustard

¼ teaspoon salt
¼ teaspoon Tabasco
1½ cups Cheddar cheese, grated
1 tablespoon onion, chopped
(optional)
2 cups spinach, cooked, drained

Drain and flake salmon, removing skin and bones. Add enough milk to salmon liquid to make 1½ cups. Add flour to melted butter in saucepan; stir with wire whisk till blended. Meanwhile, bring milk mixture to a boil; add all at once to butter-flour mixture, stirring vigorously with whisk till sauce is thickened and smooth. Season with mustard, salt and Tabasco. Mix in 1 cup cheese and onion. Place spinach in 4 individual greased casseroles; top with salmon and sauce; sprinkle with remaining cheese. Bake 425 degrees 15 minutes uncovered. Serves 4.

Encore

 Florentine—A dish made with spinach.

Broiled Pond Catfish Fillets

6 catfish fillets
Lemon pepper, garlic powder, red
and black pepper
⅓ cup butter or margarine
1 tablespoon minced parsley
⅓ cup chopped green onions
½ pound fresh shrimp, chopped,
seasoned with salt and pepper

1 cup crabmeat
1½ cups diced bread crumbs
2–3 tablespoons chicken broth
1 tablespoon dry white wine
Melted butter and lemon juice

Rinse and dry fillets. Season with lemon pepper, garlic powder, red and black pepper. Set aside. Melt butter in saucepan. Add parsley and green onions. Sauté 2–3 minutes. Add seasoned shrimp, cook until pink. Add crabmeat and bread crumbs. Add chicken broth and wine to moisten mixture. Place fillets in pan lined with foil. Broil in preheated broiler 3 minutes. Turn fillets

CONTINUED

CONTINUED

over. Baste with butter and lemon juice. Spread dressing over each fillet and broil 5 minutes longer.

PASS THE SAUCE PLEASE:
½ cup butter, melted
Juice of one lemon
1 tablespoon finely chopped
   parsley
⅛ teaspoon garlic powder

Mix butter, lemon juice, parsley and garlic powder together. Warm and serve sauce with broiled catfish. Yield: 6 servings.

Voilà! Lafayette Centennial Cookbook 1884–1984

Steamed Redfish with Creole Sauce

1 redfish (4-5 pounds)
1 can stewed tomatoes or
   equivalent of fresh stewed
   tomatoes
2 tablespoons onion, chopped
½ teaspoon salt
Salt and pepper to season
½ cup water
4 tablespoons green pepper,
   chopped
6 stuffed olives, chopped
2 tablespoons butter or margarine

Wash the cleaned redfish and dry thoroughly. Sprinkle with salt and pepper and tie in cheesecloth; steam 45 minutes to one hour depending upon the size of the fish. Remove cheesecloth, place fish in center of hot platter and pour Creole sauce over it.

Steaming can be accomplished by placing fish in a deep pan and adding a rack. Place fish on pan rack so that it does not touch water. Cover dish. Cook either in oven (medium heat) or on top of stove, being careful to observe throughout the cooking process that water is still in pan for steaming.

Put tomatoes in blender and purée. Remove and put in heavy skillet. Add remaining ingredients. Simmer over low heat for one hour. Add small amounts of water if it dries out. Serve over redfish.

Louisiana Keepsake

Bouillabaisse Marseillance
(from Versailles)

1 pound redfish	2 pounds bell pepper
1 pound lump crabmeat	1 pound sliced carrots
1½ pounds celery	1 teaspoon minced garlic
¼ cup green onions	Pinch of Saffron
½ pint oysters	2 bay leaves
2 medium onions	2 cups tomato paste
1 cup white wine (Chablis)	Salt and pepper to taste
1 gallon water	Brandy
1½ cups clarified butter	
1 pound shrimp, peeled and deveined	

Sauté celery, green onions, bell pepper, carrots, onions, and garlic in 1 cup butter for 15 minutes. Add saffron and continue to sauté for 10 minutes longer. Set aside. In a large pot, bring one gallon water to a boil. Add sautéed vegetables, 2 bay leaves, 2 cups tomato paste, 16-ounce can whole tomatoes, 1 cup white wine, salt and pepper, and continue boiling for 1 hour.

While vegetables are boiling, sauté redfish, shrimp, and oysters in ½ cup butter and add to boiling vegetables. Lower heat and cook 10 minutes. Serve in soup bowls and place individual portions of crabmeat in center of each bowl. Serves 8.

Paul Naquin's French Collection I—Louisiana Seafood

Bouillabaisse—A soup or stew made of several types of fish or shellfish. The fish is cooked with white wine or water, and usually olive oil, tomatoes and herbs.

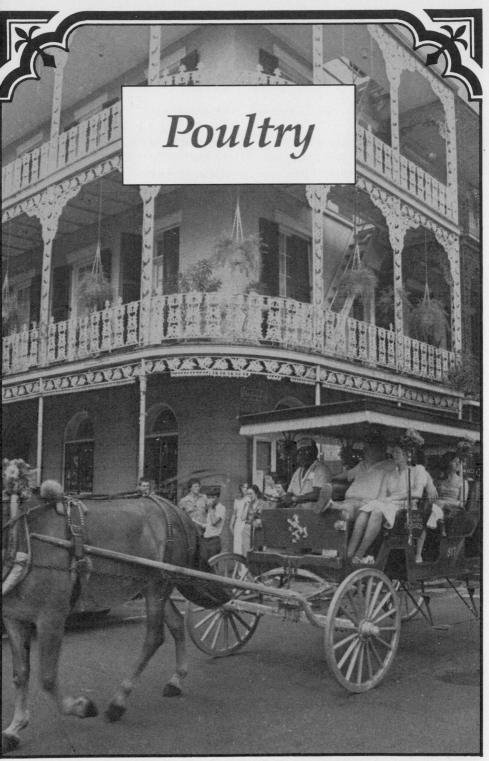

Poultry

A carriage ride through the French Quarter. New Orleans.

Poulet Blanc

3 chicken breasts (6 half breasts),
  deboned
3 tablespoons olive oil
3 toes of garlic, finely chopped
2 tablespoons lemon juice
½ teaspoon thyme
½ teaspoon salt
1 stick butter

1 tablespoon oil
4 shallots, finely chopped
5 tablespoons flour
3 cups whole milk
Black pepper
2 dashes Tabasco
Pinch of ground nutmeg

The chicken breasts have to be deboned, and this is not as formidable a task as it is thought to be. Hold the breast with the inside (or bone side) facing you and with the pointed end toward the left. Fold in half, away from you, and the bone will crack in half. Now, keep shoving the thumbs between the meat and the bones, and in a short time, and with a little practice, you'll be able to debone chicken breasts without a knife, in less than half a minute.

Place the deboned breasts between two pieces of wax paper and with the flat of your cleaver, pound the meat hard until it spreads almost double. Slice the flattened breasts into strips. Marinate for one hour in the olive oil, garlic, lemon juice, thyme, and salt. Stir a few times.

After the meat has been marinated, melt the butter in your heavy skillet, add the oil, and fry the strips of chicken for 2 minutes on each side. (Do not overcook, as chicken breasts have a tendency to get a little rubbery if cooked too long.) Remove the chicken and add the shallots to the pan; sauté until tender. Add the flour, mix well, and, stirring constantly, cook for 4 minutes. Add the milk slowly, stirring all the while and mixing well. Salt and pepper to taste and add the 2 dashes of Tabasco. When the milk begins to simmer, return the chicken to the pan and allow to simmer slowly for a few minutes until the sauce is thickened and the chicken is heated.

Add the nutmeg, stir, and the dish is ready to serve. It can be served over noodles or a slice of toast. Serves 4 to 6.

La Bouche Creole

Chicken Fricasse with Dumplings

FRICASSE:

1 cup all-purpose flour
½ cup vegetable oil
1 cup chopped onions
½ cup chopped celery, (optional)
½ cup chopped green pepper,
  (optional)

1 (2 to 3-pound) hen, cut into
  serving pieces
1 quart water
Salt and pepper to taste

Make a roux by slowly browning the flour in the oil. This process must be carefully watched and stirred constantly. When roux is golden brown, add the onion, celery, and green pepper, if desired; cook, stirring constantly, until vegetables are soft. Add chicken pieces to roux mixture, stirring and cooking about 1 minute longer. Add 1 quart water and bring to a boil, stirring frequently. Continue cooking and adding water so as to render the meat tender and to give the fricasse desired consistency. (For best results, it will require several hours of slow cooking.) If dumplings are desired, add about 1½ cups additional water and bring to a boil. Reduce heat to simmer.

DUMPLINGS:

2 cups all-purpose flour
1 teaspoon baking powder
Salt and pepper to taste
½ cup chopped green onion tops
  or fresh parsley

2 egg yolks
½ cup water

In small bowl combine flour, baking powder, seasoning and onion tops; mixing well. In separate bowl, beat egg yolks and add ½ cup water; add to flour mixture until a soft dough is formed. Drop dough by spoonsful in simmering fricasse; cook slowly, stirring very little until dumplings are cooked. Serve on hot fluffy rice.

Foods à la Louisiane

Fricassee—To cut meat, poultry or seafood into small pieces and then braise.

Cajun Fried Chicken

1 (2 to 3-pound) fryer
⅓ teaspoon red pepper
1 tablespoon yellow mustard
3 ounces Tabasco
4 tablespoons water
3 cups self-rising flour

1. Combine red pepper, yellow mustard, Tabasco and water to make a sauce. 2. Cut up fryer into frying pieces; salt chicken pieces. 3. Dip chicken in sauce and roll in flour. 4. Fry at 400 degrees for about 10 minutes on each side until golden brown. 5. Drain on paper towels. 6. Serves 4.

Louisiana Largesse

Fried Chicken

1 (3 to 3½-pound) fryer, cut up
1½ cups oil for frying
Salt to taste
Pepper to taste
1 egg beaten
1 cup Half & Half or light cream
1 cup water
½ cup flour

Wash chicken and pat dry. Season with salt and pepper. Make egg batter combining egg, cream, water, salt and pepper. Preheat oil to about 350 degrees. Dip chicken in egg batter to coat and then in flour. Fry, adding meatiest pieces first. Brown on all sides until tender, about 15 minutes.

Recipes and Reminiscences of New Orleans II

Perfect Country Fried Chicken

2 broiler-fryers, cut in serving pieces
6 tablespoons flour
1½ teaspoons salt
1 teaspoon paprika
¼ teaspoon pepper
Shortening

Toss chicken pieces in paper bag containing flour, salt, paprika, and pepper. Spread on rack to dry coating. Heat oil very hot in heavy skillet. Add chicken and brown rapidly on all sides (about 10 minutes). Reduce heat and cook slowly until tender (about 30 minutes). Turn pieces for even browning.

The Buster Holmes Restaurant Cookbook

Barbecued Chicken
(*Microwave*)

Cooking Time: 42 minutes
Utensils: Flat glass baking dish
  4-cup measuring cup
Servings: 6

1 (3-pound) fryer, cut up	1 onion, sliced
¼ teaspoon cayenne pepper	½ lemon, sliced

1. Season chicken with cayenne pepper and place in baking dish. Arrange chicken so that the meaty portions are near the outer edge of dish and boney portions in the center. Place sliced onion and lemon on top of chicken. Cover with wax paper and microwave on HIGH 8 MINUTES. Turn dish at 4 minutes.

SAUCE:

¼ cup Worcestershire sauce	1 teaspoon salt
½ cup catsup	1 teaspoon chili powder
½ cup water	½ teaspoon garlic powder
½ teaspoon Tabasco	

2. Mix Worcestershire sauce, catsup, water, Tabasco, salt, chili powder and garlic powder in a 4-cup measure and microwave on HIGH 3 OR 4 MINUTES until sauce comes to boil. Pour sauce over chicken, cover with wax paper and microwave on HIGH 30 MINUTES or until chicken is done. Turn dish every 10 minutes.

Tout de Suite à la Microwave I

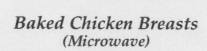

Baked Chicken Breasts
(Microwave)

Cooking Time: 11 minutes
Utensils: 2-quart dish
        8-inch square glass dish
        1-cup glass measuring cup
Servings: 4–6

**6 chicken breast halves, skinned
  and boned
1 cup dairy sour cream
2 tablespoons lemon juice
2 teaspoons Worcestershire sauce**

**½ teaspoon celery salt
1 teaspoon paprika
¼ teaspoon garlic powder
1½ teaspoons salt
¼ teaspoon red pepper**

1. Rinse and dry 6 chicken breast halves with paper towels. In a 2-quart dish combine sour cream, lemon juice, Worcestershire sauce, celery salt, paprika, garlic powder, salt and pepper. Add chicken to sour cream mixture, coating each piece well. Let stand, covered, in refrigerator overnight or at least eight hours.

**1 cup seasoned bread crumbs
¼ cup margarine**

2. Carefully remove coated chicken from sour cream mixture. Roll in crumbs, coating evenly. Arrange single layer in an 8-inch square shallow baking dish. Micromelt margarine in a 1-cup measure on HIGH (100%) 1 MINUTE and drizzle over chicken. Microwave on HIGH (100%) 10 MINUTES or until chicken is tender.

Tout de Suite à la Microwave II

Chicken Martinique

4 chicken breasts
¾ cup red wine (Burgundy)
2 tablespoons soy sauce
¼ teaspoon coarse ground black pepper
¼ teaspoon chopped basil leaves
¼ cup chopped green onion
2 pods of garlic, minced
¼ stick butter

¼ cup red wine vinegar
1 pinch curry powder
1 tablespoon Lea & Perrins sauce
Juice of ½ lemon and rind
¼ teaspoon salt
¼ cup chopped celery
1 teaspoon flour
¼ cup olive oil
½ cup water

Put vinegar, wine, butter, curry, soy sauce, Lea & Perrins, lemon juice and rinds, coarse ground pepper, basil and salt in a small pot and bring to a boil. Lower heat and simmer for 5 minutes.

Place chicken breasts in a deep glass bowl. Pour marinade over chicken and cover bowl. Let chicken marinate over 2 hours, turning and mixing every half hour to insure even marinating of chicken.

Put olive oil in a skillet. Salt and pepper chicken and brown well on both sides, approximately 15 minutes each side. Brown skin side first. Add green onions, celery, and garlic. Cook in covered skillet or pot for 15 minutes. Add ½ cup of marinade and cook slowly for additional 15 minutes. Mix flour and ½ cup water and add to chicken. Stir well and cook 15 minutes longer. Serves 4.

Paul Naquin's French Collection II—Meats & Poultry

Deviled Chicken

1 cup cooked, diced chicken
¼ cup slivered almonds
1 small onion, chopped
½ cup mayonnaise
2 or 3 hard cooked eggs
1 cup cooked rice

1 can cream of mushroom soup
Salt to taste
1 teaspoon lemon juice
¾ cup diced celery
Crushed potato chips
Paprika

Mix and place ingredients in buttered casserole or pan with crushed potato chips over top. Add paprika for color. Bake at 375 degrees for 30 to 45 minutes. Serves 6. This is a nice ladies' luncheon dish.

Cane River Cuisine

Smothered Chicken

1 (3-pound) fryer
Salt and pepper to taste
½ cup flour
½ cup vegetable oil
1 cup chopped onions
1 cup chopped celery

3 cloves chopped garlic
½ cup chopped green onions
  (reserve tops to garnish)
1 small chopped bell pepper
1 cup chopped mushrooms
1 quart water

Cut fryer into serving pieces and season with salt and pepper; set aside. In a heavy pot, make roux using oil and flour. Cook until brown. Add all seasonings except mushrooms. Sauté until done (15 minutes). Add chicken and stir well. Cook approximately 20 minutes. Add water, mushrooms and green onion tops. Cover and let simmer for approximately 1 hour. Season to taste.

The Encyclopedia of Cajun and Creole Cuisine

Brunswick Stew
(Ragôut Brunswick)

1 large hen
2 cups canned tomatoes
1 tablespoon low fat oleo
1¼ tablespoons flour
3 tablespoons low fat oleo
2 cups chopped onions
2 cloves chopped garlic
1 cup heart of celery, chopped

1 pint broth
2 cups creamed corn
1 cup chopped green onions
1 cup chopped parsley
1 cup chopped bell pepper
Salt & pepper to taste
½ cup canned mushrooms
4 hard cooked eggs, cut in half

Boil hen in enough seasoned water to make 1 pint broth. Save broth and cut chicken into small pieces. Cook tomatoes in 1 tablespoon oleo until thickened. Make a roux with flour, 3 tablespoons oleo, onions, garlic, and celery. Add broth, tomatoes, chicken, corn, green onions, parsley, bell pepper, mushrooms, and salt and pepper to taste. Cook for 1 hour, adding more broth if needed. Add eggs when cooked.

Total: 8 servings. Per serving: 333 calories.
Exchanges per serving = 3½ meats, 1 bread, 1 vegetable, 1 fat
20 grams carbohydrates, 28½ grams protein, 15½ grams fat

Cooking for Love and Life

Louisiana Chicken Sauce Piquant

2 cups (500 ml) vegetable oil or
  shortening
2 chickens, approximately three
  pounds (1.4 kg) each, cut into
  pieces
Salt to taste
Red pepper to taste
Black pepper to taste
3 pounds (1.4 kg) onions, finely
  chopped
4 cloves garlic, finely chopped

1 cup (250 ml) finely chopped
  celery
1 cup (250 ml) finely chopped
  green pepper
3 eight-ounce (227-gram) cans
  tomato sauce
2 tablespoons (30 ml)
  Worcestershire sauce
3 cups (750 ml) water, more as
  needed

Heat oil in a large cast iron pot. Season chicken with salt, red pepper and black pepper; brown in oil. Remove from pot and set aside. Pour off all but ½ cup (125 ml) oil and sauté finely-chopped onions, garlic, celery and green pepper slowly in remaining oil for about 10 minutes. Add browned chicken, tomato sauce, Worcestershire sauce and water to sautéed vegetables. Lower heat and simmer slowly, stirring occasionally to prevent sticking. Cook chicken until tender. Serve over long grain rice.

Hint: Add a small amount of roux, if a thicker sauce is desired.

'Tiger Bait' Recipes

Chicken and Asparagus Casserole

5 tablespoons flour
1 teaspoon salt
¼ teaspoon onion salt
¼ cup butter, melted
2½ cups light cream
1⅓ cups minute rice
1½ cups chicken (or turkey) broth
½ teaspoon pepper

1½ cups sharp cheese, grated
1½ cups asparagus or broccoli,
  cooked
2½ cups (or more) chicken or
  turkey, sliced
2 tablespoons slivered almonds,
  toasted

Sift flour, ½ of salt, and onion salt into melted butter. Stir in cream. Cook, stirring until thick. Pour rice into a 2-quart shallow baking dish. Combine broth, remaining salt, and pepper; pour over rice. Sprinkle ½ of cheese over rice. Top with asparagus; then chicken. Pour over sauce. Sprinkle with remaining cheese. Bake, uncovered, at 375 degrees F. about 30 minutes. Top with almonds. Freezes. Serves 4.

Pirate's Pantry

Chicken Crêpes

CRÊPE BATTER:

⅔ cups unsifted all-purpose flour   ⅛ teaspoon salt

2 eggs   1 cup milk

3 tablespoons melted, cooled
   butter

In a medium bowl, combine flour, eggs, butter, salt and ½ cup milk. Beat with rotary beater until smooth. Beat in remaining ½ cup milk until well blended. Refrigerate batter, covered, for several hours or overnight.

CHICKEN FILLING:

¼ cup butter or oleo   ½ cup dry sherry

1 (6-ounce) can sliced   ½ teaspoon salt
   mushrooms, drained   Pepper to taste

½ cup chopped green onion

2½ to 3 cups diced cooked
   chicken (one 3-pound fryer)

About 1 hour before cooking crêpes, make chicken filling. Heat butter in large skillet and add mushrooms and onion. Sauté until onion is clear, about 10 minutes. Add chicken, wine, salt and pepper. Cook over high heat, stirring frequently, until no liquid remains in skillet. Remove from heat and set aside.

SAUCE:

¼ cup unsifted all-purpose flour   ½ teaspoon salt

⅔ cup sherry   ⅛ teaspoon pepper

1 (10½-ounce) can condensed   ½ cup grated Swiss cheese
   chicken broth   Salad oil

2 cups light cream

In medium saucepan, blend flour with sherry. Stir in chicken broth, light cream, salt and pepper. Over medium heat, bring to boiling point, stirring constantly. Reduce heat and simmer, stirring once or twice, about 2 minutes. This will be a thin sauce. Add half of sauce of chicken filling. Stir until well blended. Set filling and rest of sauce aside.

To cook crêpes, slowly heat a 7-inch skillet or crêpe pan until a

CONTINUED

CONTINUED

drop of water sizzles off. Brush lightly with salad oil. Pour in about 3 tablespoons of batter, rotating pan quickly so batter will completely cover bottom of skillet. Cook over medium heat until lightly browned. Turn and brown other side. Turn out on wire rack. Repeat, being sure pan is hot enough, before cooking each crêpe. Preheat oven to 425 degrees. Place about ¼ cup of filling on each crêpe and then roll up. Arrange seam side down in single layer in buttered shallow baking dish. Pour rest of sauce over crêpes and sprinkle with grated cheese. Bake for 15 minutes until lightly browned and cheese is bubbly. Makes 15 crêpes.

Cane River Cuisine

Hot Chicken Salad Casserole

4 cups (1 liter) diced chicken
2 (10¾-ounce) (305-gram) cans cream of chicken soup or 2½ cups (625 ml) medium white sauce
2 cups (500 ml) diced celery
¼ cup (60 ml) minced onion
2 cups (500 ml) slivered almonds
1 cup (250 ml) mayonnaise
¾ cup (185 ml) chicken stock
1 teaspoon (5 ml) salt
½ teaspoon (2.5 ml) black pepper
¼ cup (60 ml) freshly squeezed lemon juice
6 hard-cooked eggs, finely chopped
1 cup (250 ml) cracker crumbs

Combine all the above ingredients except cracker crumbs and place in a 4-quart (4-liter) casserole dish. Cover with cracker crumbs. Bake at 350 degrees F (175 degrees C) for approximately 40 minutes. Serves 10. Good and not too expensive when you entertain.

'Tiger Bait' Recipes

Chicken Rosalie

12 halves chicken breasts, boned
and skinned
¼ pound margarine
12 slices ham
1 cup mushrooms
1 (10½-ounce) can cream of
chicken soup
1 (10½-ounce) can cream of
mushroom soup

½ cup white wine
1 teaspoon poultry seasoning
1 teaspoon thyme
1 teaspoon sage
1 teaspoon paprika
1 teaspoon Tabasco
Minced parsley

Sauté chicken breasts lightly in margarine. Place each on a ham slice in a 9 × 12-inch greased baking dish. In same skillet used for browning chicken, sauté mushrooms. Add remaining ingredients, mix well and spoon over chicken and ham. Sprinkle with parsley and bake at 275 degrees for 2½ hours.

Louisiana Entertains

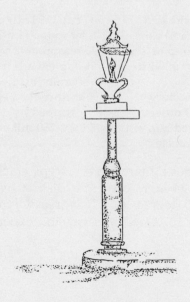

Seasoning the Turkey

Amounts depend on size of
turkey:
Mixture of salt, black pepper and
red pepper
Garlic, chopped

Bell pepper, chopped
Pecan halves
Butter, cut into pats
Celery
Parsley

1. Rinse thawed bird and pat dry. 2. Puncture all meaty parts with the point of a knife to form deep but narrow pockets all over bird. (Be sure to make many pockets all over breasts and thighs.) 3. Mix salt, black pepper and red pepper together. 4. Add chopped garlic and bell pepper to salt mixture. 5. Take small amount of this seasoning and push it down into pockets. 6. Now push 1 or 2 pecan halves into each of the slits. 7. Finish by putting a small pat of butter into each pocket. 8. Rub entire outside with salt, red and black peppers. 9. Season cavity with salt and pepper. 10. Add about ⅓ bunch fresh parsley, ⅓ bunch green onions, and 2 or 3 pieces of celery. 11. Cook turkey as desired until tender. 12. The roasting process is not complicated, but timing is important. It takes several hours, whether turkey is cooked in a covered roasting pan or barbecued on a rotisserie. 13. Use the suggested roasting time on the wrapping, but 30 minutes before the end of the suggested time, test for doneness. This can be done by inserting a meat thermometer deep into the thigh (not touching the bone). When the thermometer reaches 180 to 185 degrees the turkey is done. 14. Another way to tell is to protect the thumb and forefinger with a cloth or paper towel and pinch the thickest part of the drumstick. When done the meat will be soft to the touch and the drumstick will move easily in the socket.

Louisiana Largesse

Turkey Crunch Casserole
(Casserole de dinde croquée)

1½ pounds diced cooked turkey
2 hard cooked eggs, chopped
1 (4-ounce) can sliced mushrooms
1 cup diced celery
½ cup slivered blanched almonds

1 tablespoon chopped onion
1 (10½-ounce) can condensed
  cream of chicken soup
¾ cup low fat mayonnaise
15 crushed potato chips

Mix together first 6 ingredients. Stir soup into mayonnaise. Toss with turkey mixture. Turn into a 8×8×2-inch baking dish. Sprinkle top with potato chips. Bake at 350 degrees for 30 minutes, or until mixture is bubbling.

Total: 8 servings. Per serving: 335 calories
Exchanges per serving = 3 meats, 3 fats, ½ bread
7½ grams carbohydrates, 22 grams protein, 24 grams fat

Cooking for Love and Life

Game

Louisiana wildlife. Jungle Gardens of Avery Island, near New Iberia.

Quail Joseph

12 whole quail
2 quarts milk
Salt, red pepper and black
  pepper
1 cup flour
1 quart cooking oil
2 medium onions, chopped
12 green onions, chopped
2 tablespoons oil
3 tablespoons flour

2 cups water
2 cans sliced mushrooms, reserve
  1 cup liquor
4 chicken bouillon cubes
1 cup chopped parsley
2 cloves garlic, crushed
Salt and black pepper
2 cups cooking sherry
2 cans button mushrooms

Skin quail and place in 2-quarts of milk. Marinate overnight. Remove quail from milk and drain and dry thoroughly. Rub inside cavities and surface with black pepper, red pepper and salt. Then flour and shake off excess flour. Heat the quart of cooking oil until it begins to lightly smoke on top. Then, quick-fry quail until golden brown.

Prepare the sauce by sautéing chopped onions and chopped green onions in oil until transparent. Then add 3 tablespoons flour and cook until lightly brown. If this does not make the gravy brown enough, then Kitchen Bouquet may be added to enhance the color. Add 2 cups of water and 1 cup of liquor from the mushrooms slowly, stirring constantly. Add bouillon cubes to this. Stir and cook over low heat for approximately 30 minutes. Add the seasonings, salt and pepper to taste and add ½ cup sherry along with the mushrooms and cook for 15 minutes longer.

Now take the sauce and pour over the quail and sprinkle ½ of the cup of chopped parsley over the quail. Cover snugly with aluminum foil and bake at 350 degrees for 1 hour. Remove foil and add another cup of sherry and baste. Replace cover on pot and cook for an additional 1 hour at 250 degrees. Just before this time has ended, add the remaining wine. Cover again and cook for an additional 30 minutes. This can be served with wild rice or white rice and will serve approximately 6 to 8. Garnish with remaining parsley.

Cane River Cuisine

Quail in Herb Sauce

8 quail
Salt and pepper

½ stick butter
Flour

Salt and pepper quail and lightly dust with flour. Heat butter in a skillet and brown quail well on all sides. Cover skillet and cook on low fire for 20 minutes.

HERB SAUCE:

2 teaspoons fresh chopped
    parsley
2 tablespoons chopped green
    onion tops
1 teaspoon cornstarch

¼ teaspoon sage
½ stick butter
1 cup milk
Salt and white pepper to taste

After quail cook covered for 20 minutes, remove lid and add green onion, parsley, sage and butter. Sauté with quail for 5 minutes. Stir occasionally to mix with pan drippings. Mix cornstarch and milk and add to quail. Cook additional 10 minutes. Serve quail topped with sauce. Serves 4.

Paul Naquin's French Collection III—Louisiana Wild Game

Roast Pheasant or Chukar

Pheasant and chukar may be cooked together with great success in any number of combinations. Cook quantities according to number of guests. Suggestion: Serve 1 chukar per person, ½ large pheasant per person, or cook birds and cut and serve meat of both birds to each guest. Great combination served together.

PREPARATION:
1 gallon water
2 tablespoons salt

Soak birds in salt water for one hour. Carefully go over birds for shot and feathers which are often caught in flesh with shot. Wash and pat dry with paper towel.

COOKING:

⅛ teaspoon marjoram	Butter
Onion salt	Celery (2 or 3 stalks)
⅛ teaspoon Thyme	1 cup white wine

Heat butter in skillet or fry pan and brown birds on all sides being careful not to burn butter or birds. Remove birds from skillet. Season inside and out of each bird with the above seasonings. Place birds in a roaster or pan that can be covered with foil. Place two or three stalks of celery in pan with birds. Discard celery before serving. Add one cup white wine, cover and place in 350-degree oven for two hours. Baste birds with pan juices each ½ hour while cooking. Remove cover for last half hour and reduce heat to 250 degrees.

A compliment to these birds is a casserole of Uncle Ben's Wild Rice prepared according to directions but baked in the oven. This has to be covered very tightly with foil. Stir occasionally during baking time which is at least one hour. Before serving, spoon at least six tablespoons of drippings from the roasting pan into the rice casserole and stir in gently.

Paul Naquin's French Collection III—Louisiana Wild Game

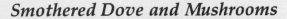

Smothered Dove and Mushrooms

8 dove
½ cup bacon drippings
Salt, pepper, and Cayenne
  pepper
1 teaspoon finely chopped garlic
2 tablespoons green onion tops,
  chopped
1 pound small-to-medium fresh
  mushrooms

2 medium onions (sliced ½-inch
  thick)
2 ounces port wine
½ stick butter
1 tablespoon flour
1 cup milk

Sprinkle inside and out of doves with salt and pepper and lightly sprinkle inside of doves with Cayenne (red) pepper. Heat bacon drippings and brown the doves on all sides. Place doves in casserole dish that can be covered. Retain bacon drippings. Slice onions, separate rings, then brown the onion rings in drippings. Remove onion and place over doves in casserole. Spread mushrooms over onions and doves. Spread chopped garlic over all.

Add butter to drippings and heat. Add flour and cook on medium high fire, stirring constantly until flour browns lightly. Lower fire and slowly add milk, stirring constantly to mix evenly. Add port wine, mix well and pour this mixture into casserole of doves. Sprinkle lightly with salt and pepper. Sprinkle green onion tops over all. Cover dish and place in a 300-degree oven for one hour. Serves 4.

Paul Naquin's French Collection III—Louisiana Wild Game

Barbequed Duck

BARBEQUE SAUCE:

½ cup leftover wine, lemon and
  butter marinade from above
1 medium clove garlic, pressed
1 teaspoon brown sugar
¼ teaspoon salt

½ teaspoon Worcestershire sauce
½ cup finely chopped onion
⅛ teaspoon fresh ground pepper
⅛ teaspoon ginger

Place all barbeque sauce ingredients in a saucepan and simmer for fifteen minutes.

2 (2 to 2½-pound) ducks
½ pound butter

½ cup Burgundy wine
¼ cup lemon juice

Cut whole ducks in half and place in pot with melted butter, wine, and lemon juice. Simmer ducks in marinade for 10 minutes and remove from heat. Keep covered for 1 hour turning every 15 minutes. Remove ducks from marinade and retain marinade. Salt and pepper both sides and place halves skin side down in large baking dish or dishes. Baste with barbecue sauce. Cover with foil and place in 300-degree oven for 45 minutes. Turn duck halves over, coat well with barbeque sauce. Cover and cook for additional 45 minutes. Lower heat to 300 degrees. Uncover and bake duck for additional 30 minutes, basting with sauce every 10 minutes.

Paul Naquin's French Collection III—Louisiana Wild Game

Chateau Teal

4 teal ducks
1 lemon
2 teaspoons salt
1 teaspoon black pepper
1 teaspoon paprika
1 teaspoon garlic salt
2 teaspoons herb seasoning
1 apple, quartered
Flour
½ stick butter plus 1 teaspoon oil

2 large onions, chopped
1 green pepper, chopped
2 pods garlic, chopped
1 package onion soup mix
2 cups water
⅓ cup orange juice
1 (4-ounce) can mushrooms stems
& pieces
3 tablespoons orange marmalade
⅓ cup red wine

Clean inside of ducks with cool running water, removing lungs and bits of inside membrane and tissue. Pat dry and rub outside with lemon slices. Season well inside and out. Stuff each teal with a quarter of an apple. Dust lightly with flour. Brown birds in butter and oil on both sides, starting with the breast, then turn over to back and brown. After browning, add chopped onion, green pepper and garlic to the pot to wilt, approximately 5–10 minutes. When vegetables are wilted, add 1 package onion soup mix and 2 cups water and turn teal over with the breasts down. Cover pot and turn fire to lowest simmer. Cook approximately 2 hours. Halfway through cooking time, add ⅓ cup orange juice. Thirty minutes before end of cooking time, add can of mushrooms and marmalade and squeeze juice of ½ lemon into pot. Adjust seasonings. Last 15 minutes add ⅓ cup red wine. Ducks are done when meat at breastbone begins to separate slightly. Serves 4.

Talk About Good II

Daddy's Baked Duck

3 ducks (preferably Mallards)
6 slices bacon
Salt to taste
Pepper to taste
1 (10¾-ounce) can cream of
   mushroom soup, undiluted

¼ cup water
1 large chopped onion
2 (4-ounce) cans sliced
   mushrooms, drained
Hot cooked rice

Preheat oven to 425 degrees. Season ducks with salt and pepper; place in a roaster pan. Place 2 slices bacon on each duck. Bake at 425 degrees F. for 20 minutes. Cover; reduce heat to 300 degrees. Cook 1–1½ hours or until tender. Cook duck and debone. Reserve stock. Skim 2 tablespoons oil from duck stock; heat in a skillet until hot. Sauté onion in hot oil until tender. Add remaining stock and cream of mushroom soup. Add ¼ cup water to soup can; add water and mushrooms to mixture. Simmer for 20 minutes. Add sliced deboned duck to mixture; simmer 30 minutes. Serve over hot, fluffy rice.

Foods à la Louisiane

Canards dans la Soupière

Wild duck, 1 per person
For each 2 ducks:
1 (10½-ounce) can beef
   consommé, full strength
½ soup can dry cocktail sherry
½ (6-ounce) can frozen orange
   juice concentrate

½ (10-ounce) jar currant or red
   plum jelly
2 tablespoons cornstarch,
   dissolved in ½ cup water
Wild or brown rice

Clean ducks. Cut in half, if necessary, to fit in large covered casserole. Pour consommé and sherry over ducks. Cover and bake in 325-degree oven for 3 hours, basting every 15 minutes. Remove ducks from liquid and take meat off bones. Discard skin; stir orange juice and jelly into liquid. Thicken with cornstarch and water. Return meat to gravy. Serve in tureen. Serve over wild or brown rice.

Revel

Stuffed Woodcock

8 woodcock	1 stick butter
Salt and pepper	2 cups white wine (Chablis)

Place birds in a deep bowl. Add wine and marinate for four hours. Turn birds occasionally to marinate evenly.

Heat butter in a skillet. Salt and pepper birds and brown them on all sides. Remove birds to baking dish. Retain butter and drippings birds were browned in.

STUFFING:

1 cup chopped onion	⅓ cup chopped celery
2 tablespoons green onion tops	1 teaspoon garlic, finely chopped
1 tablespoon parsley, finely chopped	¼ teaspoon thyme
	¼ teaspoon marjoram
3 cups cooked rice	¼ cup white wine (Chablis)

Sauté onion, celery, and green onion tops in skillet birds were browned in. Cook until soft. Add parsley, garlic, wine, thyme, and marjoram. Mix well. Add rice and mix well. Stuff birds and place in baking dish. Add ½ cup water to baking dish and cover with foil. Bake at 300 degrees. for one hour.

Paul Naquin's French Collection III—Louisiana Wild Game

Pan Fried Squirrel with Mushrooms and Onions

2 squirrels cut into serving pieces
Salt
4 tablespoons bacon fat
2 medium onions, sliced ½-inch thick
1 tablespoon tomato paste (optional)
⅛ teaspoon salt and pepper to taste
½ cup flour
Pepper
1 clove garlic, minced
¼ teaspoon Worcestershire sauce
½ stick butter
2 cups mushrooms

Soak squirrel in milk for ½ hour. Salt and pepper pieces and dredge in flour. Coat well. Brown squirrel on all sides in bacon fat. Remove squirrel from pan and set aside. Lightly brown onion slices in pan. Return squirrel to pan and mix with onions. Add garlic, Worcestershire sauce, butter, tomato paste, salt and pepper. Mix well. Cover and cook on very low fire for 40 minutes. Add mushrooms and continue cooking for 20 minutes.

Paul Naquin's French Collection III—Louisiana Wild Game

Rabbit Sauce Piquant

2 small rabbits, cut up
2 tablespoons mustard, prepared
2 tablespoons Worcestershire
3 tablespoons flour
3 tablespoons oil
1 clove garlic, chopped
5 medium onions, chopped
2 bell peppers, chopped

3 stalks celery, chopped
1 lemon, quartered
2 dill pickles, chopped
2 bay leaves
1 can mushrooms
2 cans tomato sauce
½ cup wine
Salt and pepper to taste

Mix mustard and Worcestershire together and soak rabbit in it for at least one hour. Make roux with oil and flour. Add garlic, onions, bell peppers, celery and sauté until tender. Add squeezed lemon and rind, pickles, bay leaves, mushrooms and tomato sauce. Add rabbit pieces; pour in wine and simmer 2 to 3 hours. Salt and pepper to taste.

Recipes and Reminiscences of New Orleans II

Turtle Sauce Piquant

20 pounds turtle meat
5 pounds onions
2 bunches shallots
4 bell peppers
1 bunch garlic
⅓ bunch celery
1 small bunch parsley (chop seasonings fine)
2 large cans mushrooms

4 cans cream of mushroom soup
1 pint cooking oil
6 serving spoons flour
2 cans Ro-tel whole tomatoes and peppers
Salt and pepper to taste
⅓ small bottle Lea & Perrins Worcestershire Sauce
3 tablespoons French mustard

Brown turtle meat; add onions, peppers, celery, garlic, parsley and mushroom soup. Cook until onions and seasonings cook to juice. Brown flour and cooking oil until dark brown, then add to gravy and let simmer. Let cook 4–5 hours. Add salt and pepper to taste. Add ⅓ bottle of Lea & Perrins Worcestershire sauce and 3 tablespoons of French mustard about 20 minutes before serving. Serve with rice. Serves 50.

The Encyclopedia of Cajun and Creole Cuisine

Piquant—A French word meaning lively or tangy. Most often used to describe a sauce made with roux and tomatoes.

Turtle Stew
(120-year-old recipe)

3 pounds turtle meat
3 tablespoons cooking oil or
　margarine
3 tablespoons flour
3 medium onions, chopped
2 cloves garlic, minced
2 (No. 2) cans tomatoes
1 can tomato paste
Boiling water
1 stick celery, chopped fine
1 bunch green onions, chopped
　fine

2 green bell peppers chopped fine
1 cup sherry wine
½ dozen hard-boiled eggs
Tony's Creole Seasoning or salt
　and pepper
4 bay leaves
8 whole cloves
½ teaspoon allspice, powdered
1 tablespoon sugar
¼ pound butter
1 lemon, sliced

Parboil the turtle meat. Make a brown roux of oil and flour. Add onions, garlic, bell pepper, tomato paste and tomatoes. Cook slowly 20 to 30 minutes. Add mixture to turtle meat, along with enough boiling water to cover meat. Boil down. Add celery, green onions, Tony's Creole Seasoning, wine, bay leaves, cloves, allspice and sugar.

Cook, covered, over high heat for 30 minutes. Mash egg yolks, chop the whites. Add to stew. If stew gets too thick, add a little water. Cook slowly for about 3 hours. One-half hour before serving, add sliced lemon and butter. Serves 6.

Note: To increase amount, add ½ pound of turtle meat per person.

Tony Chachere's Cajun Country Cookbook

Roux—Flour carefully browned in fat, butter or oil which Creole cooks use for thickening sauces and gravies.

Alligator Creole

This is a recipe from my first volume on Louisiana seafood for Shrimp Creole which has been altered only by substituting alligator meat for the shrimp. The alligator meat is boiled prior to using in the creole sauce so as to make it tender and also to flavor the meat. Boil the alligator meat the same way you would boil shrimp, your favorite way, or by using the boiled shrimp recipe in my book.

1 cup olive oil
¾ cup flour
2 cloves garlic, chopped
2 cups yellow onion, chopped
½ cup bell pepper, chopped
1 cup celery, chopped
2 teaspoons salt
¼ cup green onion, chopped
4 tablespoons fresh parsley, chopped

4 ripe medium tomatoes
2 (6-ounce) cans tomato paste
1 (12-ounce) can tomato sauce
¼ teaspoon black pepper
¼ teaspoon Cayenne pepper
4 pounds alligator meat (whole chops, steaks, or diced meat)

In a large heavy skillet heat one cup olive oil. Add flour and make a brown roux by constantly stirring flour and oil until flour turns to color of brown paper bag. Add onions, celery, and bell pepper and cook until soft. Add tomatoes, tomato paste, and tomato sauce. Blend. Add three cups water. Mix and simmer 30 minutes. Add alligator meat and remaining ingredients. Mix well and cook slowly for one hour. Serve over hot rice. Serves 8 to 10.

Paul Naquin's French Collection III—Louisiana Wild Game

Venison Chili

5 tablespoons salt
4 pounds ground venison
4 pounds lean ground beef
5 large onions, chopped
3 pods garlic, chopped
1 large bell pepper, chopped
2 fresh jalapeno peppers, seeded
   and chopped

4 tablespoons flour
1 teaspoon red pepper
1 (1-ounce) can ground cumin
1–1½ (3-ounce) bottles chili
   powder
5–6 cups boiling water

Sprinkle 1 tablespoon salt into bottom of largest Magnalite roaster and place over medium heat on top of stove approximately 10 minutes or until bottom begins to heat. Place all 4 pounds ground beef into roaster and spread evenly over bottom of pan. When meat begins to "fry" and begins browning, stir and break up with large spoon or fork. Continue to stir and as beef looses red color and juice accumulates in bottom of pan, add half of the venison and stir until well mixed with the beef. Add remaining venison and repeat process. Cook all meat over medium to medium-high heat until all pink color is gone. Pick out any gristle from venison as you stir meat. Add chopped onions, garlic and peppers to meat mixture and continue to stir until all vegetables are wilted and onions are transparent. Sprinkle flour over meat mixture and stir well. Add remaining 4 tablespoons salt and all ground cumin. Stir to mix thoroughly. In a large bowl, mix chili powder to 3 cups boiling water and pour into meat and vegetable mixture in roaster. Stir well and add enough remaining boiling water to bring mixture to a medium thin consistency. Turn heat on burner to medium-low and cook uncovered for several hours. Stir occasionally to prevent sticking and skim off excess oil from top as you stir. Be careful to skim only the fat and not any of the gravy. It has been my experience that the longer the chili cooks, the better the flavor. I usually cook my chili about 3–4 hours. The flavor is even better after being frozen and then thawed and reheated. Therefore, I always make at least this quantity or more, and freeze part of it. You may adjust this recipe to your needs by increasing or decreasing all ingredients proportionately. Be sure to maintain half and half balance of ground venison and ground beef.

Note: I have used other pots for this recipe, but have found that

CONTINUED

CONTINUED

when cooked in a 16-inch Magnalite roaster, the browning and cooking process is much simpler and the taste is far superior.

If you wish to use this as a dip in a chafing dish with Fritos or Doritos, cook down to a thicker consistency, or if necessary, thicken with a little cornstarch and water. Serves approximately 30.

Talk About Good II

Venison Meat Loaf

1½ pounds ground venison
2 eggs
¼ cup chopped celery
1 tablespoon fresh chopped
   parsley
½ teaspoon black pepper
½ cup seasoned bread crumbs

½ pound ground pork sausage
¾ cup chopped onion
¼ cup chopped bell pepper
1 teaspoon salt
1 teaspoon finely chopped garlic
1 (4-ounce) can tomato paste
   (optional)

Mix ground venison, pork sausage and eggs well. Add all other ingredients and mix well. Form into one large or two small loaves and place in greased baking dish. Preheat oven to 400 degrees. and place in oven uncovered for 20 to 30 minutes to brown. After browning, lower temperature to 300 degrees. Cover dish with foil and cook for 45 minutes. Can be served with your favorite brown or red gravy with rice or potatoes. This same recipe can be used for making meat balls and for stuffing bell peppers.

Paul Naquin's French Collection III—Louisiana Wild Game

Frog Legs Jesse

4 pairs medium frog legs
Salt and pepper, to taste
½ cup of flour
½ stick of butter
2½ teaspoons garlic, finely
   chopped

½ cup mushrooms, sliced
¼ cup shallots, chopped
Juice of ½ lemon

To prepare frog legs: Separate frog legs and season with salt and pepper. Dredge frog legs in flour and sauté in butter until golden brown. Add garlic and mushrooms and cook approximately 5 minutes. Add shallots and cook 3 minutes. Add lemon juice. Add brown sauce. Cover and cook over low heat for 10 to 15 minutes.

BROWN SAUCE:
1½ tablespoons clarified butter
1½ tablespoons flour
2 cups canned beef consommé

To prepare brown sauce: Melt butter in a saucepan and blend in a generous 1½ tablespoons flour, cook slowly over a low flame, stirring occasionally, until thoroughly blended and the color of brown wrapping paper. Moisten gradually with consommé, bring to a boil and cook 3 to 5 minutes, stirring constantly. Lower flame and simmer gently for 30 minutes, stirring occasionally. Skim off fat and strain the sauce through a fine sieve. Makes about 2 cups.

Recipes and Reminiscences of New Orleans II

Meats

The St. Charles Avenue Streetcar. New Orleans.

Boliche
(Stuffed Eye of the Round of Beef)

1 (3 to 4-pound) eye of the round
1 chorizo sausage, chopped
1 medium slice of cured ham,
  chopped
1 clove garlic, minced
1 large Spanish onion, chopped
½ green pepper, chopped
Salt and pepper, to taste

Paprika
¼ cup red wine
½ cup hot water
2 bay leaves
3 tablespoons bacon drippings
1½ teaspoons oregano
½ cup red wine

Cut lengthwise pocket in center of beef, leaving opposite end closed. Mix sausage, ham, garlic, onion and green pepper and stuff roast, packing well but not too tightly. Secure open end with skewers or wire. Salt and pepper beef all over and sprinkle generously with paprika and oregano. Brown well in bacon drippings. Remove and place on a piece of aluminum foil and garnish roast with bay leaves. Mix wine with some water and pour over roast. Wrap roast tightly in foil. Bake at 325 degrees until tender for about 3 hours. Test for doneness with a long pronged fork. Slice thin and serve with remaining gravy. Serves 8.

Recipes and Reminiscences of New Orleans II

Ossobuco
(Italian Veal or Beef Shanks)

4 tablespoons butter
6 veal shanks (cut into 3-inch
  pieces)
1 cup chopped onions
1 large garlic clove, chopped
2 cups Italian style tomatoes
Salt and pepper to taste
4 tablespoons olive oil

½ cup all-purpose flour
½ cup chopped celery
1 cup chopped carrots
1½ cup Maderia wine
Oregano
1½ cup chicken stock
Sweet basil

Preheat oven to 350 degrees. Heat butter and oil in Dutch oven. Dust shanks in flour and lightly brown on both sides. Remove shanks and add vegetables and sauté until wilted. Add tomatoes, chicken stock, wine and seasonings. Return shanks to Dutch oven and adjust seasonings. Cover and cook in oven for 1½ to 2 hours. Serve over pasta. Serves 6.

The Best of South Louisiana Cooking

Daube Glacée

10 pounds boneless chuck roast
1 can consommé
6 large onions
Pinch thyme
3 or 4 bay leaves
2 or 3 cloves garlic

Salt, pepper, cayenne pepper to
taste
4 ounces sherry or Madeira wine
1 package gelatin to each pint of
liquid

Rub meat with salt and pepper, and brown in fat. Place meat in large pot. Add water and consommé to cover (less liquid, if pressure cooked). Add onions, thyme, bay leaves, garlic, salt, pepper. Simmer 5–7 hours, or until meat is tender. Remove meat; strain stock. Add sherry or wine to stock. Bring to boil and remove from fire. To stock add gelatin, already softened in small quantity of water. Place meat in mold (vegetable crisper, or other large enamel pan, suggested). Pour hot stock and gelatin over meat. Skim off grease as it rises to top. Mold in refrigerator until congealed. Serve cold, unmolding in lukewarm water. Place on platter and garnish with parsley, tomato wedges, green pepper rings, etc. Serves at least 20.

River Road Recipes I

Daube Glacée—A French stew made with braised meat, vegetables, herbs and other seasonings.

Shrimp and Veal Rolls

Put this recipe at the top of your "specialty" list. It's one you'll want to serve not only to your family but to VIPs as well. While it might take a little extra effort to prepare, believe me, it's worth every minute! D-E-L-I-C-I-O-U-S!

1 stick margarine
2 cups peeled and raw diced
   shrimp
4 prime veal cutlets, thinly sliced
Salt and pepper to taste
¼ cup grated Parmesan cheese
2 tablespoons finely chopped
   fresh parsley

2 tablespoons coarsely chopped
   black olives
1 medium white onion, coarsely
   chopped
1 (10¾-ounce) can cream of
   mushroom soup

In a large skillet, melt the stick of margarine and sauté the diced shrimp *lightly*. All you want to do is turn them pink—*don't cook them*. While the shrimp are sautéing, lightly salt and pepper the cutlets and set them on several strips of waxed paper. As soon as the shrimp are pink, pour them (and the margarine) into a mixing bowl and add the cheese, parsley, olives, and onions. With a spoon, turn everything over and over until it's blended well, then spoon the mixture onto the cutlets. Try to keep the shrimp layer the same thickness throughout.

Now roll the veal *tightly* and pierce each cutlet with several toothpicks to keep it together. When all four have been rolled, place them in a baking pan. Then open the can of mushroom soup and generously spoon over each cutlet. (If you have extra shrimp mix, dribble that over the soup.) Finally, place the rolls in the oven and bake them (basting occasionally) at about 325 degrees for about 45 minutes or until the veal is tender.

Hint: You should do this meal up right! I'd prepare stuffed mushrooms as appetizers, follow it with a subtle onion soup, then serve the veal rolls with buttered Irish potatoes, green beans, and a fresh spinach salad. I'd also select a nice Rhine wine to go with the meal. And I'd top it all off with fresh strawberries and cheesecake.

The Frank Davis Seafood Notebook

Veal Parmigiana
(Microwave)

Cooking Time: 15 minutes
Utensils: Microwave browning skillet
       2-quart batter bowl
       Glass 7 × 12 baking dish
Yield: 6 to 8 servings

3 thin veal round steaks
1 cup dry bread crumbs
¼ cup Parmesan cheese
2 eggs, slightly beaten
2 tablespoons olive oil
1 cup chopped onions
1 clove garlic, crushed
2 tablespoons olive oil
1 (16-ounce) can whole tomatoes

2 (8-ounce) cans tomato sauce
1½ teaspoons ground basil
½ teaspoon thyme
1 teaspoon salt
½ teaspoon pepper
1 (8-ounce) package Mozzarella
   cheese
½ cup grated Parmesan cheese

1. Cut veal into serving-size pieces. In shallow dish, combine bread crumbs and ¼ cup Parmesan cheese. Set aside.

2. In shallow dish, place beaten egg. Salt and pepper veal, dip in eggs, then dip in crumb mixture. Set aside.

3. Preheat Microwave browning skillet on HIGH FOR 8 MINUTES. Pour 2 tablespoons olive oil into hot Microwave browning skillet. Add veal.

4. Microwave on HIGH FOR 1 MINUTE, turn over and microwave on HIGH FOR 1 MINUTE. Set aside.

5. In 2-quart batter bowl, combine onions, garlic, and 2 tablespoons olive oil.

6. Microwave on HIGH FOR 5 TO 6 MINUTES or until soft but not brown.

7. Add tomatoes, tomato sauce, basil, thyme, salt, and pepper. Mix well. Cover with plastic wrap.

8. Microwave on HIGH FOR 4 MINUTES or until hot.

9. Cut Mozzarella cheese into enough slices to cover each piece of meat. Spoon some sauce into glass 7 × 12-inch baking dish. Arrange alternate, overlapping slices of cheese and veal in the dish. Spoon remaining sauce over top of veal. Sprinkle with ½ cup Parmesan cheese.

10. Microwave on 70% POWER FOR 4 TO 5 MINUTES or until hot and bubbly. Let stand, 5 minutes before serving.

Tony Chachere's Microwave Cajun Country Cookbook

Creole Grillades and Grits

2 pounds round steak, ½-inch
thick
Flour seasoned with salt and
pepper
4 tablespoons oil
2 onions, chopped
1 bell pepper, chopped
2 ribs celery, chopped
3 cloves garlic, crushed
1 (10-ounce) can Ro-tel tomatoes
with green chilies, chopped
3 tablespoons tomato paste

1 teaspoon sugar
1 bay leaf
¼ teaspoon *each* thyme, basil and
oregano
Salt and pepper to taste
1 tablespoon Worcestershire
sauce
1½ cups beef broth
½ cup dry red wine
2 tablespoons *each* chopped
parsley and green onion tops

Trim and cut steak into serving-size pieces. Sprinkle liberally with seasoned flour. Beat with tenderizing mallet until flour is pounded in and meat is thin. Brown meat in oil in large skillet. Remove from skillet and set aside. Add onion, bell pepper, celery and garlic to skillet. Sauté until wilted. Add tomatoes, tomato paste and sugar. Simmer 4 minutes. Add bay leaf, thyme, basil, oregano, salt and pepper to taste. Add Worcestershire, broth, wine, parsley and onion tops. Bring to boil. Reduce heat, add meat. Cover. Simmer over low heat 30–40 minutes until meat is tender and gravy is thick. Serve over hot Cheese Garlic Grits. Yield: 8–10 servings.

CHEESE GARLIC GRITS:
1½ cups quick yellow grits
6 cups water
1½ teaspoons salt
1 (6-ounce) roll garlic cheese,
grated

½ cup butter
2 tablespoons heavy cream
2 eggs, beaten

Add grits to boiling salted water in large saucepan. Bring back to boil, reduce heat and cook stirring 5 minutes. Add cheese, butter, cream and eggs. Stir until cheese melts. Pour into greased 9 × 13-inch or 3-quart casserole dish. Bake in preheated 350-degree oven 30–40 minutes. Serve with grillades.

Voilà! Lafayette Centennial Cookbook 1884–1984

 Grillades—Browned beefsteaks served over grits or rice.

Grillades

1½ pounds veal steak
Flour, salt, pepper
2 tablespoons oil
⅓ cup onion, chopped
⅓ cup celery, chopped

⅓ cup bell pepper, chopped
1 (8-ounce) can tomato sauce
¼ teaspoon thyme
1 bay leaf
Seasonings to taste

Take a tender veal steak and cut into cutlets about 4-inches long and 4-inches wide. Flour, salt and pepper very lightly and fry to a golden brown. Set aside. Using fat cutlets were fried in, fry the following seasonings with tomato sauce: onion, celery, and bell pepper. Return cutlets to pan and spoon sauce over. Add water until they are covered; let simmer until meat is tender and gravy is brown. Serve with rice, spaghetti or yellow grits. In sauce for grillades, put a little thyme and bay leaf for flavoring. Serves 4–6.

Talk About Good II

Pepper Steak

1 pound round steak, 1½ inch
   thick
1 clove garlic
2 tablespoons salad oil
Salt and pepper
2 medium onions, sliced
1 cup beef stock or consommé or
   red wine

3 green peppers, cut in pieces
½ pound mushrooms, sliced
   (optional)
2 tomatoes, cut in wedges
3 tablespoons butter

Cut steak into cubes or strips. Sauté garlic in oil a few minutes; remove and brown meat. Add salt and pepper to taste. Reduce heat; add onions and ½ cup liquid of choice; cover and simmer till tender. Sauté green pepper and mushrooms, if desired, in butter 5 minutes. Add tomato wedges; cook 1 minute; season with salt and pepper. Combine with meat for 10 minutes of gentle simmering before serving. Taste; adjust seasonings. Add ½ cup liquid, if needed. Serves 4–6.

Thicken mixture with corn starch, if desired. Serve alone or over mashed potatoes, noodles or rice.

Variation: 3 tablespoons soy sauce may be added and cooked with meat.

Encore

Marinated Black Pepper Steak
(Bifteck à poivre mariné)

1 sirloin steak, 1½ to 2-inches
thick
1 cup red wine vinegar
Brown sugar substitute equal to
⅓ cup brown sugar
¼ teaspoon marjoram
1 cup minced onion

½ cup salad or cooking oil
¼ teaspoon salt
¼ teaspoon rosemary
1 clove minced garlic
4 teaspoons coarsely crushed
peppercorns

Place steak in large shallow pan. In large jar, make marinade with remaining ingredients except peppercorns. Shake well and pour over steak. Marinate several hours or overnight. Before grilling, remove steak from marinade and press both sides of steak with 2 teaspoons peppercorns per side. Grill 3 to 4 inches from coals, allowing about 15 minutes for total grilling time. (Test doneness by slitting meat near bone and noting color). To serve, cut steak diagonally across grain into thin slices.

Per 1-ounce serving: 78 calories.
Exchanges per 1-ounce serving = 1 meat, ½ fat
7 grams protein, 5½ grams fat

Cooking for Love and Life

Pepper Steak
(from La Provence)

6 (8-ounce) steaks, prime filet of
beef
1 tablespoon green peppercorns
1 pint heavy cream

2 tablespoons shallots
2 tablespoons lemon juice
Brandy
Salt and pepper

Cook steaks as desired in a pan and add to sauce when almost done.

SAUCE:

Sauté in butter, green peppercorns and shallots. Flame with brandy, add heavy cream, lemon juice, salt and pepper. Remove steaks. Reduce liquid until thickened. Pour sauce over steaks. Serves 6.

Paul Naquin's French Collection II—Meats & Poultry

Stuffed Flank Steak
(Microwave)

Cooking Time: 11 minutes
Utensils: 4-cup glass measuring cup
　　　　　1-cup glass measuring cup
　　　　　Trivet and shallow glass baking dish
Servings: 4–6

1 (2-pound) beef flank steak	**¼ teaspoon parsley, minced**
1 teaspoon salt	**¼ teaspoon basil, dried**
¼ teaspoon pepper	**¼ teaspoon marjoram, dried**

1. Pound steak to ½-inch thickness. Score meat diagonally on both sides. Mix together salt, pepper, parsley, basil and marjoram. Sprinkle on one side of meat.

¼ cup margarine	**2 tablespoons green onions and**
½ pound fresh mushrooms,	**tops, sliced thinly**
**　sliced**	**½ cup seasoned bread crumbs**

2. Micromelt margarine in a 4-cup measure on HIGH (100%) 1 MINUTE. Add mushrooms and onions. Sauté on HIGH (100%) 3 MINUTES. Stir in bread crumbs. Spread mixture over surface of meat leaving a 1-inch margin at edges. Starting at the narrow end, roll steak, jelly-roll fashion. Tie with string at 1-inch intervals or secure edge with wooden picks. Place rolled steak on a rack or trivet in a shallow dish.

¼ cup Worcestershire sauce
¼ cup margarine

3. Heat Worcestershire sauce and margarine in a 1-cup measure on HIGH (100%) 1 MINUTE. Baste top of meat with mixture. Cover with a tent of wax paper. Microwave on HIGH (100%) 6 MINUTES. Turn meat over a quarter of a turn every 2 minutes and baste generously with mixture. Remove string or picks. Slice into ½-inch thick slices.

Tout de Suite à la Microwave II

Swiss Steak

2 pounds round steak, cut into
serving pieces
4 tablespoons shortening
¼ cup flour
Salt and Cayenne pepper
1 bay leaf
1 cup chopped onions

½ cup chopped bell peppers
½ cup chopped celery
3 small chopped carrots
1 cup chopped mushrooms
1 (16-ounce) can whole tomatoes
2 cups water

Season meat well using salt and pepper. Dust in flour. In a heavy iron skillet, brown meat on all sides in oil until done. Remove and set aside. Add all seasonings. Sauté until done (approximately 5 minutes). Add water. Bring to a rapid boil, reducing heat to simmer. Add meat, tomatoes, and carrots. Cover and cook over medium heat approximately 2 hours.

The Encyclopedia of Cajun and Creole Cuisine

Baked Liver and Onions
(With bacon)

6 slices beef liver
6 slices bacon
2 large onions
¼ stick butter or margarine
½ cup dry red wine
¼ cup chopped parsley

1 bay leaf, crumbled
1 teaspoon thyme
½ cup flour
½ cup water
1 teaspoon salt
Freshly ground black pepper

Place 3 slices bacon on bottom of baking dish. Cut onions into ½-inch slices and arrange in baking dish on top of bacon. Add 3 slices bacon on top of onions and dot with butter. Add wine, parsley, bay leaf, thyme, salt, pepper and ½ cup water. Cover and bake in preheated oven (350 degrees) for 30 minutes.

Coat liver with flour, place on top of bacon and onion slices, cover and bake 30 minutes. Baste 2 or 3 times. Remove cover and bake 10 minutes. Serves 6. Try it!

Tony Chachere's Cajun Country Cookbook

Indoor Barbecued Brisket

6 pounds (2.7 kg) brisket of beef
1 tablespoon (15 ml) Liquid
  Smoke
2 teaspoons (10 ml) garlic powder
2 teaspoons (10 ml) onion salt

2 teaspoons (10 ml) celery salt
2 teaspoons (10 ml) black pepper
2 teaspoons (10 ml)
  Worcestershire sauce

Sprinkle brisket with Liquid Smoke, garlic powder, onion salt and celery salt. Allow to stand overnight, covered with foil, in refrigerator. The next morning, sprinkle with pepper and Worcestershire sauce. Cover and bake five hours at 275 degrees F (135 degrees C). Drain off grease. Set aside.

SAUCE:
1 cup (250 ml) catsup
1 teaspoon (5 ml) salt
1 teaspoon (5 ml) celery seed
¼ cup (60 ml) brown sugar
¼ cup (60 ml) Worcestershire
  sauce

2 cups (500 ml) water
1 onion, minced
¼ cup (60 ml) vinegar

Mix all ingredients for sauce and boil 15 minutes. Pour sauce over meat; bake uncovered for one hour. Serves 16.

'Tiger Bait' Recipes

Corned Beef Roll-ups

1 can corned beef
¾ pound sharp cheese
1 tablespoon mustard
1 small garlic, grated

1 medium onion, grated
1 tablespoon Worcestershire
  sauce
1 loaf thin-sliced bread

Put corned beef and cheese through food chopper. Mix in other ingredients thoroughly. Add enough mayonnaise so mixture will spread easily. Remove crust from bread and cut in halves. Spread mixture on bread and roll. Toast in hot oven. Makes 96.

Talk About Good!

Meat Pies

18 ounces cream cheese, softened
1½ pounds margarine, softened
6 to 7 cups flour
2½ pounds ground chuck,
    browned and drained
2 packages Chef Boyardee
    spaghetti sauce mix complete
    with tomato base and cheese

2 teaspoons chili powder
1 cup chopped ripe olives
2 to 3 jalapeño peppers, seeded
    and chopped fine

Blend first 3 ingredients with mixer or pastry blender. Chill thoroughly. Mix remaining ingredients. Cover and chill at least 12 hours.

Roll dough thin between lightly floured sheets of wax paper. Use biscuit cutter about 2¼ inches wide to cut circles. Put 1 teaspoon of meat mixture on circle, fold over and pinch edges together. Prick tops with fork. Freeze on cookie sheets for several hours. Remove and place in containers between layers of wax paper. Bake frozen at 425 degrees for 10 to 12 minutes or until pastry is golden brown. Yield: About 20 dozen.

Louisiana Entertains

Natchitoches Meat Pies

FILLING:

1½ pounds ground beef
1½ pounds ground pork
1 cup chopped green onions, tops and bottoms
1 tablespoon salt
1 teaspoon course ground black pepper

1 teaspoon coarse ground red pepper
½ teaspoon cayenne pepper
⅓ cup all-purpose flour

Combine ground beef, ground pork, onions and seasonings in large Dutch oven. Cook over medium heat, stirring often until meat loses its red color. Do not overcook the meat. Sift the flour over meat mixture, stirring often, until well combined with meat. Remove from heat and cool to room temperature. Place meat in a large colander to drain off excess grease and juice.

CRUST:

2 cups self-rising flour
⅓ heaping cup Crisco, not melted

1 egg, beaten
¾ cup milk

Sift flour and cut shortening into flour. Add beaten egg and milk. Form dough into a ball. Roll about ⅓ of the dough at a time on a lightly floured board or pastry cloth. Cut dough into 5 to 5½-inch circles. I use the top of an old coffee pot, which is exactly the right size. I find it easier to cut out all of the circles for the pies and place them on a cookie sheet, separated by waxed paper.

To Assemble: Place a heaping tablespoon of filling on one side of the pastry round. Dampen edge of pie containing meat with fingertips, fold top over meat and crimp with fork dipped in water. Prick with fork twice on top.

To Fry: Fry in deep fat fryer at 350 degrees until golden brown. These meat pies freeze beautifully if enclosed in plastic sandwich bags. When frying frozen meat pies, do not thaw before frying. Cocktail meatpies may be made the same way, using a biscuit cutter and 1 teaspoon of meat filling. Makes 26 to 28, 5 to 5½-inch pies.

Cane River Cuisine

Mushroom-Stuffed Meat Loaf

MIX AHEAD STUFFING:

1 pound (454 grams) fresh
  mushrooms
¼ cup (60 ml) butter or margarine
1 teaspoon (5 ml) lemon juice
1 medium onion, minced
4 cups (1 liter) soft fresh bread
  crumbs

1 teaspoon (5 ml) salt
⅛ teaspoon (0.6 ml) pepper
¼ teaspoon (1.2 ml) dried thyme
¼ cup (60 ml) minced parsley

Clean and slice mushrooms, reserving seven whole for garnishing. Sauté sliced mushrooms in butter with lemon juice and onion for three minutes. Toss in bread crumbs and next four ingredients.

MEAT MIXTURE:

2 eggs
3 pounds (1.4 kg) ground chuck
1 tablespoon (15 ml) salt
⅛ teaspoon (0.6 ml) pepper
¼ cup (60 ml) milk

⅓ cup (80 ml) catsup
1½ teaspoons (7.5 ml) dry
  mustard
Currant jelly, optional

Beat eggs; with a fork lightly mix in chuck, then remaining ingredients except currant jelly. Pack half of meat mixture into a loaf pan. Pack stuffing on top, then rest of meat. Press seven mushrooms into top. Refrigerate for several hours. About one hour and 25 minutes before serving, preheat oven to 400 degrees F (205 degrees C) and bake meat loaf for approximately one hour and ten minutes. If desired, brush top with heated currant jelly. Lift onto platter with two broad spatulas. Allow to set for 10 to 15 minutes before slicing. Makes eight servings.

'Tiger Bait' Recipes

Sauté—To fry lightly in fat in a shallow, open pan. (From the French "sauter" which means "to leap," comes sauté, "tossed in a pan.")

Bayou Boulets "Meatballs"
(Microwave)

Cooking Time: 14 minutes
Utensil: Browning dish
Servings: 4

1 cup soft bread crumbs	1½ teaspoons salt
⅓ cup milk	¼ teaspoon nutmeg
1 pound lean ground beef	¼ teaspoon allspice
1 egg slightly beaten	Pinch of pepper
3 tablespoons onion, chopped	

1. In a mixing bowl, soak bread crumbs in milk 5 minutes. Add meat, egg, onions, salt, nutmeg, allspice and pepper. Mix together thoroughly. Shape into 16 meat balls or 32 miniature balls.

1½ tablespoons butter	½ (10¾-ounce) can beef broth
1½ tablespoons flour	½ cup milk

2. Preheat browning dish 4½ minutes. Melt butter in dish and quickly brown meat balls. Cover with lid and microwave on HIGH 3 MINUTES. Turn meat balls over and continue to cook on HIGH 3 MINUTES. Remove meat balls from dish. Stir flour into butter. Add beef broth and milk slowly. Microwave on HIGH 3 MINUTES.

Put meat balls back in dish with gravy and cook on HIGH 5 MINUTES.

Tout de Suite à la Microwave I

Meatballs in Brown Gravy

MEATBALLS:

2½ to 3 pounds ground beef
1 pound lean ground pork
3 teaspoons salt
½ teaspoon red pepper
½ teaspoon black pepper

1 tablespoon ketchup
⅓ cup finely chopped onion
2 slices broken white bread,
  soaked in ⅔ cup milk
⅓ cup oatmeal

To make meatballs, place all ingredients in a large bowl and mix together well. Form balls of desired size, about 3 dozen. Roll lightly in flour. Cover bottom of large skillet with vegetable oil, heat to medium, and brown meatballs on all sides. Remove from skillet and drain on paper towels.

BROWN GRAVY:

½ cup oil
¾ cup flour
1 large onion, finely chopped
½ green pepper, finely chopped

2 cloves garlic, finely chopped
5 to 6 cups hot water
1 (14½-ounce) can beef broth
  (optional)

To prepare gravy, make a roux with oil and flour. When roux becomes a dark brown, add onion, pepper and garlic. Sauté until tender, then add hot water and beef broth. Allow this mixture to boil for 15 to 20 minutes, stirring occasionally.

Add meatballs and reduce heat to medium. Cover and cook for 1 hour. Add water if needed to thin gravy to desired consistency, stirring occasionally. Serves 14–16.

Meatballs and gravy may be served over steaming rice, but it is best over spaghetti, topped with Parmesan cheese. Petit pois add a nice finishing touch as a side dish. This freezes well and leftovers make delicious po-boys!

Louisiana LEGACY

Michael Landry's Spaghetti Sauce

2 pounds chili ground meat*
3 large onions, (chopped)
4–5 finely chopped garlic cloves
½ cup butter
½ cup olive oil
2 (16-ounce) cans whole tomatoes
  (Italian style)
1 (28-ounce) can crushed
  tomatoes
1 (6-ounce) can tomato paste
1 cup red wine
1 small carrot, finely chopped

3 bay leaves
1 tablespoon basil
1 tablespoon oregano
1 tablespoon salt
2 teaspoons black pepper
2 teaspoons garlic powder
1 tablespoon Worcestershire
  sauce
2 tablespoons sugar
Dash red pepper
1 cup sliced mushrooms

Heat oil and butter in 5-quart pot. Add onions and garlic and sauté until wilted. Add meat and cook until brown. Blend whole tomatoes in meat mixture then stir-in crushed tomatoes and tomato paste. Stir constantly on high heat for 15 minutes. Add water, wine, and carrot. Reduce heat to medium and simmer for 15 minutes. Add all seasonings and reduce heat to low and simmer uncovered for 2½ hours, stirring periodically. Fifteen minutes before serving add sliced mushrooms. Serve on cooked spaghetti with fresh grated Parmesan or Romano cheese. Serves 8 to 10.

*Can substitute ½ pound of cooked sausage for ½ pound of chili ground meat.

The Best of South Louisiana Cooking

Louisiana Creole Okra with Meat Balls

2 pounds ground round steak
2 eggs
Bread crumbs
Salt and black pepper to taste
Cooking oil
2 pounds fresh okra, sliced
 ½-inch thick

1 large white onion, chopped
2 cloves garlic, chopped
1 small bell pepper, chopped
2 ribs celery, chopped
2 cans peeled tomatoes
Red pepper to taste

Make small meat balls from mixture of meat, eggs, bread crumbs, salt, and black pepper. Brown in cooking oil in small Magnalite roaster or fryer and drain on absorbent paper. Using drippings, cook okra until tender, stirring often. Add chopped vegetables and sauté until soft. Add tomatoes and mix well before adding meat balls. Cook slowly for about 30 minutes adding hot water as needed to keep meat balls covered. Add pepper. Freezes. Serve over rice with crowder peas, cucumber salad, and corn sticks. Serves 6–8.

A great dish in the summer when fresh vegetables are plentiful. An original recipe for quick entertaining.

Pirate's Pantry

Mock Veal Cutlet

1 pound coarsely ground beef
1 teaspoon salt
¼ teaspoon pepper
1 teaspoon chili powder
1 tablespoon Worcestershire
 sauce

1 small onion, minced
2 eggs, beaten
Cracker crumbs

Mix ground beef, salt, pepper, chili powder, Worcestershire sauce and onion in mixing bowl. Cover; let chill in refrigerator for 1 hour. Form meat into club steak size pieces; place back in the refrigerator for overnight. Dip cutlets in beaten eggs, and then in bread crumbs, coating well on both sides. Fry in deep fat on medium heat until golden brown. These may be frozen and cooked when needed.

Foods à la Louisiane

Johnny Mazette
(Microwave)

Cooking Time: 31 minutes
Utensils: Clay simmer pot
Yield: 6 servings

½ pound ground beef
½ pound ground pork
½ cup chopped bell pepper
½ chopped celery
¼ cup chopped stuffed olives
1 cup chopped onions
4 tablespoons butter or margarine
1 (8-ounce) package noodles
1 (10½-ounce) can mushroom
  soup

1 (10½-ounce) can condensed
  tomato soup
1 (8-ounce) can tomato sauce
1 (3-ounce) can mushroom stems
  and pieces
1 teaspoon salt
1 cup grated American cheese

1. While chopping vegetables, soak the clay simmer pot in cold tap water for 10 minutes.

2. In bottom of clay simmer pot, combine ground beef, ground pork, bell pepper, celery, olives, onions, and butter. Mix well.

3. Microwave on HIGH FOR 6 TO 7 MINUTES or until meat is no longer pink. Drain fat. Add noodles, mushroom soup, tomato soup, tomato sauce, mushrooms, and salt. Mix well. Cover with water-soaked lid.

4. Microwave on HIGH FOR 10 MINUTES, stir, microwave on 50% POWER FOR 15 TO 20 MINUTES or until noodles are done. Top with grated cheese. Let stand, covered, until cheese is melted (about 5 minutes).

Tony Chachere's Microwave Cajun Country Cookbook

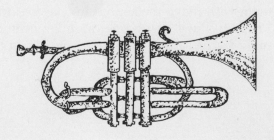

Gourmet Hamburgers

4 pounds ground meat
1 tablespoon salt
1 teaspoon black pepper
1 teaspoon lemon pepper
1 tablespoon minced onion
1 teaspoon dry mustard
4 tablespoons Worcestershire
  sauce
1 tablespoon Pickapeppa Sauce
1 tablespoon Cavender's All
  Purpose Greek Seasoning
1 tablespoon garlic powder
1 tablespoon dill weed
1 tablespoon paprika
1 tablespoon catsup
2 whole eggs
¼ pound Cheddar cheese, finely
  grated
¼ pound Swiss cheese, finely
  grated

¼ pound blue cheese, finely
  crumbled
¼ pound Gruyère cheese, finely
  grated
(Add other cheeses if desired; or
  use other cheese in place of
  above.)
2 (11-ounce) cans Cheddar cheese
  soup (undiluted)
1 tablespoon Worcestershire
  sauce
½ cup commercial barbecue
  sauce
8 English muffins, split
Mayonnaise
Mustard
Lettuce
Tomatoes
Pickles
16 crisp bacon slices

In a 4-quart mixing bowl add first 14 ingredients, and then stir until well mixed. (Adjust any special seasonings you prefer.) Make 8 hamburger patties from mixture. As you mold patties, add cheeses mixed together in center of patty and form hamburger around cheeses. Make sure patty is well molded around cheese. Cook hamburger preferably on barbecue pit over medium fire, making sure 1 side is browned lightly before turning over. (These are as good rare as they are well done.) While hamburgers are cooking, heat soup and Worcestershire sauce in a double boiler, and heat barbecue sauce. Toast English muffins after spreading them with mayonnaise and mustard. Add lettuce, tomatoes and pickles. Put 1 hamburger atop 2 muffin halves, then cheese sauce, barbecue sauce, crisp bacon slices. Serve open face. Serves 8.

Revel

Cajun Chow Mein

1 pound pork (ground)	Salt, pepper, garlic to taste
1 pound beef (ground)	1 can bean sprouts
1 green pepper, chopped	1 small can water chestnuts
2 stalks celery, chopped	1 (No. 2) can whole tomatoes
1 large onion, chopped	1 (4-ounce) can mushrooms

Sauté meat in 2 tablespoons bacon drippings; add pepper, celery, onions, mushrooms. Add No. 2 can whole tomatoes; add 1 cup water. Let come to boil and add 1 cup raw rice. Turn to simmer and cook 25 minutes. Remove cover and add can bean sprouts and 1 can water chestnuts, chopped. Let cook 10 more minutes with top on—until rice is no longer grainy. Serves 8.

Especially good for Church suppers, teen-age parties and pot luck suppers. Serves about 15 people (unless they're real hungry and then it may serve 12.)

Talk About Good!

Cold Pork Loin

1 (6-pound) pork loin roast rubbed generously with thyme and dry mustard	3 cloves garlic, pressed
	8 ounces currant or apple jelly
½ cup dry sherry	1 tablespoon soy sauce
½ cup soy sauce	2 tablespoons dry sherry
2 tablespoons ground ginger	Orange slices (optional)

Combine the ½ cup sherry, soy sauce, ginger and garlic and pour over roast. Marinate overnight.

Remove meat from marinade, which should be reserved. Bake at 325 degrees for 25 minutes per pound or until meat thermometer reaches 175 degrees, basting often with marinade. Melt jelly over medium heat. Add soy sauce and the 2 tablespoons of sherry, mixing well. Cool.

Place roast on a rack in a shallow pan. Spoon glaze over roast. As mixture runs off into pan, repeat to build up a coating. Slice and serve cold, garnished with orange slices.

Louisiana Entertains

Cajun Red Beans and Rice

Firs', cher, you take one-two pound dem red bean an' put dem in a big pot, dere. Den you wash dem bean real good an' watch out fo' dem little rock an' chuck dirt. W'en dem bean real good clean, fill up wit' planty water, fo'–five quart. Trow in nice ham bone wit planty meat lef' on, or one–two pound ham chuck. Don' fo'get to remember two–t'ree onion, fo'–five toe garlic, an' planty salt an' pepper. Now boil dat all down til dem bean planty soft an' dat gravy planty thick. Serve dem over steam rice wit' Tabasco sauce, cher. An' *bon appetit!*

2 pounds (907 grams) dried red beans
1 meaty ham bone or 1½ pounds (680 grams) ham chunks
2 large onions, chopped

4 cloves garlic, minced
1 bay leaf, optional
Tabasco to taste
Salt and pepper to taste

Translation:

Wash dried beans. Remove any foreign matter, such as stems, etc. Place in a large 4 to 6-quart (4 to 6-liter) saucepan or Dutch oven. Add 4 to 5 quarts (4 to 5 liters) water, ham, onion, garlic and seasonings. Simmer slowly for about 3 hours until beans are soft and the gravy is thick. Serve over cooked rice with Tabasco sauce. Serves 10.

'Tiger Bait' Recipes

Sausage Pilaf

1 pound pork sausage	1 cup chopped celery
½ cup chopped onions	½ cup chopped green peppers
¼ cup chopped pimentos	1 can cream of mushroom soup
1¼ cups milk	½ cup uncooked rice
½ teaspoon poultry seasoning	¼ teaspoon salt
1 cup soft bread crumbs	2 tablespoons melted butter

Brown sausage and drain off excess fat. Add celery, onions and green peppers. Cook until tender but not brown. Stir-in pimento, soup, rice, milk and seasonings. Pour into ungreased 1½-quart casserole. Bake covered in 350-degree oven for 50 minutes, stirring occasionally. Mix crumbs and butter, sprinkle evenly over casserole. Bake uncovered for 20 minutes longer. Makes 6 servings.

The Best of South Louisiana Cooking

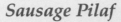 *Pilaf* or *pilau*—A dish made with meat or fish and seasoned rice.

Coony Fried Rice

1½ pounds ground beef/pork mixture	1½ cups water
	1 large bell pepper cut in large squares
1 large onion, coarsely chopped	2 cans LaChoy fried rice
2 stalks celery, chopped	Green onions tops, chopped
½ teaspoon garlic powder	Parsley, chopped
2 tablespoons soy sauce	
Salt and pepper to taste	

Brown meat. Add onions, celery, garlic powder, soy sauce, salt and pepper. Cook for 10 minutes. Add water and simmer for another 5–10 minutes. Add bell pepper and rice. Cover and cook slowly until rice is fluffy and soft. Add onion tops and parsley. Great with plain meats or fried chicken. Beef/pork mixture can be substituted with sausage. Serves 10.

Talk About Good II

Roast Pork

1 (5-pound) pork roast
½ bell pepper, chopped
½ cup chopped green onions
8 cloves chopped garlic
Salt and Cayenne pepper to taste

1 cup chopped onions
1 cup chopped celery
½ cup oil
2 cups water

With a sharp knife, cut holes in roast at 3-inch intervals. Stuff with garlic, peppers, green onions, and salt and pepper. After stuffing, salt and pepper roast well on all sides. In a heavy pot, heat oil, and brown roast well on all sides. Add onions, celery, and water. Bring to a rapid boil and reduce heat to simmer. Cook covered over medium heat approximately 3 hours.

The Encyclopedia of Cajun and Creole Cuisine

Pork Chops with Apples, Onions, and Raisins

4 pork chops, center cuts
  (1½-inches thick)
1 tablespoon cooking oil
⅓ stick butter
Salt and pepper

1 large sweet apple
1 large yellow onion
¼ cup raisins
1 ounce port wine

Use a 10 or 12-inch skillet that can be covered. Salt and pepper pork chops. Oil skillet and brown chops well on both sides. Place sliced onions over chops and cover skillet. Cook slowly for fifteen minutes. Remove cover. Place pork chops over the onions. Sprinkle raisins around pan bottom. Place wedged apple around chops, add wine, cover and simmer fifteen minutes. Turn apple wedges during cooking to assure even cooking. Remove skillet top and simmer additional five minutes to thicken sauce. Serve chops with apples, onions, raisins and sauce garnish. Serves 4.

Paul Naquin's French Collection II—Meats & Poultry

Pork Stew

½ cup all-purpose flour
½ cup vegetable oil
1 large onion, chopped
1 green pepper, chopped

6 cups water
3 pounds pork backbone, cubed
Salt and pepper to taste

In a deep heavy pot, brown flour in oil until golden brown, stirring constantly. Add onion and pepper to roux; cook on low heat until vegetables are tender. Add water; cook on medium heat for 30 minutes. Season pork with salt and pepper; add to stew. Simmer on low heat until pork is tender.

Note: Thick pork chops may be substituted for pork backbone, if desired.

Foods á la Louisiane

Creole Hogshead Cheese

1 hogs head (cut into 4 pieces,
   remove brains, ears, eyes and
   tissue)
4 hogs feet
3 pounds lean pork (fat removed)
½ sweet red pepper, or pimento,
   chopped
1 cup chopped onions

½ bell pepper, chopped
4 cloves garlic, minced
1 cup green onion tops and
   parsley, chopped
1 package plain gelatin
Tony's Creole Seasoning to taste
   (on the hot side)

Put head, feet, lean pork, garlic, bell pepper and onions in a large pot. Cover with water and boil until meat falls from bones. Remove meat and chop or grind. Cook remaining broth down to about 2 quarts or less. Strain, place meat and broth in sauce pan. Season generously with Tony's Creole Seasoning. Add gelatin softened in a little water. Cook about 15 minutes. Add onion tops, red sweet pepper and parsley. Pour into soup bowls to mold. Place in refrigerator until it sets.

Tony Chachere's Cajun Country Cookbook

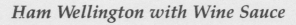

Ham Wellington with Wine Sauce

BAKED HAM:

(5 to 8-pound) fully cooked
  canned or boneless ham

¾ cup cherry preserves
2 tablespoons light corn syrup

Preheat oven to 325 degrees. Bake ham, fat side up, for 2 hours. Combine preserves and syrup. Spoon ½ of mixture on ham. Bake 10 minutes. Spoon on rest of mixture. Bake 15 minutes longer. Cool completely.

BISCUIT CRUST:

4 cups packaged biscuit mix
1 teaspoon sage
2 tablespoons prepared mustard
¾ cup Crisco

⅔ cup milk
1 (4½-ounce) can deviled ham
1 egg yolk, beaten with 1
  tablespoon water

In large bowl combine biscuit mix, sage, and mustard 2 hours before serving. Cut in shortening with pastry blender. Make well in center and add milk. Beat with fork until well mixed. Shape into ball and knead 5 minutes. On lightly floured pastry cloth, roll out ⅘ of dough to form 12 × 22-inch rectangle. Spread with deviled ham leaving 1½-inch margins. Encase cooled ham in dough, molding tightly, and pressing edges to seal. Refrigerate dough-covered ham on greased cookie sheet. Roll out remaining dough ⅛-inch thick and brush evenly with egg mixture. With sharp knife or cookie cutters cut out preferred shapes. Press cut-outs on dough-covered ham and brush with remaining egg yolk mixture. Bake 1 hour, or until crust is golden. Let stand 10 minutes before slicing.

WINE SAUCE:

3 (¾-ounce) packages mushroom
  gravy sauce mix
1 cup Port wine

2 cups water
¾ cup cherry preserves

For wine sauce make gravy according to package directions adding the Port, water, and preserves. Pass sauce with ham. Serves 10–16.

Pirate's Pantry

Boudin

2 pounds lean pork meat
1½ pounds pork liver
1 large onion, whole
½ bell pepper, unchopped
1 stalk celery
2 cloves garlic
1 large onion, chopped
2 bunches green onions, chopped (½ cup reserved)

1 bunch parsley, chopped (½ cup reserved)
6 cups cooked rice
Salt, black and red pepper to taste
Sausage casings, soaked in cold water

Simmer in covered pot the pork meat, liver, onion, bell pepper, celery and garlic in water to cover; when meat falls apart, remove meat and reserve strained broth. Discard cooked vegetables. Grind meat, onion, green onions and parsley. Mix ground meat mixture with the reserved ½ cup of green onions and ½ cup parsley and rice. Gradually add broth to make a moist dressing. Season to taste, but this dish is usually highly seasoned. Stuff into casings with sausage stuffer or form into Boudin Balls (see recipe in Hors D'Oeuvres section). Yield: 5 pounds.

The Shadows-on-the-Teche Cookbook

Boudin—A highly seasoned sausage Acadians make of pork and rice. Red boudin has more blood than white boudin.

Lamb Rack Herb'd Provence Amandine
(from Le Ruth's)

2 lamb racks, (U.S. prime choice)
   bones and cover fat off
1 teaspoon salt
2 teaspoons herbs'd provence
   (thyme, rosemary, savory,
   marjoram)

¼ pound butter
¼ cup salad oil
¼ teaspoon black pepper
2 tablespoons white wine
1 cup sliced blanched almonds
   (toasted)

Brush oil on racks and season with salt, pepper and herbs. Bone side down, roast at 475 degrees for 30 minutes for "pink" doneness. Drain pan of excess fat. Melt butter in pan. Add 2 tablespoons white wine and try to scrape up brown extract that has accumulated in bottom of roast pan. Place racks on platter. Top with almonds and pour sauce over almonds. Sprinkle with parsley. Serves 2.

Paul Naquin's French Collection II—Meats & Poultry

 Amandine—A dish served or topped with almonds.

Vegetables

Cypress Lake. Lafayette.

Southern Snap Beans

4 slices salt pork
2 tablespoons minced green
onion

Salt and pepper to taste
2 pounds beans, snapped
2 or 3 large red potatoes

In heavy pot, brown salt pork. Add onion, salt and pepper, about 1½ cups water and the beans. Cover and simmer 10 minutes, stirring occasionally.

Cut each potato into about 6 pieces and add. Simmer covered until potatoes are done, stirring once or twice.

Two (1-pound) cans of snap beans, partially drained, may be substituted for the fresh. Serves 6–8.

Plantation Country

Green Beans Horseradish

2 (No. 303) cans whole green
beans
1 large onion, sliced
Several bits of ham, bacon or salt
meat
1 cup mayonnaise
2 hard-cooked eggs, chopped
1 heaping tablespoon horseradish
1 teaspoon Worcestershire sauce

Salt to taste
Pepper to taste
Garlic salt to taste
Celery salt to taste
Onion salt to taste
1½ teaspoons parsley flakes
1 lemon, juiced

Cook beans with meat and sliced onion for 1 hour or more. Blend mayonnaise with remaining ingredients and set aside at room temperature. When beans are ready to serve, drain and spoon mayonnaise mixture over beans. Serves 8. These are excellent, leftover, cold. The green beans are so different.

River Road Recipes I

New Crop White Beans

1½ pounds new crop dried white (Navy) beans
2½ quarts water
⅓ pound cooked ham scraps
3 tablespoons chopped onion
1½ tablespoons chopped bell pepper

4 tablespoons bacon drippings
2 tablespoons chopped green onion
1 tablespoon minced parsley
1 teaspoon black pepper
2 teaspoons salt
Steaming rice

Wash beans in a colander under cold running water. Discard defective ones. Place in a 4-quart pot with water and ham. Bring to a boil, reduce heat to medium, cover and cook 30 minutes, adjusting heat upward if necessary to assure an active bubbling cooking. Add onion and bell pepper and cook over medium heat for 30 more minutes. Add bacon drippings, green onion, parsley, salt and pepper, and stir. Simmer covered, another 30 minutes, or until soft and creamy. Serve over rice with smoked pork sausage. Serves 18.

In the Fall, everyone anticipates the arrival of the "new crop" of white beans, sold in some stores by the pound from a large bin. These will cook to tender, flavorful goodness quickly, needing no pre-soaking or longer cooking time as their shelf counterparts might. "New crop" isn't a brand name, but a form of the dried navy bean which is newly-processed. If you don't get them this way, you can still cook delicious beans by pre-soaking overnight and allowing for longer cooking, 1–2 hours more. White beans are the favorite along the bayou.

Louisiana LEGACY

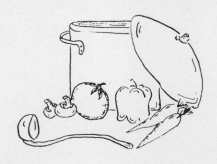

Lima Bean Casserole

2 cups dried lima beans	1 teaspoon red pepper
1 teaspoon salt	2 tablespoons fat
½ to 1 pound ground meat	2 cups tomatoes
½ cup onion rings	1 tablespoon chili powder
1 clove crushed garlic	½ cup grated sharp cheese

Cook beans for 1 hour beginning with cold water. Add salt the last half hour. Drain and reserve 1 to 2 cups liquid. Brown beef, onion, garlic and pepper in fat. Add tomatoes, chili powder, lima beans and cheese. Put in a greased baking dish. Add enough of the reserved liquid to barely cover beans. Bake in a 350-degree oven for 1 hour.

The Cotton Country Collection

Broccoli Casserole

¼ pound butter	1 package frozen broccoli
1 cup chopped onions	1 can cream of chicken soup
½ cup chopped celery	1½ cups cooked rice
½ cup chopped green onions	Salt and Cayenne pepper to taste
1 cup grated Cheddar cheese	Seasoned Italian bread crumbs

In a medium-size pot, cook broccoli according to directions. Drain well. Mix broccoli with cheese and soup. Stir in rice; set aside. In a large skillet, sauté onions and celery in butter until done—5 minutes. Add to broccoli rice mixture. Place all ingredients in a casserole dish. Top with bread crumbs. Bake at 325 degrees for 1 hour.

The Encyclopedia of Cajun and Creole Cuisine

Buccaneer Broccoli au Gratin

2 bunches fresh broccoli (about 4
  stems per bunch)
8 cups water
1¼ tablespoons salt
1 teaspoon lemon juice
1½ cups potato rolls (about 4;
  French bread may be
  substituted)

¾ pound creamy super sharp
  cheese
6 tablespoons butter

Prepare fresh broccoli by cutting where stem and flowerets meet. Wash and drain flowerets. Bring water, salt, and lemon juice to a vigorous boil. Add broccoli and boil, uncovered, for 2 minutes. Cover, turn off heat, and leave in pot 5 minutes. Drain. Broccoli will be firm; do not overcook. Place rolls in preheated 350-degree oven. Toast 10 minutes. Rolls should be brown and crisp on outside and soft on inside. Let cool. Trim outer crust and roll with rolling pin to make bread crumbs. Cube remainder of roll into bite sized pieces.

SAUCE:
¼ pound butter
1 tablespoon flour
½ cup milk
¼ pound hot pepper cheese

8 ounces French onion dip
¼ teaspoon cayenne pepper
Bread crumbs

Make a white sauce with butter, flour, and milk. Add hot pepper cheese and stir until melted. Add French onion dip and stir until smooth and thick. Add cayenne pepper. Remove from stove and fold in bread crumbs. Line bottom of a 3-quart casserole with a layer of broccoli and a layer of sauce, and sprinkle with ½ the super sharp cheese. Repeat layering, ending with cheese. Top with potato roll bread crumbs and dot with butter. Bake, covered, in preheated 350-degree oven for 10–15 minutes, or until cheese is completed melted and bubbly. Serves 10.

Pirate's Pantry

Au gratin—A dish covered in bread crumbs, butter and cheese, then browned.

Carrots and Celery Au Beurre Tarragon

½ ounce corn oil
⅔ stick butter
3 medium ribs celery, split and in 2-inch lengths

6 medium carrots, cut in 2-inch lengths
2 teaspoons tarragon

Heat oil on medium heat in a large skillet or fry pan that can be covered. Add butter and melt. Place carrots in pot and cover. Cook on low heat for fifteen minutes. Turn carrots during cooking to cook evenly. Add celery and tarragon and cook for twenty minutes. Gently turn carrots and celery during last twenty minutes of cooking, two times, to cook evenly. Serves 6 to 8.

Paul Naquin's French Collection II—Meats & Poultry

 Au Beurre—Cooked or sautéed in butter.

Off Beat Carrots

6 carrots, pared and diced
½ cup mayonnaise
2 tablespoons horseradish
2 tablespoons grated onion

½ teaspoon salt
¼ teaspoon black pepper
½ cup buttered bread crumbs

Cook carrots until tender. Drain and put into a 1½-quart baking dish. Combine mayonnaise, horseradish, onion, salt and pepper. Mix well and stir into the carrots. Top with bread crumbs. Bake at 300 degrees in preheated oven about 15 to 20 minutes. Serves 4.

Turnip Greens in the Bathtub

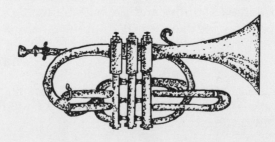

Cheese Onion Bake

1 large yellow onion, minced fine
3 tablespoons butter
2 cups scalded milk, cooled to
   room temperature
1 beaten egg
½ teaspoon salt
¼ teaspoon Cayenne
Dash Tabasco

1⅔ cups coarsely crumbled soda
   crackers
½ cup melted butter
¾ teaspoon curry powder
1 cup grated sharp Cheddar
   cheese
3 tablespoons Parmesan cheese
Paprika

Sauté onion in 3 tablespoons butter. Combine milk, egg, salt, Cayenne, and Tabasco. Set aside. In another bowl, mix cracker crumbs with ½ cup melted butter and curry powder.

Spread ½ of the cracker mixture in a glass baking dish. Top with sautéed onions, then sprinkle with ½ cup of the Cheddar cheese. Cover with milk mixture. Top with remaining ½ of the cracker mixture and the rest of the Cheddar cheese. Sprinkle with Parmesan and paprika for color.

Casserole may be refrigerated at this point. Return to room temperature, and bake at 375 degrees for 25 minutes. Remove from oven, and let stand for a few minutes to set. Serve hot in squares. Serves 6 as a brunch dish or as a side dish with steak.

Le Bon Temps

Zucchini-Corn Casserole

1½ pounds zucchini or yellow
   crookneck squash
1 medium onion, finely chopped
½ green pepper, finely chopped
2 tablespoons vegetable oil
2 eggs, beaten
½ cup grated Cheddar cheese

1 (16-ounce) can cream style
   white shoe peg corn
½ teaspoon salt
½ teaspoon garlic salt
¼ teaspoon pepper
¼ teaspoon dried rosemary

Slice zucchini and steam until just tender. Let cool. Sauté onion and pepper in oil until limp. Add eggs, cheese and seasonings to corn. Fold into zucchini along with sautéed onion and pepper. Pour into buttered casserole and place in pan of hot water. Bake at 350 degrees for 45 minutes or until firm. Crumbled bacon or cubed ham makes a nice addition. Serves 6–8.

Revel

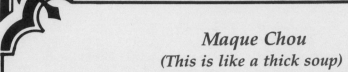

Maque Chou
(This is like a thick soup)

2 cups boiled, peeled shrimp*
12 tablespoons bacon fat or oil
  (reserve 4 tablespoons)
1 cup flour
2 large bell peppers, chopped
4 large white onions, chopped
6 ribs celery, chopped
½ bunch green onions, chopped
1 cup parsley, chopped
12 ears fresh corn *or* 2 cans
  creamed corn and 1 can whole
  kernel corn, drained

4 tablespoons tomato paste
1 teaspoon seasoned salt
1 teaspoon celery salt
2 teaspoons regular salt
2 bay leaves
2 chicken bouillon cubes
2 cups hot water
2 (14½-ounce) cans chicken broth
Dash of thyme, Beau Monde,
  Accent, Tabasco
Red pepper

Make roux using 8 tablespoons bacon fat or oil and 1 cup flour. When brown, add onions, bell peppers and celery. Sprinkle with red pepper to taste. Cover and cook down well until tender. Add 1 teaspoon celery salt and green onions. Remove from fire. If using fresh corn, cut and scrape from cob. As indicated, canned corn may be substituted. Sauté corn in 4 tablespoons bacon fat or oil. Add tomato paste, 2 teaspoons regular salt, 1 teaspoon seasoned salt. Combine corn mixture with roux and vegetables, adding the water and bouillon cubes, chicken broth and bay leaves. While simmering, add liberal dash of thyme, Beau Monde, Accent and Tabasco. Add additional salt if necessary. Simmer ½ hour. Just before serving, add cooked shrimp and parsley. Makes 3 quarts. Freezes well.

  If you want a less thick soup, add more chicken broth.

*Instead of boiling, the shrimp may be sprinkled with lemon juice, salt, pepper, cayenne, and Tabasco and sautéed in margarine until pink.

Turnip Greens in the Bathtub

Maquechou
(Microwave)

Cooking Time: 23 minutes
Utensil: 3-quart casserole
Servings: 6

10 ears fresh corn or
2 (16-ounce) cans whole corn,
  drained or
4 cups frozen corn kernels,
  defrosted

1. For fresh corn: Cut top part of kernels from cob with sharp knife. Use back of knife and rub over cob to press out milk. For canned corn: Use electric can opener!

¼ cup butter or bacon fat
1½ cups onion, chopped
½ cup green bell pepper,
  chopped
1 clove garlic, minced

2. Micromelt fat in a 3-quart dish. Sauté onion, bell pepper and garlic on HIGH 3 MINUTES or until tender.

1 (10-ounce) can Ro-tel tomatoes,
  chopped, with liquid
1 teaspoon salt

3. Add corn, tomatoes and salt. Cover with wax paper. Cook on HIGH 20 MINUTES. Stir once or twice. Cooking time will be shorter for canned corn.

Variation: For *Seafood Maquechou* add 1 pound cooked shrimp or crawfish during the last 5 minutes of cooking.

Maquechou (pronounced mock shoe) is Indian-style stewed corn and tomatoes.

Tout de Suite à la Microwave I

197

Choux Glorieux
(Glorified Cabbage—Simple Method)

1 medium head cabbage
¾ stick butter
1 onion, chopped fine
1 can cream of mushroom soup

½ pound Velveeta cheese
Bread crumbs
Salt and red pepper to taste

Chop cabbage fine and boil until very tender in salted water. Wilt onion in butter. When wilted, add cheese in hunks and allow to melt over low heat. When cheese has melted, add mushroom soup. Still over low heat, blend in soup with cheese mixture. When blended, add boiled cabbage and mix well. Add bread crumbs until of proper casserole consistency, about ¾ to 1 cup. Season to taste. Put in a 1½ or 2-quart casserole, sprinkle bread crumbs on top and bake at 350 degrees about 20–30 minutes or until bubbly and hot.

Talk About Good!

Spinach Cucumbers

4 cucumbers
1 (10-ounce) package frozen
   chopped spinach
2 minced shallots
⅓ to ½ cup mayonnaise
4 tablespoons sour cream

½ to 1 teaspoon lemon juice
2 egg yolks, hard-boiled and
   grated
Salt and pepper
Dill weed

Cook spinach according to directions on package. Drain thoroughly. Peel cucumbers and slice lengthwise. Scoop out seeds, making a boat. Salt and pepper the cucumbers. Cover with dill weed. Place on platter, cover and chill. In bowl mix well-drained, cooked spinach, shallots, mayonnaise, sour cream, lemon juice, salt and pepper. Check seasonings. Fill cucumber boats with spinach mixture. Dust with grated egg yolk. Serve chilled. May be cut in small sections to serve as hors d'oeuvres.

Turnip Greens in the Bathtub

Eggplant Fritters II

1 medium prepared eggplant	1 teaspoon sugar
1 beaten egg	½ cup flour
½ teaspoon vanilla	Dash salt
½ teaspoon baking powder	Confectioners sugar

Peel and slice eggplant. Steam until tender and drain. Mash and beat until smooth. Add remaining ingredients to prepared eggplant and mix well. Drop by spoonful into deep hot fat, 375 degrees and fry until brown turning once. Drain on paper towel. Powder with confectioners sugar. Serves 6.

MICROWAVE:
In 2-quart casserole, place 2 tablespoons water and ½ teaspoon salt. Add peeled and cubed eggplant. Cover. Cook on high for 6 minutes. Stir after 3 minutes. Drain and mash. Add remaining ingredients to prepared eggplant and mix well. Follow rest of the above recipe.

Recipes and Reminiscences of New Orleans II

Eggplant Romano
(from Ralph & Kacoo's)

3 eggs, slightly beaten
1 cup milk
Salt and pepper to taste
8 large eggplants, slice ¼-inch
  thick
2 cups flour
Cooking oil
1 large onion, chopped
3 cloves garlic, minced
2 (16-ounce) cans whole tomatoes

3 tablespoons catsup
1 tablespoon Worcestershire
  sauce
1½ teaspoon salt
1 teaspoon black pepper
1 teaspoon oregano
1 teaspoon Italian seasoning
1½ pounds thin sliced cheese
2 pounds extra-thin sliced ham
¼ pound Romano cheese

Mix the eggs and the milk together in a mixing bowl. Salt and pepper the eggplant slices to flavor them. Dip them into the egg-milk mixture. Place them in the flour and fry in the cooking oil over moderate heat until a light brown. In a medium skillet over moderate heat, sauté the onions and garlic until they are soft, about 5 to 7 minutes. Mash the whole tomatoes. Mix the tomatoes and onion-garlic-butter mixture in a large pot. Add the catsup, Worcestershire, salt, pepper, oregano, and Italian seasoning. Let this sauce simmer for 1½ hours, stirring periodically. When the sauce is cooked, preheat the oven to 350 degrees. Take an 8 × 12-inch pan that is 2½-inches deep and cover the bottom with the tomato sauce. Place one layer of the eggplant into the pan, one layer of sliced cheese, one layer of the sliced ham. Sprinkle the grated cheese on top of the ham. Repeat 3 or 4 times until the pan is full. Bake at 350 degrees for 15 minutes. Serve hot. Serves 12 to 18.

La Meilleure de la Louisiane

Vegetable Pear Casserole
(Casserole de légumes avec poires)

10 ounces lean ground meat	1½ teaspoon salt
½ cup chopped onion	½ teaspoon black pepper
1 tablespoon chopped green pepper	4 teaspoons low fat oleo
2 cups chopped vegetable pears	1 tablespoon parsley
	6 tablespoons bread crumbs

Spray grease a skillet. Brown meat. Add onion, green pepper, vegetable pears, and seasonings. Cook slowly until well done, about 30 minutes. Remove all excess fat. Grease casserole dish with low fat oleo, and fill with mixture, mixing parsley in. Top with bread crumbs. Bake at 350 degrees for 20 minutes.

Total: 4 servings. Per serving: 193 calories
Exchanges per serving = 2 meats, 1 vegetable, ½ fat
12½ grams carbohydrates, 17 grams protein, 8½ grams fat

Cooking for Love and Life

Mirliton—A pale green squash often used in Creole recipes. It is also called a vegetable pear.

Stuffed Baked Eggplant Or Mirlitons

3 large mirlitons or medium-size eggplants	½ cup butter
¼ cup celery	½ cup chopped onions
1 tablespoon pimento	¼ cup bell pepper
1 cup white crabmeat	1 cup cooked chopped shrimp
Salt, pepper, garlic powder	½ cup bread crumbs
	¼ cup chopped green onions

Cut eggplants in half and steam until tender. Cool, scoop out and keep shells intact. Brown vegetables in melted butter. Add shrimp, crabmeat and pulp of eggplant. Season well. Stir together and cook 10 minutes. Add bread crumbs and green onions. Add more melted butter if too dry. Stuff shells of eggplant. Sprinkle top with bread crumbs. Bake at 350 degrees until hot.

The Best of South Louisiana Cooking

Mushroom Streudel

1 pound mushrooms, minced
1½ sticks butter
1 tablespoon oil
½ cup minced yellow onion
1 cup minced green onions
¼ teaspoon Tabasco
½ cup sour cream

2 tablespoons minced fresh dill,
  or 1 tablespoon dried dill
½ teaspoon salt
¼ teaspoon pepper
6–8 filo leaves (a Greek pastry
  dough packaged in paper-thin
  leaves)

Preheat oven to 350 degrees. Place mushrooms, a handful at a time, in a tea towel and squeeze out moisture. In a skillet, heat 3 tablespoons butter and oil; sauté mushrooms with onions until moisture has evaporated, about 15 minutes. Remove skillet from heat and stir in Tabasco, sour cream, dill, salt, and pepper; cool.

Keep filo leaves moist by placing them under a damp tea towel. Melt remaining butter. On a sheet of waxed paper, place one filo leaf and brush gently with butter. Place a second filo leaf directly over the first and brush with butter. Spread a 1-inch wide strip of mushroom mixture along one of the long sides of the leaves to contain filling and roll up leaves jelly-roll fashion. Place roll, seam-side down, on a buttered baking sheet. Make remaining rolls and brush them with butter. Bake 45 minutes until crisp and golden. Allow rolls to cool 5 minutes. Cut on an angle in 1-inch slices. Makes 4 dozen.

Jambalaya

Mushrooms Florentine

¼ cup butter
¼ cup chopped onion
1 pound fresh mushrooms
2 (10-ounce) packages frozen
  chopped spinach, cooked and
  drained

1 cup grated Mozzarella,
  Monterey Jack, or Romano
  cheese
1 teaspoon salt
¼ teaspoon garlic salt

In a medium skillet melt the butter. Add the onion and mushrooms and sauté for 5 minutes. Stir in the remaining ingredients and transfer the mixture to a 9 × 9-inch baking dish. Bake the casserole at 350 degrees F. for 20 minutes. Serves 6–8.

La Bonne Cuisine

Champignon au Crème

2 pounds mushrooms, sliced	2 cups whipping cream
1 stick butter	Salt and pepper to taste
1 can consommé	8 patty shells

Sauté mushrooms in butter. Boil consommé and whipping cream for 10 minutes. Add mushrooms, salt, and pepper. If sauce is too thin, add some beurre manie (softened butter and flour mixed together to form a paste).

Note: This is great as a first course or can be used as a luncheon dish as is. One pound cooked shrimp or 1½ cups cooked chicken may also be added.

Opera on the Halfshell

 Champignons au crème—Mushrooms in cream.

Seafood Stuffed Mushrooms

1 pound shrimp	½ cup plain bread crumbs
½ pound crabmeat	2 tablespoon sherry
1 stick butter	¼–½ teaspoon Tabasco
⅓ cup chopped parsley	1 pod garlic
⅓ cup chopped green onions	1½ pounds fresh mushrooms
3 tablespoon flour	Salt to taste
¼ cup heavy cream	

Peel shrimp and devein. Chop them into small chunks. Melt butter and add parsley and green onions, saute for about 5 minutes and add shrimp. Cook for another 5 minutes, then stir in flour. When mixed, add cream and stir, then bread crumbs, Tabasco, garlic and salt. Remove from heat and stir in crabmeat and sherry. Adjust seasoning. Make sure you have enough salt to compensate for the blandness of the mushrooms. Wash the mushrooms and remove the stems. Stuff each one and put in a baking pan. Bake at 350 for 15–20 minutes.

Variation: You may stir in ¾ cup shredded Swiss cheese before stuffing.

La Bonne Louisiane

Okra and Tomatoes Creole

½ small onion, chopped
1 tablespoon bacon grease or salad oil
½ cup fresh okra, washed and sliced
1 teaspoon flour
1 tomato, cut in pieces
½ teaspoon sugar
Salt and pepper to taste

In heavy medium-size saucepan or skillet, slightly brown onion in bacon grease, about 1 minute on medium heat. Dredge okra in flour and add to onion. Continue cooking until okra is slightly brown, about 5 minutes. Add tomato to mixture. Add sugar. Cook partly covered over slow heat about 25 minutes stirring occasionally to keep from sticking. Add seasoning. Serves 1–2.

Quickies for Singles

Stuffed Bell Peppers

14 white bread slices
1 (6-ounce) can tomato paste
2 teaspoons salt
1 teaspoon pepper
3 eggs, beaten
3 slices bacon, cut into pieces
3 slices ham, cubed
½ cup milk
½ cup green pepper seeds
½ cup chopped green pepper
2 tablespoons Crisco shortening
½ cup margarine
10 large green peppers, halved
1 cup soft breadcrumbs

Soak bread in enough water to moisten; combine bread, tomato paste, salt, pepper, eggs, bacon, ham, milk, green pepper seeds and green pepper. Mix well. In a large black skillet melt Crisco; when melted, add mixed ingredients. Cook on low heat, stirring occasionally until mixture dries somewhat. Add margarine and keep on stirring from bottom of skillet. Cook on low heat for 1 hour. Remove from heat. Preheat oven to 250 degrees. Stuff cooked mixture into halved green peppers. Sprinkle breadcrumbs over top. Place peppers in a large baking pan. Bake at 250 degrees for 50 to 60 minutes. Serves 12–16.

Foods à la Louisiane

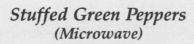

Stuffed Green Peppers
(Microwave)

Utensils: Medium size mixing bowl
          7 × 11-inch oblong casserole dish
Time: 25 minutes
Servings: 8

**4 medium green peppers, washed
  and halved
1 pound lean ground beef
⅔ cup Italian bread crumbs
1 egg**

**½ cup tomato sauce
2 tablespoons water
¾ teaspoon salt
½ teaspoon cayenne pepper
¼ cup green pepper, chopped**

1. In medium mixing bowl, mix beef, bread crumbs, egg, to-mato sauce, water, salt, pepper and green pepper. Fill pepper halves with beef mixture.

**½ (8-ounce) can tomato sauce
1 (15½-ounce) jar Ragu spaghetti
  sauce**

2. Pour tomato sauce and Ragu sauce over peppers. Cover with plastic wrap. Micro on 70% POWER 25 MINUTES. Let stand 10 minutes.

Southern Spice à la Microwave

Stuffed Bell Pepper

4 large green peppers
½ pound butter
2 cups chopped onions
½ cup chopped celery
½ cup chopped parsley
½ pound ground beef
½ loaf fresh bread

½ pound shrimp peeled and
    deveined
3 eggs
Salt and pepper to taste
1 clove garlic
½ cup bread crumbs

Preheat oven to 350 degrees. Cut peppers lengthwise removing seeds and stems, and wash. Boil in slightly salted water; do not overcook. Remove and drain well. In a large sauté pan, melt butter. Add onions, celery, parsley, garlic and sauté for 15 minutes, or until done. Add ground meat and shrimp and cook for 20 minutes longer. Wet bread under faucet, squeeze out all liquid and add to sautéed ingredients. Add eggs and salt and pepper; stir well to blend bread into meat. Remove and fill peppers with mixture, top with bread crumbs, place on a baking dish. Add ½ cup water at bottom of dish and bake until brown.

The Encyclopedia of Cajun and Creole Cuisine

Spanish Rice

2 tablespoons oil
1 large onion, chopped
½ medium bell pepper, chopped
2 cups long grain rice

1 (16-ounce) can tomatoes
3 cups water
Salt and pepper, to taste
1 teaspoon vinegar

Sauté onion and bell pepper in oil until tender. Add rice and fry until lightly brown, stirring occasionally. Add tomatoes and fry a little longer. Add water, vinegar, salt, pepper and cover. Let cook over low fire until fluffy, stirring occasionally. Serves 8.

Variation: 2 tablespoons capers in liquid.

Recipes and Reminiscences of New Orleans II

Baked Louisiana Sweet Potatoes (Yams)

Scrub and dry (cured) yams. Trim the ends, rub lightly with oil and place on a cookie sheet in a preheated 400-degree oven. Bake 15 minutes, reduce the heat to 375 degrees, and continue to bake until potatoes are soft, about 1½ hours. Do not wrap the yams in foil, or they will steam instead of baking and will lose their sweet syrupy flavor. Sweet potatoes baked in the microwave do not have the same rich flavor of those baked in a conventional oven.

Plantation Country

Grand Yams

1 small sweet potato	2 tablespoons orange juice
1 tablespoon brown sugar	1 tablespoon butter
Dash of salt and cinnamon	¼ cup miniature marshmallows

Peel and cut sweet potato in small chunks. Boil in salted water to cover, about 15 minutes. Place drained potato in small buttered baking dish. Sprinkle with brown sugar, salt and cinnamon. Pour orange juice over. Dot with butter. Top with marshmallows. Bake 15 minutes in 450-degree oven. Serves 1.

GRAND CARROTS:
Use recipe above using 2 small thinly sliced carrots in place of sweet potato. Orange juice and cinnamon are optional.

Quickies for Singles

Yam/Bourbon Casserole

3 (17-ounce) cans Trappey's yams
½ cup brown sugar
Rind of one large orange, grated
½ cup fresh orange juice
⅓ cup bourbon whiskey or
  sherry
½ stick butter
1 teaspoon salt

Place yams in a buttered casserole (1 layer thick), sprinkle with sugar, add orange juice, rind, and bourbon or sherry. Dot with butter, cover and bake at 350 degrees for 45 to 50 minutes until all the juice has cooked into the yams. Yield: 6–8 servings.

Note: This recipe can also be used by mashing the yams before putting into casserole, mixing the butter, sugar, rind, orange juice and bourbon or sherry together.

The Shadows-on-the-Teche Cookbook

Natalie's Potatoes

6 medium potatoes, red
⅓ cup chopped onion
¼ cup margarine plus 2
  tablespoons
1½ cups sour cream*
2 cups shredded Cheddar cheese
1 teaspoon salt
½ teaspoon black pepper

Boil potatoes, drain, cool and peel. Grate potatoes, placing them in buttered 9 × 14-inch casserole. Make the following sauce to pour over them:

SAUCE:
Sauté onions in ¼ cup margarine. Add sour cream and shredded cheese to melt. Add other ingredients. Heat thoroughly and pour over cooked and grated potatoes. Dot with 2 tablespoons margarine. Bake 35 minutes in 350 degree oven. Makes 8 to 10 servings. May be frozen prior to baking.

*If I have only one carton of sour cream (8 ounces) on hand, I rinse the carton with ½ carton of milk which works very well.

Turnip Greens in the Bathtub

Squash Morelle
(Microwave)

Cooking Time: 24 minutes
Utensils: 2-quart glass or ceramic casserole
Servings: 6

2 pounds yellow squash, sliced
1 cup onions, chopped
1 teaspoon butter

1. Place squash and onions in a 2-quart casserole dish. Dot with butter and cover tightly with plastic wrap. Microwave on HIGH (100%) 16 MINUTES. Shake dish once or twice to rearrange contents. (Shaking eliminates removing the cover.) Drain and mash.

2 eggs, beaten   **1 tablespoon sugar**
½ cup sour cream   **1½ teaspoons salt**
2 tablespoons butter, softened   **½ cup Mozzarella cheese**

2. Mix together eggs, sour cream, butter, sugar, salt and cheese and stir into squash. Microwave on HIGH (100%) 4 MINUTES.

½ cup ground almonds

3. Sprinkle on ground almonds and microwave on HIGH (100%) 4 MINUTES more.
An interesting and tasty dish for dinner parties.
Tout de Suite à la Microwave II

Butternut Squash Soufflé

2 cups cooked, mashed butternut   **½ cup milk**
squash   **¾ to 1 cup sugar**
3 eggs, beaten   **½ teaspoon ground ginger**
⅓ cup melted butter   **½ teaspoon coconut extract**

Mix all ingredients together. Pour into lightly greased 1½-quart casserole and bake 1 hour at 350 degrees.
Louisiana Entertains

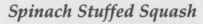

Spinach Stuffed Squash

3 boxes frozen chopped spinach
  thawed with liquid squeezed
  out
2 sticks butter
1 small regular onion, chopped
1 small bunch green onions,
  chopped
1 large stalk of celery, chopped
⅓ cup chopped parsley
2 cloves garlic, minced
1 egg, beaten

1 cup Italian bread crumbs
⅓ cup grated Parmesan
½ teaspoon thyme
1 teaspoon black pepper
1 teaspoon onion salt
½ teaspoon garlic salt
½ teaspoon Beau Monde
8 large/10 small yellow squash
Salt to taste
½ cup bread crumbs
½ stick butter

Cut squash in half lengthwise and steam them until just half cooked with about 1½ inches water in the pot. Remove from pot and set aside to cool. Melt the butter in a sauce pan and sauté the celery, onions, green onions and parsley until wilted. Stir in the next 9 ingredients, then the spinach. Scoop out the seeds from the squash and discard. Stuff the squash halves with the spinach mixture; sprinkle each one with extra bread crumbs and dot each one with butter. Bake at 350 degrees for 20–25 minutes. Serves 8–10. The stuffing freezes well, and is good stuffing for mushrooms.

La Bonne Louisiane

Spinach Mold

1 package frozen chopped
  spinach
1 envelope unflavored gelatin
¼ cup cold water
2 teaspoons minced onion
½ teaspoon salt
½ teaspoon white pepper

½ cup mayonnaise
1 to 2 tablespoons horseradish,
  depending on taste
2 teaspoons lemon juice
Dashes of Tabasco
1 cup sour cream

Cook and drain spinach thoroughly, removing all liquid. Soak gelatin in cold water, and dissolve over hot water in a double boiler. Mix spinach, gelatin, and all ingredients except sour cream in a food processor or blender. Pour into a greased two-cup mold, and chill until firm.

When ready to serve, unmold and spread sour cream on top. Serve with crackers or Melba rounds. Serves 8.

Le Bon Temps

Spinach and Artichoke Casserole

4 (10-ounce) packages frozen
  chopped spinach
2 tablespoons butter
2 tablespoons flour

¾ cup milk
Salt and pepper to taste
½ teaspoon garlic salt
2 (14-ounce) cans artichoke hearts

Cook spinach according to directions on the package, and drain well. Make a white sauce by melting butter in saucepan; add flour, cooking and stirring constantly for 1 minute. Gradually add milk, and cook until sauce thickens. Season with salt, pepper, and garlic salt. Mix white sauce with drained, cooked spinach. Split artichoke hearts in half and layer in bottom of greased 10-inch casserole. Pour spinach mixture over artichokes. Top with sour cream topping (below).

TOPPING:
1 cup sour cream
1 cup mayonnaise
Juice of ¼ lemon

Mix all ingredients together and spread on top of spinach mixture. Bake at 375 degrees for 35 minutes. Yield: 8 to 10 servings.

From A Louisiana Kitchen

Spinach Pauline

2 (10-ounce) packages frozen
  chopped spinach, cooked and
  well drained
6 tablespoons finely minced
  onion
¼ cup melted margarine
1 teaspoon salt
¾ teaspoon black pepper

6 tablespoons heavy cream or
  evaporated milk
6 tablespoons grated Parmesan
  cheese
2 tablespoons cream cheese
Tabasco sauce, if desired
Italian bread crumbs

Cook spinach according to package directions in unsalted water. Drain. Sauté onions in margarine. Add drained spinach, salt and pepper to taste. Pour in milk. Add cheeses and Tabasco sauce. Mix well. Before serving, place in baking dish and top with buttered Italian bread crumbs and bake at 375 degrees for 10 to 15 minutes. Freezes well. Serves 4 to 6.

River Road Recipes II

Zucchini, Mushrooms and Artichokes

1 pound fresh mushrooms, sliced
3 medium zucchini, sliced
1 onion chopped
6 tablespoons butter
2 tablespoons flour
1 cup milk

1 can artichokes, quartered
½ cup green onions, chopped
¾ cup grated Swiss cheese
½ teaspoon salt
¾ cup seasoned bread crumbs
2 tablespoons butter

Sauté onions in 4 tablespoons butter. When soft, add mushrooms and zucchini and stir fry until zucchini is half done. Remove from pan and stir flour and 2 tablespoons butter into pan. Add milk and cook for 5 minutes. Put zucchini, mushrooms and drained artichoke hearts back in the pan and add Swiss cheese. Salt and pepper to taste. Pour all into a buttered casserole and sprinkle with bread crumbs. Dot with 2 tablespoons extra butter; bake at 350 degrees for 20–25 minutes. Serves 6 to 8.

La Bonne Louisiane

Cakes, Cookies, Candies

Mardi Gras. New Orleans.

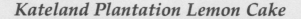

Kateland Plantation Lemon Cake

2 tablespoons very soft butter or
  margarine
¼ cup fine dry bread crumbs
3¾ cups sifted cake flour
2½ teaspoons baking powder
1 teaspoon salt
½ pound plus 4 tablespoons
  butter or margarine, softened

2½ cups sugar
5 eggs, at room temperature
3 tablespoons grated lemon peel
1¼ cups milk, at room
  temperature
⅔ cup sugar
⅓ cup lemon juice

Spread the 2 tablespoons soft butter evenly in a 10-inch tube pan and dust with bread crumbs. (This forms a lovely crust when the cake is baked). Sift flour, baking powder and salt together. Beat remaining butter, 2½ cups sugar, eggs and lemon peel at high speed for 3 minutes. Stir in by hand flour mixture alternately with milk, beating after each addition until batter is smooth. Spoon carefully into prepared pan, smooth the top, and bake at 325 degrees for 1¾ hours or until top springs back when lightly pressed with finger tips. Loosen cake at tube edge; turn out onto a wire rack.

To glaze, combine the ⅔ cup sugar and lemon juice in a saucepan. Heat slowly, stirring constantly, just until the sugar is dissolved. Brush some of the glaze onto the sides of the hot cake, then drizzle the remaining glaze evenly over the top. Cool. Freezes well.

Louisiana Entertains

Praline Cake

1 yellow cake

Pour cake batter into 2 greased and floured 13×9×2-inch pans. Bake at 350 degrees F. for about 30 minutes, or until done. Remove from oven and cool.

PRALINE TOPPING:

1 (1-pound) package light brown sugar	**½ cup butter, melted**
2 tablespoons flour	**1 teaspoon vanilla**
2 eggs, beaten	**1½ cups pecans, coarsely chopped**

In skillet mix light brown sugar, flour, and eggs in melted butter, and cook for 3 minutes over low heat. Remove from heat and stir in vanilla and pecans. Spread evenly over surface of cooled cakes. Bake for about 8 minutes at 400 degrees F. to set the frosting. Cool and cut into 1½-inch strips. Make 60 bite-sized servings.

Pirate's Pantry

Grand Marnier Cake

1 package butter recipe golden cake mix	**4 eggs**
	¾ cup milk
1 regular size instant vanilla pudding mix	**⅓ cup Grand Marnier liqueur**
	½ cup chopped pecans
1 stick butter	**Confectioners sugar**

Have butter at room temperature. Mix cake mix and pudding. Add other ingredients and beat 4 minutes until smooth. Bake in greased Bundt pan at 325 degrees for 60 minutes or until done. When cake is cool, sprinkle with confectioners sugar.

Talk About Good II

Bobbie's Blackberry Cake

1 cup butter or margarine
2 cups sugar
3 eggs
3 cups flour
2 teaspoons baking soda
1 teaspoon cinnamon
1 teaspoon ground cloves
2 cups blackberries with juice or
   1 (17-ounce) can blackberries in
   juice

ICING:
1½ cups brown sugar
1½ cups granulated sugar
1½ cups milk
1 tablespoon shortening
2 tablespoons butter or margarine

Preheat oven to 350 degrees F. Grease and flour 3 round cake pans. Cream butter and sugar. Add eggs. Combine flour, soda, cinnamon and cloves and add to creamed mixture. Blend in blackberries. Pour into cake pans and bake for 25 to 30 minutes. Allow to cool in pans 10 minutes, then invert on racks to cool completely. Ice when cool. To prepare icing, combine sugars and milk in a saucepan. Cook, stirring constantly, until mixture forms a very soft ball in cold water. Remove from heat, add shortening and butter. Cool to lukewarm, then beat until thick and creamy. Spread icing between layers, on top and sides of cake. Serves 12–16.

Fresh blackberries make the difference with this one. A richly-flavored cake with a frosting that's out of this world. (In fact, the icing would "make" any cake!)

Louisiana LEGACY

Hot Fudge Sundae Cake

1 cup Gold Medal flour
¾ cup sugar
2 tablespoons cocoa
2 teaspoons baking powder
¼ teaspoon salt
½ teaspoon milk
2 tablespoons salad oil

1 teaspoon vanilla extract
1 cup chopped nuts
1 cup brown sugar
¼ cup packed cocoa
1¾ cups hottest tap water
Favorite ice cream

Heat oven to 350 degrees. In ungreased 9×9 pan, stir together flour, sugar, 2 tablespoons cocoa, baking powder and salt. Mix in milk, oil and vanilla with fork until smooth. Stir in nuts. Spread evenly in pan. Sprinkle with brown sugar and ¼ cup cocoa. Pour hot water over batter. Bake 40 minutes. Let stand 15 minutes, then cut into squares. Invert onto dish. Spoon on ice cream and then sauce that is formed on bottom of cake pan. Serves 8.

The Best of South Louisiana Cooking

Zebra Cakes

1 cup sugar
3 (8-ounce) packages cream
   cheese, softened
5 eggs

1 tablespoon vanilla
1 (4-ounce) package of Baker's
   German Sweet Chocolate,
   melted and cooled

Mix sugar and softened cheese well in a bowl. Add the eggs separately, beating thoroughly after each one. Add vanilla. Remove two cups of this mixture and combine in another bowl with the melted chocolate. Pour the remaining cheese mixture into a 9-inch square pan which has been well buttered. Put the chocolate mixture on top of the plain mixture by dropping from a large spoon. Then zig-zag spatula through the mixture. Bake for 45 minutes at 350 degrees. Cool; then chill. Cut in squares and place in cup cake papers for individual servings. Very pretty and popular!

Opera on the Halfshell

Little Dixie Pound Cake

6 tablespoons sugar
3 tablespoons soft butter
1 egg
2½ tablespoons buttermilk

1 pinch of baking soda
6 tablespoons flour
¼ teaspoon vanilla
¼ teaspoon orange extract

Beat sugar and butter with mixer until light and fluffy. Beat in egg. Add half the buttermilk and drop the small pinch of baking soda into the buttermilk. Beat vigorously. Blend in half the flour. Stir in remaining buttermilk and beat again. Beat in remainder of flour. Add vanilla (and orange extract, if desired) and blend well. Pour into a well-greased and flour-dusted 1½-pint baking dish and bake at 350 degrees for 30 minutes. Dust with powdered sugar, if desired. Serves 1–3.

Quickies for Singles

Summer Light Cheese Cake
(Gâteau aux ananas et fromage pour l'été)

1 (13-ounce) can evaporated milk
4 ounces soft low fat cream
   cheese
1 (15¼-ounce) can crushed
   pineapples in own juice,
   (reserve juice) drained

1 package diet gelatin (any flavor)
Sugar substitute equal to ½ cup
   sugar
1 teaspoon vanilla extract
1 teaspoon rum flavoring
½ cup graham cracker crumbs

Pour milk into a large bowl and freeze until crystals begin to form, then whip. Let cream cheese soften to room temperature. Add enough water to pineapple juice to make 1 cup, then heat to boiling. Dissolve gelatin in boiling pineapple juice. Allow to cool until thick but not set. Add cream cheese, sugar substitute, vanilla and rum flavoring. Beat well. Fold in crushed pineapples and whipped evaporated milk. Line a 9 × 12-inch pan with graham cracker crumbs, and fill with mixture. Chill.

Total: 8 servings. Per serving: 148 calories
Exchanges per serving = 1 bread, 1 meat
15 grams carbohydrates, 9 grams protein, 5½ grams fat.

Cooking for Love and Life

Praline Cheesecake

2 pounds cream cheese, room
  temperature
6 eggs, room temperature
2 cups sugar

¼ cup water
2 teaspoons vanilla
2 cups light cream
⅓ cup Kahlua liquer

In a sauce pan heat the sugar and ¼ cup water, and cook over medium heat until sugar has turned golden brown and has liquified. Pour in the cream and cook until the sugar has dissolved. Set this aside and let cool. In a large bowl, cream the cream cheese until fluffy. Mix in the vanilla and then the eggs, 1 at a time, until well blended. Add the cooled praline mixture and mix well. Stir in the Kahlua and pour the batter in a springform pan lined with graham cracker crust. (Recipe follows.) Bake at 400 degrees for 15 minutes, then at 300 degrees for 1 hour. Turn off the oven, crack the door and leave in the oven for 30 minutes. Refrigerate for at least 4 hours before removing from pan.

CRUST:

1 cup graham cracker crumbs
¼ cup melted butter

¼ cup sugar
¾ cup ground pecans

Mix all ingredients together and press in the bottom of a spring form pan and bake at 375 degrees for 8–10 minutes. Lightly grease the sides of the pan before filling.

La Bonne Louisiane

Black Forest Cake
(from Chef "Shorty" Lenard)

MERINGUE DISCS:

1 cup egg whites
1 small pinch cream of tartar
2 cups plus 2 tablespoons sugar

1 teaspoon vanilla
4½ ounces slivered almonds, finely chopped

Cut 4 (9-inch) parchment paper discs. Place on cookie sheets and grease discs. (The same paper discs may be used many times; just be sure to grease them each time.) Whip egg whites until foamy and add cream of tartar. Continue whipping egg whites until stiff enough to follow the beater around. With mixer on low speed, blend sugar and vanilla in whites. Add sugar about ⅓ cup at a time. If you stir it too much, the sugar will melt the whites. Fold in almonds with a wooden spoon. Use rubber spatula and gently spread meringue on discs. Be sure the meringue is not higher in the center. Cook for 2½ hours at 225 degrees; then turn off the ovens and leave inside at least 6 hours with the doors closed so that the discs can dry thoroughly.

CHOCOLATE FILLING:

3 egg whites
¾ cup sugar
3 tablespoons cocoa

3 ounces German sweet chocolate, melted
3 sticks butter, very soft

Whip egg whites over hot, but not boiling water. Add sugar and whip until stiff. Add cocoa. Take off fire. Add German chocolate; then fold in butter. Let chocolate mixture get cold enough to spread. Then use a rubber spatula and smooth it right on top of each disc and set in the refrigerator to chill.

WHIPPED CREAM ICING:

3 cups whipping cream
⅓ cup sugar
2 tablespoons vanilla

3 ounces German sweet chocolate, grated

Whip cream very stiff. Add sugar and vanilla. Remove meringue and chocolate discs from refrigerator. To build the cake, simply ice the first disc with whipped cream, place the second on

CONTINUED

CONTINUED

top of this and ice it, and so on until all 4 layers are arranged. Then ice the sides and top with remainder of whipped cream and sprinkle grated German chocolate on top. Store in refrigerator or freezer.

Suggestions: start the cake in the early evening. First, break off six one-inch squares from a 4-ounce package of the chocolate to grate later for top of cake. Rewrap the rest and save to melt in top of double boiler when making chocolate filling later. Remove butter from refrigerator so it will soften. Preheat ovens. Make meringue; put each one on a cookie sheet and bake one above the other in double ovens. If you have only 1 oven, it might be necessary to mix and bake just 2 at a time. (There *must* be room for the heat to circulate, or the meringues will melt.) After they are baked, turn off the ovens and leave them in there overnight. After putting the meringues in the ovens, mix the chocolate filling and leave it at room temperature. It will be the right consistency to spread the next morning.

Confectioner's sugar blends with whipping cream better than granulated sugar.

When you run out of confectioners' sugar, blend 1 cup granulated sugar and 1 tablespoon cornstarch in blender on medium-high or in food processor for 2 minutes.

Revel

Heavenly Hash Cake

2 eggs
1 cup sugar
¾ cups self-rising flour
1 cup pecans, chopped

8 tablespoons margarine
1½ cups miniature marshmallows
1 teaspoon vanilla
3 tablespoons cocoa

Cream sugar and margarine. Add eggs and other ingredients except marshmallows. Bake in buttered 9×9× ×2-inch pan, 350 degrees for 30 to 35 minutes. Test with toothpick. While cake bakes make icing.

ICING:
2 tablespoons cocoa
2 tablespoons margarine
½ box powdered sugar

2 to 4 tablespoons evaporated
milk (icing will be thin)

Remove cake from oven and while cake is hot pour marshmallows over cake to cover. When completely cooled put icing on cake in pan. Cut in 36 squares (1½ inches each).

Recipes and Reminiscences of New Orleans I

Easy Chocolate Brownies

4 (1-ounce) squares unsweetened
chocolate
⅔ cup salad oil
2 cups sugar
4 eggs

1½ cups flour
1 teaspoon double acting baking
powder
1 teaspoon salt
1 cup chopped pecans

Set oven at 350 degrees and grease large, oblong pan. Melt over hot water the chocolate and salad oil. Beat in sugar and eggs. Sift together and stir in the dry ingredients. Add nuts. Spread in pan; bake 35 to 40 minutes. A slight imprint will be left when top is touched lightly with finger. Cool slightly and cut into squares.

River Road Recipes I

Verlie's Fudge Brownies

1 cup margarine (Fleischman's)
2 cups sugar
4 eggs
2 teaspoons vanilla

2 cups all-purpose flour
8 tablespoons cocoa
1 cup chopped pecans

Cream margarine and sugar in a large mixing bowl. Add eggs and vanilla. Mix in flour, cocoa and pecans. Pour onto a greased and floured 11 × 16 × 1-inch deep cookie sheet or jelly roll pan. Bake in preheated 350-degree oven for 20 minutes. Ice while cake is hot and cut into squares. Leave in pan until cool.

ICING:

½ cup margarine
1 (l-pound) box confectioners
  powdered sugar, sifted

6 tablespoons cocoa
1 teaspoon vanilla
Milk or hot water

Blend margarine, sugar, cocoa and vanilla in mixing bowl. Add milk or hot water until icing is of smooth consistency for spreading on hot cake. Yield: 60 servings.

Voilà! Lafayette Centennial Cookbook 1884–1984

Leprechauns

1 pound raisins
1 cup Irish Whiskey
½ pound pecans, halved
½ pound diced pineapple,
  candied
½ pound cherries, candied
¼ cup margarine

½ cup light brown sugar
2 eggs
1½ cups flour
1½ teaspoons soda
1½ teaspoons cinnamon
1½ teaspoons nutmeg

Soak raisins, pineapple and cherries overnight in Irish Whiskey. Cream margarine, gradually add sugar, beat well and add eggs, one at a time. Beat well after each addition. Sift flour and spices. Add to margarine mixture. Add raisins, pecans and fruit. Blend well. Drop by teaspoonful on buttered cookie sheet. Bake in 325-degree oven about 15 minutes. Makes about 120.

Recipes and Reminiscences of New Orleans II

Butter Pecan Turtle Cookies

2 cups all-purpose flour
1 cup firmly packed brown sugar
½ cup butter, softened
1 cup whole or chopped pecans

⅔ cup butter
½ cup firmly packed brown sugar
1 cup chocolate chips

Preheat oven to 350 degrees. In a 3-quart bowl combine flour, 1 cup brown sugar, and ½ cup softened butter. Mix at medium speed, scraping sides of bowl often for 2 to 3 minutes or until well-mixed and particles are fine. Pat firmly into an ungreased 13×9×2-inch pan. Sprinkle pecans evenly over unbaked crust and press in lightly.

In a heavy 1-quart saucepan combine ⅔ cup butter and ½ cup brown sugar. Cook over medium heat, stirring constantly, until entire surface of mixture begins to boil. Boil 1 minute, stirring constantly.

Pour caramel mixture over pecans and crust. Bake near the center of the oven for 18 to 22 minutes, or until entire caramel layer is bubbly and crust is light golden brown. Remove from oven, and immediately sprinkle with chocolate chips. Allow chips to melt slightly (1 to 2 minutes), then swirl chips as they melt. Leave some whole for a marbled effect, and do not spread. Cool completely, and cut into desired size. Makes about 75 bite-size squares.

Le Bon Temps

Pecan Cocoons

1 cup butter
4 tablespoons powdered sugar
2¾ cups flour

4 teaspoons vanilla
1 cup finely chopped pecans
1 tablespoon ice water

Mix all ingredients together. Work dough well with the hands until it can be handled like pie pastry. Break into small pieces and roll between the hands into cocoons. Place on ungreased cookie sheet 1 inch apart. Bake at 350 degrees until very delicate brown. Remove from oven and roll in powdered sugar while still hot. When cool, roll in powdered sugar again. Yield: approximately 3 dozen.

Recipes and Reminiscences of New Orleans I

Candy Bar Cookies
(Microwave)

Utensils: Medium size mixing bowl for flour
           2 small bowls
Time: 9 minutes
Servings: 36 cookies

¾ cup oleo
¾ cup powdered sugar
2 tablespoons evaporated milk

1 teaspoon vanilla
¼ teaspoon salt
2 cups all-purpose flour, sifted

1. In medium mixing bowl, cream oleo. Add powdered sugar gradually. Cream well. Add evaporated milk, vanilla and salt. Mix well. Stir in flour until mixed thoroughly. Divide dough in half. To each half add 3 tablespoons flour. Stir. Put one half of dough between two pieces of wax paper. Roll out dough to about 12 × 8-inch rectangle. Cut into about 3 × 1½-inch rectangles or 2-inch squares. Use glass bottom of oven as a cookie sheet. Butter bottom of oven. Place the complete first batch of cookies in circles in oven. If your oven wattage is 650, Micro on HIGH 5 MINUTES. Let cool slightly. Remove with spatula. Set aside. If your oven is between 650–700, Micro on HIGH 4 MINUTES. If your oven is 700 or over wattage, Micro on 90% POWER 5 MINUTES. Repeat with second batch of cookies.

CARAMEL FILLING:

½ pound or 28 caramel candies
¼ cup evaporated milk
¼ cup oleo

1 cup powdered sugar, sifted
1 cup pecans, chopped

1. In small bowl, put caramels and evaporated milk. Micro on HIGH 2 MINUTES. Stir. Add oleo, powdered sugar and pecans. Stir well. Put a small scoop of caramel mixture on each cookie.

CHOCOLATE FILLING:

1 (6-ounce) package semi-sweet
  chocolate pieces
⅓ cup evaporated milk

2 tablespoons oleo
1 teaspoon vanilla
½ cup powdered sugar, sifted

1. In small bowl, put chocolate pieces and evaporated milk. Micro on HIGH 2 MINUTES. Stir in oleo, vanilla and powdered sugar. Mix well. Put a small amount over caramel on each cookie. You may top each cookie with a pecan half.

You will love these!

Southern Spice à la Microwave

Peanut Butter Sighs
(Microwave)

Cooking Time: 3 minutes 30 seconds
Utensils: 7 × 11-inch glass baking dish
          Flat glass dish or paper plate
Servings: 45 squares

**1 (8-ounce) jar natural peanut   1 pound confectioners powdered
  butter, no salt   sugar
1 cup margarine**

1. Place peanut butter and margarine in a 7 × 11-inch baking dish. Cover with wax paper and microwave on HIGH (100%) 2 MINUTES, until margarine and peanut butter melt. Blend together. Add powdered sugar stirring to mix. Press smoothly into bottom of dish.

**1 (12-ounce) package semi-sweet
  chocolate chips**

2. Place chocolate chips in a flat dish to melt on HIGH (100%) 1 MINUTE 30 SECONDS. Spread over top. Cool in refrigerator and cut into squares.

Tout de Suite à la Microwave II

Pralines

**2 cups sugar   ¾ cup butter
1 teaspoon baking soda   1½ teaspoons vanilla
1 cup buttermilk   1½ cups chopped pecans**

In heavy large saucepan, cook sugar, baking soda, buttermilk, and butter to soft ball stage (240 degrees on candy thermometer). Stir frequently while cooking. When mixture reaches soft ball stage, remove from heat and beat until mixture lightens in color and thickens (about 5 minutes). Stir in vanilla and pecans. Drop by tablespoons on wax paper. Yield: 3 dozen small pralines.

From A Louisiana Kitchen

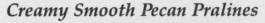

Creamy Smooth Pecan Pralines

2 cups sugar
½ cup white Karo syrup
½ cup water

2 cups pecan halves
½ stick margarine
1 tablespoon vanilla

Combine sugar, syrup, water and pecans in a heavy 3-quart saucepan. Stir over medium heat until sugar is dissolved and mixture comes to a boil. Cook, stirring occasionally, until mixture reaches soft ball stage (small amount forms soft ball when dropped into cold water). Remove saucepan from heat, add margarine and vanilla.

Allow candy to cool. Whip until mixture gradually changes to lighter color and becomes creamy. Drop by tablespoonful on buttered cookie sheet. Push mixture from tablespoon with a teaspoon to hasten dropping before praline becomes too firm to shape.

Tony Chachere's Cajun Country Cookbook

 Pralines—Confections made with pecans (or almonds, but not in Louisiana).

Louisiana Pralines Microwave

2 cups sugar
2 cups pecan halves
¾ cup buttermilk

2 tablespoons butter
⅛ teaspoon salt
1 teaspoon soda

Combine first 5 ingredients in a 4-quart glass casserole. Microwave on HIGH for 12 minutes, stirring every 4 minutes. Add soda, stirring well as it foams. Microwave on HIGH 1 minute longer; beat mixture until thickened and looses its gloss (about 1 minute). Drop candy by teaspoonfuls onto waxed paper; let stand until firm.

Note: You may need to adjust cooking time with your microwave oven. Soft failures are just as delicious to eat as firm pralines.

Foods à la Louisiane

Orange Pecan Pralines

3 cups sugar	1 teaspoon vanilla
⅔ cup milk	1 tablespoon butter
⅓ cup evaporated milk	1 cup chopped pecans
Grated rind of one orange	2 drops yellow food coloring
Dash salt	2 drops red food coloring

Combine sugar, milk, orange rind and salt in a large saucepan. Bring to a boil and cook over medium heat, stirring occasionally until soft ball stage (235 degrees F.) Remove from heat. Add vanilla, butter, pecans and food coloring. Beat until mixture has thickened. Drop by spoonfuls onto waxed paper. Yields 3 dozen pralines.

Make plenty of these beauties; they go fast!

Louisiana LEGACY

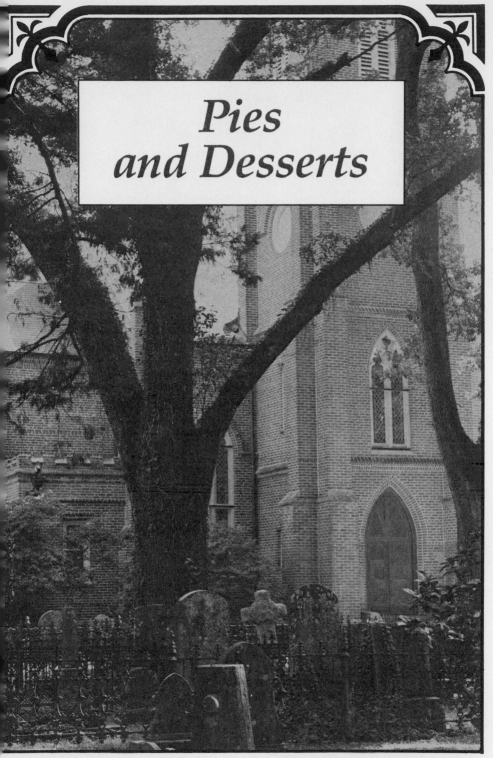

Pies
and Desserts

Grace Episcopal Church. St. Francisville.

Fig Pie
(With Whipped Cream)

3½ cups flour	3 eggs, separated
1 cup butter	2 tablespoons cornstarch
½ cup ice water	2 tablespoons sherry
30 figs	1 cup cream
½ cup water	Juice of 2 lemons
1½ cups sugar	Pinch of salt

1. Make a pie crust of flour, salt, and butter mixed together. 2. Add ½ cup ice water and mix lightly. 3. Refrigerate for 24 hours. 4. Next day roll the dough, line 2 pie tins, and bake in a 400-degree oven until lightly browned. 5. Cut figs into small pieces. 6. Add ½ cup water and sugar and cook over a low heat for 8 minutes. Set aside. 7. Combine beaten egg yolks with cornstarch. 8. Add sherry, lemon juice and a little water and mix well. 9. Add cream and mix again. 10. Pour on the fig mixture and cook in a double boiler for 5 minutes. Cool slightly. 11. Beat egg whites until stiff and fold into fig mixture. 12. Pour the mixture into pie shell and brown in hot oven. 13. Top with whipped cream.

Louisiana Largesse

Grasshopper Pie

14 finely crushed Hydrox cookies	½ cup milk
2 tablespoons melted butter	2½ jiggers green creme de
1 (10-ounce) package	menthe
marshmallows or about 24	2 jiggers creme de cocoa
large marshmallows	1 cup whipping cream, whipped

Prepare pie crust with crushed cookies and butter. Bake at 400 degrees for 5 minutes. Cool. Melt marshmallows in milk in double boiler, stirring constantly so mixture will be smooth. Cool and add creme de menthe and creme de cocoa. Refrigerate until it begins to thicken, stirring occasionally to keep from separating. Carefully fold in whipped cream until smooth and pour into chocolate crumb crust. Garnish as desired with whipped cream, chocolate bits, toasted almonds, cherries or fresh mint.

Cane River Cuisine

Brandy Alexander Pie

1 envelope unflavored gelatin	¼ cup Cognac
½ cup cold water	¼ cup crème de cacao
⅔ cup sugar	2 cups whipped cream
⅛ teaspoon salt	1 (9-inch) graham cracker crust*
3 eggs, separated	Chocolate curls for garnish

Sprinkle gelatin over the cold water in saucepan. Add ⅓ cup of the sugar, salt and egg yolks. Heat over low temperature until gelatin dissolves and mixture thickens. Do not boil. Remove from heat.

Stir in liqueurs and chill until mixture mounds slightly. Beat egg whites until stiff. Gradually beat in remaining sugar and fold this into the thickened gelatin mixture. Fold in 1 cup of the whipped cream. Turn into crust and chill several hours. Garnish with remaining whipped cream and chocolate curls. Serves 6–8.

*A pastry crust is equally suitable.

Recipes and Reminiscences of New Orleans I

Black Bottom Pie

CRUST:
1 package chocolate wafers,
   ground
¼ cup margarine, melted

1. Combine crumbled wafers and butter and mix well. (Reserve a little to sprinkle over top of pie.) 2. Press into bottom of pie plate and bake for 10 minutes at 350 degrees.

FILLING:

1 (1-pound) package	1 cup whipping cream, whipped
marshmallows	1 (7-ounce) package coconut
1 cup milk	Pinch of salt

1. Slowly melt marshmallows in milk until well blended. 2. Chill marshmallow and milk mixture until cool. 3. Carefully fold in the whipped cream and coconut. 4. Add dash of salt. 5. Fill shell and sprinkle a little of the crumb mixture over the top.

Louisiana Largesse

Nadine's Buttermilk Pie

3 cups sugar
6 teaspoons flour
1½ cups buttermilk, divided
5 eggs, beaten

1½ sticks margarine, melted
2 teaspoons vanilla
2 (9-inch) unbaked pie shells
½ teaspoon nutmeg

Preheat oven to 425 degrees F. Mix sugar, flour and ¾ cup buttermilk. Add beaten eggs, then the rest of the buttermilk, and mix well. Fold in melted butter. Add vanilla. Pour into pie shells. Bake at 425 degrees F. for 10 minutes, then turn oven down to 350 degrees F. and bake until firm, about 30 minutes. Sprinkle nutmeg on top of each. Serves 12.

In any custard pie such as this, prevent a soggy crust by brushing the uncooked shell with a slightly-beaten egg white, then bake at 425 degrees F. for about 10 minutes. Fill and bake according to recipe.

Louisiana LEGACY

Strawberry Pie

1 quart fresh strawberries	3 tablespoons corn starch
¾ cup water	1 cup whipped cream
1 cup sugar	1 (9-inch) pastry shell (baked)
1 teaspoon lemon juice	

Place all but 1 cup of berries in the bottom of a baked pastry shell. Spread out well, and set aside. In a saucepan, simmer the other cup of berries in ¾ cup of water for 5 minutes. Add sugar and blend well. Add corn starch. After mixture thickens, add lemon juice. Cook until clear. Pour sauce over berries in shell. Chill in refrigerator, and top with whipped cream.

The Encyclopedia of Cajun and Creole Cuisine

Five Layer Pie

2 eggs, separated	1 (6-ounce) package semi-sweet
½ teaspoon vinegar	chocolate chips
¼ teaspoon salt	¼ cup water
1 teaspoon vanilla	1 cup whipping cream
½ cup sugar	¼ cup sugar
1 (9-inch) baked pie shell	

Separate eggs and set yolks aside. Combine egg whites, vinegar, salt, and ½ teaspoon of vanilla in mixing bowl. Beat until soft peaks form. Gradually add ½ cup sugar and beat until stiff peaks form. Spread meringue over bottom and up sides of baked pie shell. Bake at 325 degrees for 15 to 20 minutes, or until light brown. Cool. Melt chocolate chips in top of double boiler. Blend in reserved egg yolks and water, stirring until smooth. Spread 4 tablespoons of this mixture over cooled meringue. Chill remaining chocolate mixture until it begins to thicken. In mixing bowl, beat whipping cream until soft peaks form. Add ¼ cup sugar and the other ½ teaspoon vanilla, beating until stiff peaks form. Spread ½ of whipped cream over chocolate layer. Fold chilled chocolate mixture into remaining whipped cream. Spread this over whipped cream layer in pie. Refrigerate until ready to serve.

Note: This is a favorite.

From A Louisiana Kitchen

Pecan Pie

1 cup light corn syrup
1 cup light brown sugar
3 eggs
2 teaspoons vanilla

¼ teaspoon salt
1 stick butter
1 cup pecans

Mix all but the pecans together until smooth then add pecans. Pour into an unbaked pie shell. Cook at 350 degrees for 50–60 minutes.

La Bonne Louisiane

Pecan Pie III

¾ cup sugar
2 tablespoons flour
1 teaspoon salt
1 cup dark corn syrup
2 eggs

½ cup evaporated milk
1 cup pecans
1 teaspoon vanilla
2 tablespoons butter

Mix sugar, flour and salt in 1½-quart bowl. Stir in corn syrup and melted butter. Beat in eggs, one at a time. Mix in milk, pecans and vanilla. Pour into a 9-inch unbaked pie crust. Bake 50 minutes at 375 degrees.

Talk About Good!

The Best Pecan Pie

1 stick butter
1 cup light Karo
1 cup sugar
3 large eggs, beaten
½ teaspoon lemon juice

1 teaspoon vanilla
1 dash of salt
1 cup chopped pecans
(8 or 9-inch) unbaked pie shell

Brown butter in saucepan until it is golden brown, *do not burn;* let cool. In separate bowl add ingredients in order listed; stir. Blend in browned butter well. Pour in unbaked pie shell and bake at 425 degrees F. for 10 minutes, then lower to 325 degrees for 40 minutes.

The Cotton Country Collection

Pecan Slice Torte

CRUST:
1 cup flour
½ cup butter

Mix to a paste the flour and butter. Press on bottom of buttered 9 × 9-inch square pan. Bake 15 minutes at 350 degrees, until a very light brown.

FILLING:

2 eggs, slightly beaten	2 tablespoons flour
1½ cups brown sugar	¼ teaspoon baking powder
¾ cup coconut	½ teaspoon salt
1 cup chopped nuts	1 teaspoon vanilla

While crust is baking, mix filling ingredients in order given above. Pour this filling on the baked crust and again bake at 350 degrees for 20 minutes. Remove from oven and cool. When cool, spread the icing.

ICING:

2 tablespoons butter	1 tablespoon lemon juice
1½ cups powdered sugar	½ cup finely chopped nuts
3 tablespoons orange juice	

Mix icing ingredients. Spread on torte. Sprinkle top with nuts. Let this cool in the pan you bake it in. Cut in small squares to serve, as it is very rich and delicious. Makes 16 or more servings.

River Road Recipes II

 Torte—A rich pastry or small cake.

Chocolate Yummy

CRUST:
1 cup flour
1 stick margarine, melted
1 cup pecans, finely chopped

Mix all ingredients well. Spread crust in a 9½ × 13½-inch baking dish. Bake at 350 degrees F. for 20 minutes. Cool.

FILLING:
1 cup Cool Whip
1 cup confectioners sugar
1 (8-ounce) package cream cheese
1 (3-ounce) package each
   chocolate and vanilla instant
   pudding

3 cups milk
3 cups Cool Whip
1 Hershey bar, frozen, grated

Mix Cool Whip, sugar, and cream cheese. Spread over cooled crust. Mix puddings with milk. Let set for a few minutes to thicken. Pour over cream cheese layer and top with Cool Whip. Sprinkle with Hershey. Serves 10.

   A dessert men love!

Pirate's Pantry

Bread Pudding

6 cups stale French bread
4 eggs
1 quart milk, scalded
½ cup butter, melted
2 cups sugar
¼ cup bourbon

½ cup raisins
½ cup chopped pecans
2 teaspoons vanilla
1 cup shredded coconut
   (optional)

Soak the bread, which has been broken into small pieces in the milk. Cream well the butter and sugar, and add the eggs one at a time. Stir in the vanilla, then the raisins, pecans and bourbon. Mix the soaked bread and pour into a 3-quart Pyrex pan. Bake at 350 degrees for 40–50 minutes. This is best served warm.

La Bonne Louisiane

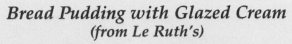

Bread Pudding with Glazed Cream
(from Le Ruth's)

½ stick butter, softened
4 eggs
½ loaf stale poor boy bread cut
   into slices 1-inch thick
1 tablespoon vanilla
1 quart milk
2½ cups sugar
¾ cup raisins
¼ teaspoon mace

TOPPING:
½ cup whipping cream or sour
   cream
⅓ cup sugar
½ stick butter

Spread soft butter over 12-inch round baking pan. Mix eggs, sugar, milk, vanilla and mace. Stir in raisins. Add bread and allow to soak 10 minutes. Pour into pan. Bake at 375 degrees. until pudding is almost firm. Remove from oven. Increase oven temperature to 425 degrees. Carefully pour liquid whipping cream over top (no substitutes) then sprinkle with ⅓ cup sugar and pieces of butter. Return to oven and bake 10 to 15 minutes to allow cream to set. Serves 6 to 8.

Paul Naquin's French Collection II—Meats & Poultry

Jambalaya Bread Pudding

1 loaf French bread (1½ feet long)	2 tablespoons vanilla
1 quart milk	1 teaspoon cinnamon
3 eggs, beaten	1 cup raisins
2 cups sugar	3 tablespoons butter

Preheat oven to 375 degrees. In a large bowl, break bread into bite-size pieces. Cover with milk and soak 1 hour. Mix well. Add eggs and sugar. Stir in vanilla, cinnamon, and raisins. Melt butter in a 13×9×2-baking dish, tilting to coat all sides. Pour in pudding and bake 1 hour. Serves 12.

SAUCE:

1 stick butter	1 egg, beaten
1 cup sugar	¼ cup bourbon

In top of a double boiler, melt butter and sugar. Gradually whisk egg. Cool slightly. Add bourbon. If serving right away, pour warm sauce over pudding. If not, warm sauce slightly before serving and serve in a sauce boat.

Jambalaya

Baked Cup Custard

4 eggs	1 teaspoon vanilla extract
½ cup sugar	1 quart milk
¼ teaspoon salt	

Beat eggs, sugar, salt, and vanilla together. Scald milk over low heat and add slowly to the egg mixture, stirring constantly. Pour caramel syrup or desired flavoring into baking molds or small Pyrex molds, then pour custard mixture on top of that. Place molds in pan of water in slow oven at 300 degrees F. and bake about 1 hour. Test with a knife, which will come out clean when custard is set. When cooled, unmold into serving dishes.

SYRUP:

Melt 1 cup sugar. When cooled, use 1 teaspoon per custard mold to coat bottom of mold before adding custard. One teaspoon whiskey may be added to this as flavoring if desired.

Louisiana Keepsake

Trifle

A British dessert. I think the version we use is Irish, but all trifles are variations on the same theme.

For your convenience, why not do this in wine glasses rather than the traditional bowl? Besides being quite pretty, there is no hitch in the service.

Sherry
Whipped cream
3 or 4 macaroons
Candied cherry or a bit of
    angelica

3 cups of rather thin stirred
    custard
18 ladyfinger halves
Currant jelly

Spread jelly on flat side of ladyfingers. Line glasses with these, 3 to a glass, jelly side facing in.

Dribble 2 teaspoons of sherry over ladyfingers in each glass. Pour custard to fill. Cover top with a dusting of macaroon crumbs and decorate with cherry or angelica, or both.

The Asphodel Plantation Cookbook

Trifle—A sweet dish made with wine or liqueur-soaked sponge cake or macaroons, with whipped creams and fruit jams.
Angelica—An herb grown in moist climates. Candied angelica, which is made from the plant's stalks, is used with other candied fruits for decoration.

Floating Isle

3 egg yolks
¾ cup sugar
1 large can evaporated milk
1 can water
Pinch of salt

2 teaspoons vanilla extract
3 tablespoons corn starch
3 egg whites
1 tablespoon sugar

Combine egg yolks and ¾ cup of sugar. Add milk, water, salt, vanilla extract and corn starch and cook until the mixture begins to thicken. Beat egg whites and one tablespoon of sugar until stiff. Pour custard mixture over egg whites mixture and gently streak it through. Cool before serving. Serves 4–6.

Recipes and Reminiscences of New Orleans I

Strawberry Cream Flan

PASTRY:

2 cups flour
2 tablespoons sugar
¼ teaspoon salt

1 cup butter, softened
2 egg yolks

Mix lightly flour, sugar and salt. Work butter in with finger tips. Add egg yolks; blend to a smooth dough. Using a double thickness of aluminum foil, make a rectangle 8×16 with the 2 long edges of foil meeting underneath. Roll out pastry on foil to match size. Place on baking sheet; make 1-inch sides to rectangle, with pastry and foil, carefully shaping corners. Chill; prick all over with fork; bake 425 degrees 20 minutes or till golden brown. Cool before removing foil.

FILLING:

½ pint heavy cream
2 tablespoons powdered sugar
½ cup light rum

2 pints strawberries, hulled
½ cup sugar
½ cup currant jelly

Whip cream; add powdered sugar and 2 tablespoons rum. Sprinkle berries with remaining rum and sugar to taste. Spread cream in baked shell, reserving some to pipe around edge. Stand berries in cream, close together, points up. Melt jelly over hot water; spoon berries to glaze. Pipe remaining cream around edge of dessert. Refrigerate till served. Serves 8.

Serve promptly; does not keep well.

Encore

Baked Alaska In Filo Dough

4 sheets Filo dough
1 pint strawberry ice cream
½ stick melted butter
¼ cup strawberry preserves

1 pound cake
1 pint vanilla ice cream
3 tablespoons sugar mixed with 3
    tablespoons chopped pecans

Preheat oven to 500 degrees. Slice pound cake into 3 pieces length-ways. Spread cake with preserves and then ice cream. Then add another slice of cake and repeat same procedure. Freeze. Spread 2 sheets of Filo dough and cover with other 2 sheets. Brush with butter. Sprinkle pecans over butter. Center frozen cake on Filo and fold Filo over, enclosing cake. Turn ends of dough under cake as you enclose it. Brush with butter. Bake for 1 to 2 minutes. Slice and serve immediately.

The Best of South Louisiana Cooking

Crêpes Suzette

1⅛ cups sifted flour
4 tablespoons sugar
Salt (pinch)
3 eggs
1½ cups milk
1 tablespoon melted butter
1 tablespoon Cognac
1 teaspoon butter

½ cup butter
½ cup powdered sugar
1 teaspoon orange rind, grated
Juice of 1 orange
¼ cup Grand Marnier or
    Cointreau
¼ cup brandy

Sift together sifted flour, sugar and salt. Combine eggs (beaten) and milk. Stir into dry ingredients until smooth. Stir in butter and Cognac. Let stand for 2 hours.

In a frying pan, heat sweet butter. Pour in 1 tablespoon of batter to cover bottom of pan with a thin layer. Rotate pan to spread batter evenly. Cook one minute on each side. Stack crêpes one on top of the other, separated by wax paper.

Cream butter and powdered sugar and orange rind. Add orange juice and ¼ cup Grand Marnier or Cointreau. Spread on crêpes and fold or roll them up. Arrange on hot serving dish. Sprinkle with sugar and ¼ cup warmed brandy. Ignite and serve flaming. Serves 6.

Recipes and Reminiscences of New Orleans I

French Banana Éclair

1 cup water	1 cup flour
½ cup butter	4 tablepoons sugar
½ teaspoon salt	4 eggs

Bring water, butter, and salt to boil in large saucepan over medium heat. Combine flour with sugar and add all at once, stirring vigorously with spoon until dough forms ball and leaves sides of pan. Remove from heat. Beat in eggs, one at a time, and continue beating until dough is stiff and glossy. Set aside about a third of dough for top. On greased 15 × 10 × 1-inch jellyroll pan, form remaining ⅔ of dough into one long oblong, about 7 inches wide. Spoon reserved dough into mounds along the top of the oblong. Bake at 400 degrees for 30 minutes. Remove from oven. With a sharp knife, make slits along sides of éclair 2 inches apart to let steam escape. Return to oven and continue baking 10 minutes longer. Remove to cooling rack. Slice off top of éclair. Remove any soft dough inside. Cool thoroughly and fill (see recipe below).

FILLING:

4 cups whipping cream,	6 to 8 bananas
4 tablespoons sugar	4 tablespoons cream de cocoa

Whip cream in mixing bowl until soft peaks form. Gradually add sugar, whipping until stiff. Mash enough bananas to make about 2 cups. Add cream de cocoa to mashed bananas and fold into whipped cream. Fill éclair shell with half of whipped cream and banana mixture. Slice remaining bananas over whipped cream. Cover sliced bananas with remaining whipped cream. Replace top of éclair and drizzle with glaze (see recipe below).

GLAZE:

½ cup powdered sugar	1 teaspoon vanilla
2 tablespoons cocoa	6 to 8 tablespoons boiling water
2 tablespoons butter, melted	½ cup chopped pecans

Combine powdered sugar, cocoa, melted butter, and vanilla in small bowl. Stir in enough boiling water to make a thin glaze. Drizzle over filled éclair. Sprinkle with chopped pecans. Chill until serving time. Slice crosswise to serve; each slice may be cut in half. Yield: 16 to 20 servings.

Note: This dessert is something to look at as well as delicious.

From A Louisiana Kitchen

Lemon Tequilla Soufflé
(from Versailles)

2½ ounces lemon juice
3 ounces white wine
⅔ cup sugar

6 egg yolks
1½ ounces Tequilla
1½ cups whipped cream

Combine sugar with one cup water in a sauce pan and boil gently until mixture begins to thicken (syrup stage). Remove and let cool thoroughly. When above mixture is cold, combine with the egg yolks, wine, lemon juice and tequilla. Cook this mixture over a low flame, whisking constantly until the foam goes down. Taste to be sure eggs are cooked. Place in refrigerator and stir occasionally to cool. When cool fold in 1½ cups whipped cream and place in freezer.

To serve: Place soufflé in hollowed-out lemons, placed on a bed of shaved ice and freeze. When about to serve, garnish with whipped cream from a tube and a mint leaf. Serves 6.

Paul Naquin's French Collection II—Meats & Poultry

Cherry Jubilee Parfait

36 large black pitted cherries
2 tablespoons sugar
2 cups cherry brandy or plain
  brandy

Vanilla ice cream
Sugar cubes
Lemon extract or orange extract

Heat cherries and sugar till juice thickens slightly; cool; add brandy. Saturate sugar cubes with lemon or orange extract. Place ice cream in parfait glasses; pour some of syrup from cherries over ice cream. Place 4 or 5 cherries on top of ice cream; place sugar cube on a mound of ice cream among but not touching cherries. Hold tip of lighted match to cube to light just before serving. Serves 8–10.

Nice for festive occasions; serve with cookies.

Encore

Cherries Jubilee—A dessert dish of cherries cooked in syrup, served often over vanilla ice cream. The dish is set aflame with brandy as it is served.

Fresh Peach Crisp

1 cup flour
½ cup sugar
½ cup firmly packed light brown
 sugar
¼ teaspoon salt
½ teaspoon cinnamon

½ cup margarine
4 cups sliced fresh peaches
¼ teaspoon almond extract
2 tablespoons water
¼ teaspoon ground nutmeg
Whipping cream

Combine first 5 ingredients. Cut in margarine with a pastry blender until mixture resembles coarse corn meal. Set aside. Combine peaches, almond extract and water. Spoon into a greased 9-inch square baking dish. Sprinkle flour mixture over peaches. Sprinkle nutmeg on top. Bake covered in a 350-degree oven for 15 minutes. Remove cover and bake 35–45 minutes longer or until the topping is brown. Serve warm with whipped whipping cream. Serves 6–8.

Revel

Peaches Eudora

1 cup fresh peaches, peeled and
 sliced
½ tablespoon flour
½ teaspoon orange liqueur,
 vanilla or almond extract
6 tablespoons sugar

2 tablespoons butter, melted
¼ cup flour
Dash of salt
1 tablespoon shortening
1 tablespoon milk
1 tablespoon butter, melted

Mix first 5 ingredients lightly and pour in small baking dish. For pastry, stir ¼ cup flour and salt together. Cut in shortening with fork till thoroughly mixed in small pea-size bits. Add milk. Roll thin; cut in strips and place over filling. Pour 1 tablespoon melted butter over all. Bake in 350-degree oven 25 minutes or until golden brown. Serves 1–2.

Good with ice cream or whipped topping.

Quickies for Singles

Bananas Foster

2 tablespoons brown sugar
1 tablespoon butter
1 ripe banana, peeled and sliced
  lengthwise

Dash cinnamon
½ ounce banana liqueur
1 ounce white rum
1 large scoop vanilla ice cream

Melt brown sugar and butter in flat chafing dish. Add banana and sauté until tender. Sprinkle with cinnamon. Pour in banana liqueur and rum over all and flame. Baste with warm liquid until flame burns out. Serve immediately over ice cream. Yields 1 serving.

Brennan's New Orleans Cookbook

Strawberry Supreme

8 ounces cream cheese, softened
¾ cup sugar
10 ounces frozen strawberries
  thawed in their liquid
1 (8-ounce) can crushed
  pineapple, drained

1 cup chopped nuts
3 small or 2 large bananas, sliced
1 (12-ounce) carton whipped
  dessert topping
6 whole strawberries for garnish

In a large mixing bowl, cream sugar and cream cheese. In a separate bowl mix together strawberries and strawberry liquid, pineapple, nuts and bananas. Fold into cream cheese mixture. Add whipped dessert topping. Fold until well-blended. Pour into 9 × 13-inch dish (or 2 smaller dishes). Garnish top with whole or sliced strawberries. Freeze. Defrost slightly before serving as salad or dessert. Yield: 48 servings.

Voilà! Lafayette Centennial Cookbook 1884–1984

Sour Cream (No Cook) Homemade Ice Cream

2 cans condensed milk
2 (8-ounce) cartons sour cream

1 quart homogenized milk
1 teaspoon vanilla

Mix above ingredients and add fruit of your choice. Freeze in ice cream freezer. Suggestions: 1 quart strawberries, blended; 1 pint strawberries with 2 or 3 bananas; 4–6 fresh peaches; 1 quart fresh-blended figs; 1 quart fresh-blended blackberries. (Fresh fruit should be sweetened to taste—about ½ cup). Canned fruit such as crushed pineapple can be used with juice and no sugar added. For chocolate ice cream, add 12 ounces of chocolate syrup.

Foods à la Louisiane

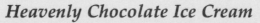

Heavenly Chocolate Ice Cream

25 ounces (10–12 bars) Milky Way
   candy, cut into pieces
1 (14-ounce) can sweetened
   condensed milk
1 (5.5-ounce) can chocolate syrup
3 quarts milk (for a creamier ice
   cream replace part of milk with
   1 pint Half & Half cream)

Combine candy and condensed milk in large saucepan. Cook over low heat, stirring constantly, until candy melts. Cool, stirring occasionally. Add 1 quart of milk (or a combination of Half & Half and milk) to the candy mixture. Beat until well blended. Pour mixture into freezer can of a 4-quart ice cream freezer. Stir in chocolate syrup. Add remaining milk to fill line (or within 4 inches from top).

Freeze according to freezer directions. From one chocolate lover, like myself, to another. Yield: 1 gallon.

Microwave shortcut: Place candy and condensed milk in 8-cup glass measure. Microwave on HIGH (100%) 3 MINUTES. Stir mixture 1 time during cooking time. Cool and continue to follow recipe.

Voilà! Lafayette Centennial Cookbook 1884–1984

Mint Sherbet
Monroe's famous sherbet

6 tablespoons mint leaves
6 oranges, juiced
2 lemons, juiced
Grated rind of 1 lemon
2 cups sugar
2 cups water
Green food coloring, optional
1 stiffly beaten egg white
½ pint heavy cream

Soak chopped mint leaves in the orange and lemon juices along with the grated lemon rind for at least 30 minutes. Boil the sugar and water for 5 minutes, without stirring. Pour the hot mixture into the fruit juices. When cold, strain. Add a few drops of food coloring, if desired. Add the egg white and cream. Freeze in an electric or hand freezer.

The Cotton Country Collection

Lagniappe

The Louisiana Pelican, the state bird. Louisiana Purchase Gardens and Zoo, Monroe.

Ambrosia
(Ambrosia)

1 cup grapefruit sections (each cut in half)
2 cups apples cut in bite-size pieces
2 cups orange sections (each cut in half)
20 pitted cherries, sliced in half

2 cups sliced bananas
½ cup shredded coconut (use fresh or coconut without sugar added)
80 small (mini) marshmallows
½ cup sour cream

Wash, peel, and section grapefruit and oranges. Put in large bowl. Wash, core, and cut apples. Add to above. Mix well. (This will prevent apples from getting dark). Wash, pit, and slice cherries and add to above mixture. Peel and slice bananas and add to above. Add coconut, marshmallows and sour cream. Mix all together. (If this recipe is prepared ahead, do not add marshmallows until ready to serve).

Total: 16 servings. Per serving: 81 calories
Exchanges per serving = 1 fruit, ½ fat, ¼ bread
14 grams carbohydrates, ½ gram protein, 2½ grams fat

Cooking for Love and Life

Curried Fruit

1 (13½ ounce) can pineapple chunks
1 (29-ounce) can sliced peaches
1 (29-ounce) can sliced pears
1 (10-ounce) jar Maraschino cherries

1 can bing cherries (optional)
1 cup brown sugar
4 tablespoons cornstarch
1 tablespoon curry
1 stick oleo
1 tablespoon Brandy or sherry

Drain fruit. Put in casserole pan. Mix brown sugar, cornstarch and curry powder. Sprinkle over fruit. Melt oleo and pour over fruit. Cover casserole and bake 30 minutes in 350-degree oven. Uncover and bake 10 minutes more. Just before serving add Brandy or sherry. Serves 10–12.

Plantation County

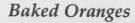

Baked Oranges

6 small oranges	Whole cloves
Sugar	Butter
Salt	Water

Soak oranges 12 hours in water to remove bitterness from skin; weight down to hold under water. Slice in halves or thirds depending on size of oranges. Place in flat casserole. Cover with sugar and a little salt. Place 2 whole cloves and pat of butter on each slice. Pour 1 inch water in casserole. Cover tightly with foil. Bake 300 degrees 2 hours or till tender. Yield: 12–18 slices.

Perfectly delicious; eat rind and all. Good with any fowl, game or pork.

Encore

Sugar Glazed Pecans
(Microwave)

Cooking Time: 6 minutes
Utensils: 1½-quart casserole
Yield: 1 pound

½ cup butter or margarine	1 pound (about 4 cups) pecan
1 cup packed brown sugar	halves
1 teaspoon cinnamon	

1. In 1½-quart casserole, place butter.
2. Microwave on 70% POWER FOR 1 to 1½ MINUTES or until melted. Stir in brown sugar and cinnamon.
3. Microwave on HIGH FOR 2 MINUTES or until bubbly. Add nuts and mix to coat each piece.
4. Microwave on HIGH FOR 3 to 5 MINUTES or until hot and bubbly. Spread out onto wax paper and let cool slightly. Serve hot or cold.

Tip: Other nuts may be used in place of pecans.
Tony Chachere's Microwave Cajun Country Cookbook

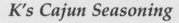
K's Cajun Seasoning

Quick to fix; eliminates search for numerous cans and jars of spices—they are all mixed here in one spicy blend for quick, tasty seasoning.

1 (26-ounce) box salt	**2 tablespoons Accent**
3 tablespoons black pepper	**2 tablespoons dried parsley flakes**
2 tablespoons garlic powder	**4 tablespoons cayenne pepper**
1 teaspoon onion powder	**2 tablespoons chili powder**
1 teaspoon nutmeg	

Mix all in large bowl. Fill a shaker for daily use; store remainder in tightly covered container.

Quickie Tip: Brang some o' dis K's Cajun Seasoning to your frans, cher; d'ell ahpreeciate dat a'planty!

Quickies for Singles

Modica
(Seasoned Breadcrumbs)

Use stale bread. If you have a blender or a food processer, great!! That's the fast and easy way to make breadcrumbs. Otherwise, use a grater and grate bread until fine. One slice of bread is about ½ cup of crumbs. To one cup of breadcrumbs add:

¼ to ⅓ cup grated Italian cheese (the cheese makes it *good*)	**1 leaf basil, chopped, optional**
1 or 2 pods of garlic, minced	**1 teaspoon parsley, finely chopped**
¼ teaspoon oregano	**Salt and pepper**
2 teaspoons onion, finely chopped	

Combine all ingredients and store in the refrigerator. Use this mixture in meatballs, artichokes, cabbage balls, or wherever a recipe calls for seasoned breadcrumbs.

Chesta e Chida

Creole Cream Cheese Master Recipe

**3 half-gallons (5.6 liters)
  pasteurized whole milk
1 quart (1 liter) buttermilk**

Place whole milk and buttermilk in large bowl and cover with cloth. In about 24 hours, milk mixture will separate from whey, leaving curds. Line colander with 6 thicknesses cheesecloth. Place in bowl and pour curds in, allowing whey to drain into bowl. When thick cheese occurs, pour into container and refrigerate. Yield: About 1 quart (1 liter).

Note: Do not use homogenized milk.

Favorite New Orleans Recipes

Creole Mayonnaise

**1½ cups oil
1 egg
3 tablespoons chopped onion
1 tablespoon Creole mustard
3 tablespoons vinegar, *or* lemon
  juice**

**¼ teaspoon paprika
Tabasco to taste
1 teaspoon prepared yellow
  mustard
1 teaspoon salt**

In blender or food processor, place ¼ cup oil. Add remaining ingredients and blend on high speed until smooth. Immediately add remaining oil, a little at a time, until all is used. Makes 2 cups.

Jambalaya

251

Hollandaise Sauce

4 egg yolks   ½ pound butter, melted
2 tablespoons lemon juice   ¼ teaspoon salt

In top half of double boiler, beat egg yolks and stir in lemon juice.
Cook very slowly in double boiler over low heat, never allowing
water in bottom pan to come to a boil. Add butter a little at a time,
stirring constantly with a wooden spoon. Add salt and pepper.
Continue cooking slowly until thickened. Yields 1 cup.

Brennan's New Orleans Cookbook

 *Hollandaise*—A rich sauce made with egg yolks, butter and le-
mon juice or vinegar.

New Orleans Tartar Sauce

1 cup mayonnaise (freshly made   ⅛ teaspoon red pepper
   with olive oil)   2 tablespoons chopped dill pickle
1 teaspoon powdered mustard   2 tablespoons capers, drained
2 tablespoons parsley, minced   and chopped
½ clove garlic, put through press   1 tablespoon minced green onion
1 teaspoon onion, grated   tops

Combine all ingredients, mix well, and serve with filet of trout
and other seafood.

Louisiana's Original Creole Seafood Recipes

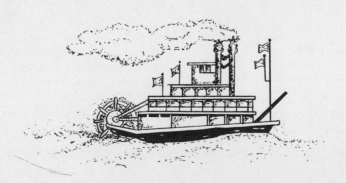

Jezebel Sauce

1 (18-ounce) jar pineapple
preserves
1 (18-ounce) jar apply jelly
1 (5-ounce) jar horseradish

1 (1⅛-ounce) can dry mustard
1 tablespoon cracked black
pepper (optional)

Blend in mixer, or by hand. Serve with ham. This keeps in refrigerator for several weeks.

This makes a nice Christmas or other occasion remembrance. Package in small attractive jars and wrap in colored cellophane.

Turnip Greens in the Bathtub

Praline Parfait Sauce

⅓ cup boiling water
⅓ cup brown sugar

1 cup white corn syrup
1 cup chopped pecans

Bring water to a boil. Add sugar, then add the corn syrup. Cook slowly until the mixture comes to a boil. Add the pecans. When cool, pour into a jar or similar container and refrigerate. Mixture will thicken when cool. Pour over ice cream.

Recipes and Reminiscences of New Orleans I

Parfait—A layered dessert with whipped cream, ice cream and fruit syrup, or a frozen mixture of egg whites, water and whipped cream.

Granddad's Barbeque Sauce

1 cup fresh lemon juice
1 stick butter
¼ cup salt
½ pint vinegar
½ clove garlic, chopped
2 cups tomato sauce

½ bunch celery, chopped fine
1 (14-ounce) bottle ketchup
1 teaspoon black pepper
½ cup sugar
1 bottle (10-ounce) Worcestershire
1 quart water

Bring all ingredients to boil; reduce heat. Cook slowly till fairly thick.

Encore

Tabasco Jelly

3 cups (750 ml) sugar
1 cup (250 ml) water
⅓ cup (80 ml) lemon juice
4 to 6 tablespoons (60 to 90 ml)
  Tabasco sauce

⅓ cup plus one tablespoon (95
  ml) liquid pectin
Red food coloring, if desired

Bring first 4 ingredients to a boil. Add pectin, let come to a boil, and boil for 1 minute. Add food coloring, if desired, to make a prettier jelly. Pour into jars.

'Tiger Bait' Recipes

Hot Pepper Jelly

¾ cup bell pepper, ground
6½ cups sugar
¼ cup hot red peppers, ground

1½ cups vinegar
½ teaspoon salt
1 bottle Certo (2 packs)

Grind peppers, keep juice. Put juice, sugar, salt and vinegar in kettle. Bring to boil. Boil and stir 5 minutes. Let cool 10 minutes. Add Certo. Pour into jars. After 10 minutes turn upside-down for five minutes to distribute seeds evenly. Yields approximately 6 (8-ounce) jars.

Recipes and Reminiscences of New Orleans II

Olives Agria e Ducci
(Sweet and Sour Olives)

1 pound black olives
1 medium onion, sliced
2 tablespoons sugar

½ cup vinegar
Oil for frying

Wash olives and drain well. In skillet, sauté onion in oil and add olives, cook for 2 or 3 minutes. Remove from heat and add remainder of ingredients. Be careful when adding vinegar as it will ignite. Bring to boil. Cool. Place in sterile jar and store in the refrigerator. Delizioso in salads or as an antipasto.

Chesta e Chida

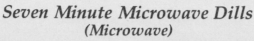

Seven Minute Microwave Dills
(Microwave)

1 quart (2–3 inch) whole
   cucumbers or ¼-inch unwaxed
   cucumber slices
1 clove garlic, peeled
½ teaspoon dried dill weed or 1
   head fresh dill

⅛ teaspoon turmeric
1 hot pepper, optional
1½ cups water
½ cup cider vinegar
2 tablespoons salt, uniodized

Fill sterile 1-quart canning jar with washed and dried cucumbers, garlic, dill weed, turmeric and hot pepper, if desired. In a 4-cup Pyrex measuring cup combine water, vinegar and salt. Microwave on HIGH (100%) 4 MINUTES until boiling. Pour liquid over cucumbers until covered. Add additional water if necessary. Cover jar loosely with plastic wrap. Microwave on HIGH (100%) 3 MINUTES. Cap, leaving plastic wrap in place. Cool and eat! Store in refrigerator for maximum crispness. Will keep 1 year. Yield: 1 quart.

Voilà! Lafayette Centennial Cookbook 1884–1984

Bread and Butter Pickles II

Combine and let stand 3 hours:

6 quarts thinly sliced cucumbers
6 onions, thinly sliced
1 cup salt

Drain well in colander.

In large pot, combine:
1½ quarts vinegar
6 cups sugar
½ cup mustard seed

1 tablespoon celery seed
½ teaspoon cayenne pepper

Bring to boil. Add cucumbers and onions. Heat to simmering. Do not boil. Pack while hot. Best if chilled before serving. These are very crisp pickles. Yields 8-9 pints.

Plantation Country

Mirliton Pickles

10 medium-sized mirlitons
10 turning-red bell peppers
1 tablespoon mustard seed
2 teaspoons ground tumeric
4 teaspoons salt

2½ cups cider vinegar
2½ cups sugar
¼ teaspoon ground cloves
Medium-sized onions, to make
  same amount as peppers

1. Peel and cut mirlitons into sticks 2. Slice peppers and onions, salt and set aside for several hours. 3. Drain and wash. 4. Place all ingredients in a saucepan. 5. Let come to a boil, but *don't* boil. 6. Pack in sterilized jars, seal and process for 10 minutes (don't boil) in water bath canner. 7. Makes 10 pints.

Louisiana Largesse

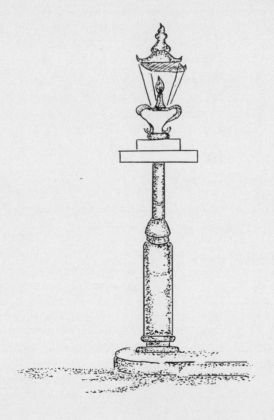

GLOSSARY

À la, au, and *aux*—French terms meaning served in a certain style. These words can also be translated as "with" or "in."

Angelica—An herb grown in moist climates. Candied angelica, which is made from the plant's stalks, is used with other candied fruits for decoration.

Amandine—A dish served or topped with almonds.

Andouille—A highly seasoned, hard, smoked sausage, made by the French Acadians especially for use in gumbo.

Au Beurre—Cooked or sautéed in butter.

Au gratin—A dish covered in bread crumbs, butter and cheese, then browned.

Bearnaise—A hollandaise sauce flavored with wine, shallots and herbs.

Bechamel sauce—A mixture of butter, flour, mile and some seasonings.

Beignets—Small, square French pastries fried like doughnuts and covered with powdered sugar.

Bienville—Oysters baked with a roux-based sauce.

Boudin—A highly seasoned sausage Acadians make of pork and rice. Red boudin has more blood than white boudin.

Bouillabaisse—A soup or stew made of several types of fish or shellfish. The fish is cooked with white wine or water, and usually olive oil, tomatoes and herbs.

Bouillon—A hearty stock made from seasoned beef or poultry.

Boulets or *boulettes*—meat balls.

Café—The French word for coffee.

Café au lait—Coffee with milk.

Café Brulot—An after-dinner drink made with coffee and spiced with brandy, cinnamon, sugar, lemon and/or orange rind.

Cala—A sweet rice cake which originated in New Orleans.

Canapé—A cracker or small, thin piece of bread or toast spread with cheese, meat, or relish, and served as an appetizer.

Champignons au crème—Mushrooms in cream.

Cherries Jubilee—A dessert dish of cherries cooked in syrup, served often over vanilla ice cream. The dish is set aflame with brandy as it is served.

Consommé—A term used to describe either a clear beef stock or a soup made with several kinds of meat, vegetables, spices and herbs.

Couche-couche—Also spelled "coush-coush" or "cush-cush." A crusty Creole bread dish made with corn meal. It is often served with milk and sugar or with cane syrup and crisp bacon.

Courtbouillon—A fish soup or stew cooked with vegetables and served over rice.

Crawfish—Also spelled crayfish, but rarely by Louisianians. A fresh water crustacean resembling a lobster, but considerably smaller.

Creole—A type of French, Spanish, Indian and African cuisine which originated in the Gulf States, especially Louisiana. The word also refers to a red sauce which is often used in Creole cookery. The sauce is made of tomatoes, peppers and other spices, and it is usually served over rice.

Crêpes—Small, thin pancakes.

Daube Glacée—A French stew made with braised meat, vegetables, herbs and other seasonings.

Éclair—A cream puff covered with chocolate and filled with custard or whipped cream.

En papilloté—A dish that has been made using a thin parchment paper or foil made for baking.

Entrée—Refers to the main course with regard to supper. Used in reference to lunch, it is one of the subordinate dishes.

Étouffée—Stewed or braised. Usually crawfish or shrimp cooked slowly with vegetables.

Filé—A kind of powder made from sassafras leaves, it is added to gumbo just before serving to thicken the liquid.

Fillet or *filet*—A boneless piece of meat cut into long, thin strips.

Florentine—A dish made with spinach.

Fricassee—To cut meat, poultry or seafood into small pieces and then braise.

Gougère—A pastry mixed with cheese which originated in Burgundy, France.

Grillades—Browned beefsteaks served over grits or rice.

Grits—Coarsely ground corn cooked with water for breakfast or dinner.

Gumbo—A Creole dish similar to a soup or stew and served over rice. Some sources say that the word gumbo comes from the African word for okra, which is frequently used as a thickener for the dish. Others tell that the Choctaw word "konbo," meaning "sassafras," is the origin of the name. (Sassafras is used to make filé, another thickening agent often used in gumbo.)

Hollandaise—A rich sauce made with egg yolks, butter and lemon juice or vinegar.

Hors D'Oeuvres—Small appetizers served before lunch or dinner.

Hush puppies—Fried cornmeal fritters. They usually accompany seafood.

Jambalaya—A Creole dish of seasoned rice mixed with meat or seafood in which rice is the main ingredient.

Julienne—To cut into narrow, thin strips.

Lagniappe—A term which means an extra bonus, or something added "for good measure."

Mirliton—A pale green squash often used in Creole recipes. It is also called a vegetable pear.

Mornay—A traditional French sauce made with white sauce and one or more kinds of melted cheese.

Mousse—A French term which refers to light, airy dishes prepared with whipped cream or egg whites.

Okra—Long, green vegetable pods commonly used as gumbo ingredient.

Oysters Rockefeller—A dish of oysters on the half-shell with a purée of spinach, onions or shallots, and celery. According to one source, the dish is named Rockefeller because of its richness.

Parfait—A layered dessert with whipped cream, ice cream and fruit syrup, or a frozen mixture of egg whites, water and whipped cream.

Pilaf or *pilau*—A dish made with meat or fish and seasoned rice.

Piquant—A French word meaning lively or tangy. Most often used to describe a sauce made with roux and tomatoes.

Poulet—French for chicken.

Pralines—Confections made with pecans (or almonds, but not in Louisiana).

Quiche—A French tart filled with unsweetened custard and flavored with cheese, bacon, meat or seafood.

Rémoulade—A piquant cold sauce for cold poultry, meat or shellfish, made of mayonnaise with chopped pickles, capers, anchovies, and herbs.

Roux—Flour carefully browned in fat, butter or oil which Creole cooks use for thickening sauces and gravies.

Sauté—To fry lightly in fat in a shallow, open pan. (From the French "sauter" which means "to leap," comes sauté, "tossed in a pan.")

Shallots—Mild onion-like herbs which are formed in small clusters rather than in large bulbs. Sometimes called scallions or green onions.

Soufflé—A light, puffed dish made with eggs, which may contain cheese, fruit, fish, minced meat or vegetables.

Torte—A rich pastry or small cake.

Trifle—A sweet dish made with wine or liqueur-soaked sponge cake or macaroons, with whipped creams and fruit jams.

INDEX

260

INDEX

261

INDEX

INDEX

INDEX

INDEX

Catalog of Contributing Cookbooks

Chretien Point on Bayou Bourbeau. Near Sunset.

CATALOG OF CONTRIBUTING COOKBOOKS

All recipes in this book have been submitted from the Louisiana cookbooks shown on the following pages. Individuals who wish to obtain a copy of any particular book can do so by sending a check or money order to the address listed. Prices are subject to change. Please note the postage and handling charges that are required. Louisiana residents add tax only when requested. Retailers are invited to call or write to same address for wholesale information.

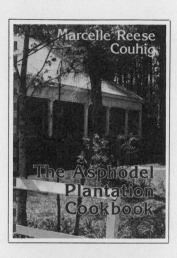

THE ASPHODEL PLANTATION COOKBOOK

Pelican Publishing Company
P. O. Box 189
Gretna, LA 70053   (504) 368-1175

Marcelle Reese Couhig shares in this charming book recipes served at the plantation tables as well as those characteristic of the fantastic cuisine of Louisiana. These are home-tested recipes that aren't found in ordinary places, are fairly easy to prepare, and wonderful to eat! Also available in a unique Cook Box.

$6.95 Retail price
$1.00 Postage and handling
$ .42 Tax for Louisiana residents
Make check payable to Pelican Publishing Company
ISBN 0-88289-194-4

THE BEST OF SOUTH LOUISIANA COOKING

By Bootsie J. Landry
103 Ridona   (318) 232-5903
Lafayette, LA 70508   (318) 234-3815

Bootsie Landry specializes in foods made famous in South Louisiana. She depicts international cooking with a southern flair. Within this book are foods of the Lebanese, French, Mexican, Greek, Jewish, Spanish, Creole and other styles loved in South Louisiana.

$10.95 Retail price
$ 1.85 Postage and handling
$ .65 Tax for Louisiana residents
Make check payable to *The Best of South Louisiana Cooking*
ISBN 0-9610982-0-1

270

BRENNAN'S NEW ORLEANS COOKBOOK

Pelican Publishing Company
P. O. Box 189
Gretna, LA 70053   (504) 368-1175

Brennan's Restaurant has inspired this profusion of praise—no small feat in a city that has always been a gourmet's paradise. This cookbook combines recipes for their finest dishes with a fascinating history of the Brennan family and how it founded a fantastically successful French restaurant devoted to creole cuisine.

$11.95 Retail price
$ 1.00 Postage and handling
$ .72 Tax for Louisiana residents
Make check payable to Pelican Publishing Company
ISBN 0-88289-382-3

BUSTER HOLMES RESTAURANT COOKBOOK

Pelican Publishing Company
P. O. Box 189
Gretna, LA 70053   (504) 368-1175

Buster Holmes Restaurant has been the place to go for a good hearty meal in the New Orleans French Quarter since 1944. Now Buster shares 174 of his famous creole soul recipes—everything from his renowned red beans and rice to "Buster's Garlic Chicken" and "Louisiana Mud Pie.".

$8.95 Retail price
$1.00 Postage and handling
$ .54 Tax for Louisiana residents
Make check payable to Pelican Publishing Company
ISBN 0-88289-374-2

CANE RIVER CUISINE

Service League of Natchitoches, Louisiana
P. O. Box 2206
Natchitoches, LA 71457   (318) 352-7990

A beautiful Louisiana cookbook, *Cane River Cuisine* contains fourteen full color photographs illustrating delicious food in historical settings. Many of the 800 recipes have been handed down through families of Cane River and reflect the French, Spanish, and Indian heritage of the Natchitoches area. Recipes to delight every taste.

$11.95 Retail price
$ 1.50 Postage and handling
Make check payable to Service League of Natchitoches
ISBN 0-9607674-0-1

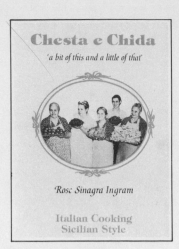

CHESTA E CHIDA
by Rose Sinagra Ingram
P. O. Box 31895
Lafayette, LA 70503   (318) 984-3395

Chesta e Chida (key-sta-ah-key-da) meaning a bit of this and a little of that, is a unique historical collection of traditional recipes of the Italian Sicilian people. Interspersed with the recipes are bits of information about traditions and customs of these people.

$6.95 Retail price
$1.50 Postage and handling
Make check payable to Rose S. Ingram

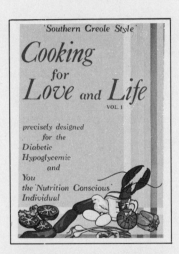

COOKING FOR LOVE AND LIFE
Recipes for Life, Inc.
P. O. Box 4718
Lafayette, LA 70502   (318) 234-1295

Par excellence! A unique book. Each recipe precisely calculated for number of servings, calories, carbohydrates, proteins, fats and exchanges. How to equate other recipes with Exchange Lists provided. Also, list of "Free Foods," Seasonings, Hints for Home, Beauty Hints, Finding Your Ideal Weight, Canning, Freezing, etc. Over 300 recipes. A must for every household.

$12.95 Retail price
$ 1.00 Postage and handling
$ .65 Tax for Louisiana residents
Make check payable to Recipes for Life, Inc.

COTTON COUNTRY COLLECTION
Junior League of Monroe, Louisiana
P. O. Box 7138
Monroe, LA 71211   (318) 322-3863

This beautiful book has received rave reviews from national publications such as *The New York Times, The Washington Post* and *Good Housekeeping.* Over 1100 recipes in 492 pages. Spiral bound. Over 350,000 copies sold. Gift wrap in brown kraft paper, brown sateen ribbon and hand-picked Louisiana cotton boll available for same price.

$12.95 Retail price
$ 1.55 Postage and handling
Make check payable to *Cotton Country Collection*
ISBN 0-9602364-0-6

ENCORE
Shreveport Symphony Women's Guild
P. O. Box 4344
Shreveport, LA 71104   (318) 868-2107

The *Encore* is a reasonably-priced hardback cookbook. Recipes are from guest artists as well as patrons of the Shreveport Symphony. Proceeds from the sales benefit the Shreveport Symphony Orchestra. The recipes are some of the finest Shreveport has to offer.

$6.50 Retail price
$1.00 Postage and handling
Make check payable to *Encore Cookbook*

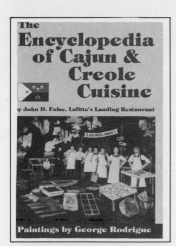

THE ENCYCLOPEDIA OF CAJUN AND CREOLE CUISINE
Cuisine Promotions, Ltd.
13441 Tiger Bend
Baton Rouge, LA 70817   (504) 291-5136

A collection of over 350 South Louisiana recipes, containing 12 George Rodrigue prints in this unique tabulated 410-page cookbook. The "Personal Taste" section makes an excellent feature for those of varying palates.

$12.00 Retail price
$ 2.00 Postage and handling
$ .60 Tax for Louisiana residents
Make check payable to Cuisine Promotions, Ltd.
ISBN 0-9613251-0-0

FAVORITE NEW ORLEANS RECIPES
Pelican Publishing Company
P. O. Box 189
Gretna, LA 70053   (504) 368-1175

Contains mouth-watering New Orleans dishes of all kinds. It is written in three languages in honor of the three cultures that have existed in Louisiana since 1718. (Inquire from publisher about Spanish, French and Trilingual editions.) The variety of recipes will appeal to novice or gourmet cooks.

$4.95 Retail price
$1.00 Postage and handling
$ .30 Tax for Louisiana residents
Make check payable to Pelican Publishing Company
ISBN 0-88289-198-7

Louisiana Farm Bureau Women

FOODS À LA LOUISIANE
Louisiana Farm Bureau Federation
P. O. Box 15361
Baton Rouge, LA 70895 (504) 922-6200

Over 700 family-favorite recipes from the Louisiana Farm Bureau Women's Group originating from their best memories. Authentic recipes focusing on the state's resources. Large seafood section including recipes for crawfish, crab, shrimp, oysters, fish. Features Creole and Cajun cuisine. Five roux preparations—including microwave. Helpful hints included. 376 pages.

$7.95 Retail price
Make check payable to Louisiana Farm Bureau Federation
ISBN 0-918544-61-0

FOREWORD BY PAUL PRUDHOMME

THE FRANK DAVIS SEAFOOD NOTEBOOK
Pelican Publishing Company
P. O. Box 189
Gretna, LA 70053 (504) 368-1175

Frank Davis gives tips on proper handling of seafood, plus detailed standard cooking methods and cooking tricks. According to noted New Orleans chef Paul Prudhomme, Frank Davis is a "number one" authority of cooking and eating the fresh fish of Louisiana.

$14.95 Retail price
$ 1.00 Postage and handling
$ .90 Tax for Louisiana residents
Make check payable to Pelican Publishing Company
ISBN 0-88289-309-2

written by Holly Berkowitz Clegg
expressly for
Goudchaux/Maison Blanche

FROM A LOUISIANA KITCHEN
by Holly B. Clegg
Goudchaux's
P. O. Box 3478
Baton Rouge, LA 70821-3478 (504) 389-7000

Contains over 400 recipes—all tested and easy to follow. Featured in the 240 pages is a special section called *Chocolate Favorites*. Selections include wonderful entertaining recipes to fabulous desserts, simple dishes to ones that are very impressive—all Holly's very favorite recipes.

$9.95 Retail price
$1.50 Postage and handling
$ .60 Tax for Louisiana residents
Make check payable to Goudchaux's
ISBN 0-9610888-0-X

274

JAMBALAYA
Junior League of New Orleans, Inc.
4319 Carondelet Street
New Orleans, LA 70115   (504) 895-6653

Official Cookbook of the Louisiana World's Exposition (1984 World's Fair). An outstanding collection of Louisiana recipes from shrimp gumbo to bread pudding. Hardbound, color throughout. Featured in *Ladies' Home Journal*, *Town and Country*, and *Louisiana Life*. Perfect gift to anyone interested in southern cooking.

$11.95 Retail price
$ 2.00 Postage and handling
$ .22 Tax for Louisiana residents
Make check payable to Junior League of New Orleans Publications
ISBN 0-9604774-2-X

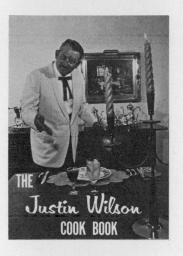

THE JUSTIN WILSON COOK BOOK
Pelican Publishing Company
P. O. Box 189
Gretna, LA 70053   (504) 368-1175

Justin Wilson's unique collection of Cajun recipes (and humor) will surely set your imagination on the right track. There are recipes for everything from the perfect roux to "Eggplant Appetizer à la Justin" to "Turtle Etouffee" to "Snap or String Beans au Vin."

$5.95 Retail price
$1.00 Postage and handling
$ .36 Tax for Louisiana residents
Make check payable to Pelican Publishing Company
ISBN 0-88289-019-0

LA BONNE CUISINE
Episcopal Churchwomen of All Saints', Inc.
P. O. Box 23065
Harahan, LA 70183   (504) 737-1416

As *Town & Country* magazine says (December 1983), "*La Bonne Cuisine* is New Orleans cooking at its finest." It contains over 550 recipes and a special 33-page "Bonus Section of Recipes" from famous New Orleans restaurants. Beautiful photographs of this lovely city divide the food sections. A winner!

$9.95 Retail price
$1.50 Postage and handling
$ .30 Tax for Louisiana residents
Make check payable to *La Bonne Cuisine*
ISBN 0-9606880-0-5

LA BONNE LOUISIANE
by Michelle Odom
805 Edison
Baton Rouge, LA 70806

Written from a great love of Louisiana foods and also to record some of grandmother's old family recipes. A. Hays Town, Sr., gave permission to use his collection of Louisiana oil paintings to illustrate the book. 98 recipes in 83 pages.

$8.95 Retail price
$1.50 Postage and handling
$ .54 Tax for Louisiana residents
Make check payable to *La Bonne Louisiane*

LA BOUCHE CREOLE
Pelican Publishing Company
P. O. Box 189
Gretna, LA 70053   (504) 368-1175

Leon Soniat has collected here authentic Creole recipes including many familiar—and not-so-familiar—New Orleans dishes. Interwoven with the recipes are the author's recollections of an earlier New Orleans. Interesting reading as well as excellent recipes.

$9.95 Retail price
$1.00 Postage and handling
$ .60 Tax for Louisiana residents.
Make check payable to Pelican Publishing Company
ISBN 0-88289-242-8

LA MEILLEURE DE LA LOUISIANE
Pelican Publishing Company
P. O. Box 189
Gretna, LA 70053   (504) 368-1175

Here is a grand cookbook with a little lagniappe. In more than 300 pages, Jude Theriot offers over 600 recipes representing a comprehensive picture of the culinary arts of cuisines of Louisiana. As a bit of lagniappe, Theriot reviews the best of Louisiana restaurants, lounges, plantations, antebellum homes and festivals.

$10.95 Retail price
$ 1.00 Postage and handling
$ .66 Tax for Louisiana residents
Make check payable to Pelican Publishing Company
ISBN 0-88289-407-2

LE BON TEMPS
Young Women's Christian Organization
201 St. Charles Street
Baton Rouge, LA 70802   (504) 383-7761

This is a Louisiana menu cookbook featuring settings and party menus for twelve occasions. It is 88 pages in length.

$4.95 Retail price
$ .70 Postage and handling
$ .30 Tax for Louisiana residents
Make check payable to *Le Bon Temps*
ISBN 0-9608282-0-6

THE LOUISIANA CRAWFISH COOKBOOK
Rt. 1, Box 62
Lettsworth, LA 70753   (504) 492-2281

A tribute to the progress made by the crawfish from the back bayous, this book explains the delicate crustation and challenges the creativity within the art of cooking. "Pearls from Paw," offering Cajun wisdom and humor, are interspersed among unique, superb crawfish recipes. A gift of sophisticated delight with a Cajun flair.

$12.95 Retail price
$ 1.50 Postage and handling
$ .65 Tax for Louisiana residents
Make check payable to *Louisiana Crawfish Cookbook*
ISBN 0-9613409-0-8

LOUISIANA ENTERTAINS
Rapides Symphony Guild
P. O. Box 4172
Alexandria, LA 71301   (318) 442-9709

This beautiful cookbook contains 500 recipes in 273 pages. It is written in a party menu format, featuring special wine selections. Spiral bound. Cross-referenced index. Chosen to be Official Cookbook 1984 World's Fair.

$11.95 Retail price
$ 1.25 Postage and handling
$ .36 Tax for Louisiana residents
Make check payable to *Louisiana Entertains*
ISBN 0-9603758-0-5
ISBN 0-9603758-1-3

LOUISIANA KEEPSAKE

Petit Press
P. O. Box 4053
Baton Rouge, LA 70821   (504) 383-3270

The *Louisiana Keepsake* book is a signed, limited
annual edition in daily planner calendar form. It celebrates in colorful pictures and words Louisiana's
renowned food, fairs, festivals and folklife in English
and French. Part of proceeds go to Creative Resources,
a non-profit foundation for the gifted/talented.

$10.00 Retail price
$ 1.50 Postage and handling
$ .60 Tax for Louisiana residents
Make check payable to Petit Press
ISBN 0-9610174-8-1

LOUISIANA LARGESSE

State-Times & Morning Advocate
P. O. Box 588
Baton Rouge, LA 70821   (504) 388-0146

A superb state-of-the-art Louisiana cookbook combining some of the great classics with the newest creative cuisine from the Baton Rouge area, where cooking
is the eighth lively art. Edited by Food Editor, Pat
Baldridge, with more than 30 full-color photographs
by Art Kleiner. 178 pages.

$12.00 Retail price
$ 1.75 Postage and handling
$ .46 Tax for Louisiana residents
Make check payable to Capital City Press

Louisiana LEGACY

Thibodaux Service League, Inc.
P. O. Box 305
Thibodaux, LA 70302   (504) 446-9818

Beautiful cooking from bayou country, *Louisiana
LEGACY* offers nearly 500 twice-tested recipes in
a 288-page hardbound volume with spiral binding.
Clear, sharp type on substantial paper, clearly-written,
standardized recipes, extensive glossary, and a well-
developed index create a quality publication. Strik-
ing art and interesting copy make it a winner!

$11.95 Retail price
$ 2.00 Postage and handling
Make check payable to *Louisiana LEGACY*
ISBN 0-9608800-0-3

LOUISIANA'S ORIGINAL CREOLE SEAFOOD RECIPES

Creole Foods of Opelousas, Inc.
P. O. Box 1687
Opelousas, LA 70570

Toll free   1 (800) 551-9066
In Louisiana 1(800) 321-1816

A complete coverage of all Louisiana's bountiful seafood recipes. 190 pages and over 200 recipes.

$8.95 Retail price
$1.00 Postage and handling
Make check payable to Creole Foods
ISBN 0-9604580-4-2

OPERA ON THE HALF SHELL

Pelican Publishing Company
P. O. Box 189
Gretna, LA 70053   (504) 368-1175

Opera and good food go hand-in-hand in the minds of singers. This interesting cookbook includes favorite recipes of singers, musicians and others involved in the production of opera including opera lovers. This delightful book should appeal to all who have developed a taste for our regional fare.

$9.95 Retail price
$1.00 Postage and handling
$ .60 Tax for Louisiana residents
Make check payable to Pelican Publishing Company
ISBN 0-88289-373-4

PAUL NAQUIN'S FRENCH COLLECTION - LOUISIANA SEAFOOD - VOLUME I

F. Paul Naquin
P. O. Box 14594
Baton Rouge, LA 70898   (504) 292-9553

Famous Louisiana style! A blend of Creole, Cajun, New Orleans, and continental French cooking techniques and recipes. Written so beginner cooks can understand and perform with great results. Experienced chefs and gourmets will be amazed. Complete planned meals, selected wines and serving tips included.

$7.95 Retail price
$1.00 Postage and handling
Make check payable to F. Paul Naquin

279

PAUL NAQUIN'S FRENCH COLLEC-TION- MEATS & POULTRY - VOLUME II

F. Paul Naquin
P. O. Box 14594
Baton Rouge, LA 70898   (504) 292-9553

   Louisiana influence and style again turns all types of meats and poultry into great cooking and dining experiences. Includes baked, broiled, sauteed, pan-fried meat and poultry dishes. Has appetizers, salads, soups and desserts to go with entrees. Also includes wine selections and planned dinners.

$7.95 Retail price
$1.00 Postage and handling
Make check payable to F. Paul Naquin

PAUL NAQUIN'S FRENCH COLLEC—TION - LOUISIANA WILD GAME - VOLUME III

F. Paul Naquin
P. O. Box 14594
Baton Rouge, LA 70898   (504) 292-9553

   Tested and re-tested game recipes of all types of large and small game. Information on field-dressing game after the hunt and carving game after cooking. Recipes are easy with clear step-by-step directions. Great old Louisiana game dishes. Appetizers, salads, desserts and wine selections included.

$7.95 Retail price
$1.00 Postage and handling
Make check payable to F. Paul Naquin

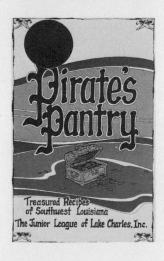

PIRATE'S PANTRY

Junior League of Lake Charles, Louisiana
P. O. Box 3066
Lake Charles, LA 70602   (318) 436-3048

   Treasured Recipes of Southwest Louisiana. Contains charming illustrations of natural and historic scenes in the area with a special section on seafood and wildlife. 400 pages. 800 taste-tested recipes. Has been endorsed as "The Official Cookbook of Contraband Days," a festival honoring Jean Lafitte.

$11.95 Retail price
$ 2.05 Postage and handling
Make check payable to *Pirate's Pantry*
ISBN 0-9607524-0-4

PLANTATION COUNTRY
Women's Service League
P. O. Box 904-QR
St. Francisville, LA 70775

In 325 pages of over 700 kitchen-tested recipes, here is a blend of plantation cooking from the main kitchen to the back woods. A culmination of our French, English, and Spanish heritage. Full of charts and tips.

$9.95 Retail price
$1.50 Postage and handling
Make check payable to Women's Service League
ISBN 0-9609422-1-1

QUICKIES FOR SINGLES
Fellowship Church
136 South Acadian Thruway
Baton Rouge, LA 70806   (504) 387-0884

An alternative for singles who are tired of TV dinners, leftovers, and hamburgers-on-the-run, here are over 200 quick-to-fix, small-serving recipes. "Quickie Tips" throughout the book give hints to save time, avoid waste, enhance nutrition. "The Single's Cupboard" lists basic kitchen necessities. Great for singles!

$4.95 Retail price
$l.05 Postage and handling
Make check payable to Fellowship Church
ISBN 0-937552-03-8

RECIPES AND REMINISCENCES OF NEW ORLEANS, VOLUME I
Ursuline Convent Cookbook
P. O. Box 7491
Metairie, LA 70010   (504) 834-3956

Volume I is the most authentic Creole cookbook with 10 full sections prefaced by historical sketches of the Creoles whose recipes through the years have come to constitute a heritage of superb food. This book has 200 pages with over 400 recipes.

$7.95 Retail price
$1.00 Postage and handling
$ .64 Tax for Louisiana residents
Make check payable to Ursuline Convent Cookbook
ISBN 0-9604718-0-4

RECIPES AND REMINISCENCES OF NEW ORLEANS, VOLUME II

Ursuline Convent Cookbook
P. O. Box 7491
Metairie, LA 70010   (504) 834-3956

Volume II is a melange of some of the best recipes of noted New Orleans dishes served up with lively and well-authenticated bits of Louisiana history and spiced with tales concerning the ethnic groups who gave piquant flavor to the Crescent City and to its cuisine. This book has almost 400 pages with over 600 recipes.

$11.95 Retail price
$ 1.50 Postage and handling
$ .95 Tax for Louisiana residents
Make check payable to Ursuline Convent Cookbook
ISBN 0-9604718-1-2

REVEL

Junior League of Shreveport, Inc.
P. O. Box 4648
Shreveport, LA 71104   (318) 868-7866

First four sections are a collection of parties, menus, and traditions, presented in vivid color and superb graphics covering Spring, Summer, Autumn and Winter. Fifth section contains 600 thrice-tested recipes. Index allows reader to easily locate recipes, parties, or menus. As professional in appearance as it is in content.

$11.95 Retail price
$ 1.50 Postage and handling
Make check payable to Books Unlimited
ISBN 0-9602246-1-0

RIVER ROAD RECIPES

Junior League of Baton Rouge
4950-B Government Street
Baton Rouge, LA 70806   (504) 924-3000

First published in 1959, *River Road Recipes* has been recognized in national newspapers and magazines and on national television as the best selling community cookbook in America. The 650 triple-tested recipes are spiral-bound in 262 pages representing the basics of traditional Louisiana cuisine.

$9.00 Retail price
Make check payable to *River Road Recipes*
ISBN 0-9613026-0-7

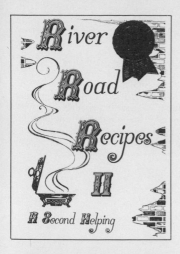

RIVER ROAD RECIPES II - A SECOND HELPING

Junior League of Baton Rouge
4950-B Government Street
Baton Rouge, LA 70806   (504) 924-3000

Published in 1976 as a companion cookbook to
River Road Recipes, this best-seller contains an additional 606 triple-tested recipes on 256 pages. Featuring
recipes from seafood to party food, *River Road Recipes II - A Second Helping* continues the tradition of
Louisiana's Creole and Cajun cooking.

$9.00 Retail price
Make check payable to *River Road Recipes*
ISBN 0-9613026-1-5

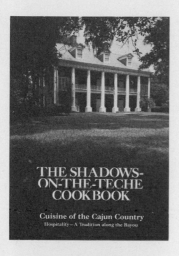

THE SHADOWS-ON-THE-TECHE COOKBOOK

The Shadows Service League
P. O. Box 254   (318) 369-0481
New Iberia, LA 70560   (318) 369-6446

The second printing of *The Shadows-on-the-Teche
Cookbook* consists of 384 pages, containing 677 recipes,
some old, some new, all tried and true. The laminated
covers portray the front and back of the present Shadows. Cajun country cuisine is an art. We are proud to
share our culinary history.

$12.95 Retail price
$ 1.75 Postage and handling
Make check payable to *The Shadows-on-the-Teche
Cookbook*
ISBN 0-9609994-1-8

SOUTHERN SPICE À LA MICROWAVE

Pelican Publishing Company
P. O. Box 189
Gretna, LA 70053   (504) 368-1175

Margie Brignac, a microwave specialist, demonstra-
tor, and columnist, has successfully adapted her favorite
recipes and shares them here. Now you can enjoy the
tastes of French, Acadian, and Creole cooking while
experiencing the timesaving convenience of the microwave.

$8.95 Retail price
$1.00 Postage and handling
$ .54 Tax for Louisiana residents
Make check payable to Pelican Publishing Company
ISBN 0-88289-318-1

Le LIVRE de la CUISINE de LAFAYETTE

TALK ABOUT GOOD!

Junior League of Lafayette
P. O. Box 52387 OCS
Lafayette, LA 70505　　　　　　(318) 988-1079

A delightful cookbook which includes 450 pages of
1200 recipes. Nationally recognized for its introduction
of fine foods of Acadiana. Features a special section
on seafood and game. Cross-indexed. Over 400,000
copies sold. A perfect gift for all occasions, a delight
for the cook and the collector.

$8.00 Retail price
$1.50 Postage and handling
Make check payable to Junior League of Lafayette
ISBN 0-686-15971-3

Talk About Good II
Le Livre de Cuisine des Acadiens

TALK ABOUT GOOD II

Junior League of Lafayette
P. O. Box 52387 OCS
Lafayette, LA 70505　　　　　　(318) 988-1079

Talk About Good II, published in 1980, is a unique book of Cajun tradition with 720 gourmet recipes
and full color reproductions by internationally ac-
claimed local artist, George Rodrigue. It is new and
completely different from the first *Talk About Good*.

$9.00 Retail price
$1.50 Postage and handling
Make check payable to Junior League of Lafayette
ISBN 0-686-26155-0

'TIGER BAIT' RECIPES

Louisiana State University Alumni Federation
Post Office Box 17170-A, LSU
Baton Rouge, LA 70893　　　　　　(504) 388-6624

'Tiger Bait' is a composite of recipes submitted by
alumni of Louisiana State University, kitchen-tested
and edited by LSU Home Economics alumni. Contains
over 600 recipes including metric measurements. Illustrated by some of Louisiana's well-known artists. All
recipes included were judged as excellent by Home
Economist testing.

$7.75 Retail price
$1.00 Postage and handling
Make check payable to *'Tiger Bait' Recipes*

TONY CHACHERE'S CAJUN COUNTRY COOKBOOK

Creole Foods of Opelousas, Inc.
P. O. Box 1687
Opelousas, LA 70570

Toll free   1 (800) 551-9066
In Louisiana 1 (800) 321-1816

A collection of Tony's favorite recipes, featuring seafood and wild game. A 200-page cookbook with over 250 recipes.

$8.95 Retail price
$1.00 Postage and handling
Make check payable to Creole Foods
ISBN 0-9604580-1-8

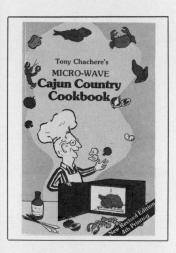

TONY CHACHERE'S MICRO-WAVE CAJUN COUNTRY COOKBOOK

P. O. Box 1687
Opelousas, LA 70570

Toll free   1 (800) 551-9066
In Louisiana 1 (800) 321-1816

Tony's favorite Cajun recipes are converted for microwave use. Seafood, wild game and Cajun-style dishes. 180 pages and over 200 recipes.

$8.95 Retail price
$1.00 Postage and handling
Make check payable to Creole Foods
ISBN 0-9604580-0-X

TOUT DE SUITE À LA MICROWAVE I

Tout de Suite à la Microwave, Inc.
P. O. Box 30121
Lafayette, LA 70503   (318) 984-2903

A gourmet's cookbook of French, Acadian, and Creole recipes. Spiral bound, 200 recipes, 224 pages. It features delicious Louisiana roux, gumbo, crawfish stew, etouffee, pralines, and more—all for microwave cooking. Easy-to-follow instructions and utensils required for each recipe. Over 250,000 sold in five years.

$9.95 Retail price
$1.50 Postage and handling
$ .50 Tax for Louisiana residents
Make check payable to Tout de Suite à la Microwave, Inc.
ISBN 0-9605362-0-5

285

TOUT DE SUITE À LA MICROWAVE II

Tout de Suite à la Microwave, Inc.
P. O. Box 30121
Lafayette, LA 70503   (318) 984-2903

This is a delightful cookbook of Mexican, Italian and French recipes. Spiral bound, 221 recipes, 232 pages. Good sections on drying flowers, roasting a turkey, preparing enchiladas, lasagna, Mexican candy, bread pudding, chocolate mousse and more—all in the microwave. 140,000 in print.

$9.95 Retail price
$1.50 Postage and handling
$ .50 Tax for Louisiana residents
Make check payable to Tout de Suite à la Microwave, Inc.
ISBN 0-9605362-1-3

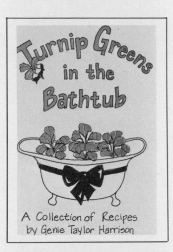

TURNIP GREENS IN THE BATHTUB

by Genie T. Harrison
2335 Olive Street
Baton Rouge, LA 70806   (504) 343-6633

Turnip Greens in the Bathtub is a collection of recipes gathered over 35 years from friends and family, reaching from Georgia to North Dakota, but mostly from Louisiana, the adopted state of the author. The cookbook consists of 303 pages and 537 recipes.

$8.95 Retail price
$1.00 Postage and handling
$ .27 Tax for Louisiana residents
Make check payable to *Turnip Greens in the Bathtub*

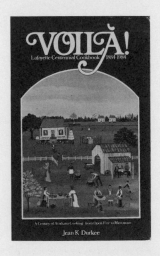

VOILÀ!

Lafayette Centennial Cookbook
P. O. Box 30121
Lafayette, LA 70503   (318) 984-2903

Voilà! A Century of Acadiana "Cajun" Cooking from Open Fire to Microwave. Beautiful 5-color hard cover, spiral bound, 264 pages, 417 recipes. Kitchen-tested recipes, index, 20 pen-and-ink drawings, conventional recipes plus microwave shortcuts by Jean Durkee, the author of *Tout de Suite a la Microwave I and II.*

$11.95 Retail price
$ 2.00 Postage and handling
$ .60 Tax for Louisiana residents
Make check payable to Voilà! Lafayette Centennial Cookbook
ISBN 0-9605362-2-1

THE QUAIL RIDGE PRESS
"BEST OF THE BEST" COOKBOOK SERIES

The cookbooks in the Quail Ridge Press "Best of the Best" series are each considered the most complete survey available of that state's particular cooking style and flavor. They are compiled by searching out a comprehensive cross-section of the leading cookbooks in the state, and then requesting the authors, editors, and publishers of these books to select their most popular recipes. The volumes listed below have been completed as of 1994.

**Best of the Best
from Alabama**
288 pages, (28-3) $14.95

**Best of the Best
from Arkansas**
288 pages, (43-7) $14.95

**Best of the Best
from Florida**
288 pages, (16-X) $14.95

**Best of the Best
from Georgia**
320 pages, (30-5) $14.95

**Best of the Best
from Kentucky**
288 pages, (27-5) $14.95

**Best of the Best
from Louisiana**
288 pages, (13-5) $14.95

**Best of the Best
from Mississippi**
288 pages, (19-4) $14.95

**Best of the Best
from Missouri**
288 pages, (44-5) $14.95

**Best of the Best
from North Carolina**
288 pages, (38-0) $14.95

**Best of the Best
from Pennsylvania**
320 pages, (47-X) $14.95

**Best of the Best
from South Carolina**
288 pages,(39-9) $14.95

**Best of the Best
from Tennessee**
288 pages, (20-8) $14.95

**Best of the Best
from Texas**
352 pages, (14-3) $14.95
Hardbound, (34-8)
$16.95

**Best of the Best
from Virginia**
320 pages, (41-0) $14.95

**Best of the Best
from New England**
(Available Fall 1994)

All books plastic-ring bound, unless noted otherwise. ISBN Prefix: 0-937552-; suffix noted in parentheses under each title. *See next page for complete listing of Quail Ridge Press Cookbooks.*

"Best of the Best" Cookbook Series:

Best of the Best from Alabama $14.95   28-3

Best of the Best from Arkansas $14.95   43-7

Best of the Best from Florida $14.95   16-X

Best of the Best from Georgia $14.95   30-5

Best of the Best from Kentucky $14.95   27-5

Best of the Best from Louisiana $14.95   13-5

Best of the Best from Mississippi $14.95   19-4

Best of the Best from Missouri $14.95   44-5

Best of the Best from North Carolina $14.95   38-0

Best of the Best from Pennsylvania $14.95   47-X

Best of the Best from South Carolina $14.95   39-9

Best of the Best from Tennessee $14.95   20-8

Best of the Best from Texas $14.95   14-3

Best of the Best from Texas (hardbound) $16.95   34-8

Best of the Best from Virginia $14.95   41-0

Best of the Best from New England (Fall of 1994)   50-X

The Quail Ridge Press Cookbook Series:

ISBN SUFFIX

The Little New Orleans Cookbook (hardbound) $8.95   42-9

The Little Gumbo Book (hardbound) $8.95   17-8

The Little Bean Book (hardbound) $9.95   32-1

Gourmet Camping $9.95   45-3

Lite Up Your Life $14.95   40-2

Hors D'Oeuvres Everybody Loves $5.95   11-9

The Seven Chocolate Sins $5.95   01-1

A Salad A Day $5.95   02-X

Quickies for Singles $5.95   03-8

Twelve Days of Christmas Cookbook $5.95   00-3

Country Mouse Cheese Cookbook $5.95   10-0

ISBN Prefix: 0-937552-. All books are plastic-ring bound unless otherwise noted. To order by mail, send check, money order, or Visa or MasterCard number with expiration date to:

QUAIL RIDGE PRESS
P. O. Box 123 / Brandon, MS 39043

Please add $2.00 postage for any amount of books sent to one address. Gift wrap with enclosed card add $1.50. Mississippi residents add 7% sales tax. Write or call for free catalog of all QRP books and cookbooks.

Phone orders call toll free: 1-800-343-1583